COMMITMENT, EDUCATIVE ACTI

For Eustás Ó Héideáin, O.P.

Commitment, Educative Action and Adults

Learning programmes with a social purpose

Denis O'Sullivan
University College Cork

Avebury

Aldershot · Brookfield USA · Hong Kong · Singapore · Sydney

Published by
Avebury
Ashgate Publishing Limited
Gower House
Croft Road
Aldershot
Hants GU11 3HR
England

Ashgate Publishing Company
Old Post Road
Brookfield
Vermont 05036
USA

Set using TEX in Adobe Stone 11 on 13pt

British Library Cataloguing in Publication Data

O'Sullivan, Denis
    Commitment, Educative Action and Adults:
    Learning Programmes with a Social Purpose
    I. Title
    374

ISBN 1 85628 292 9

Printed and Bound in Great Britain by
Athenaeum Press Ltd, Newcastle upon Tyne.

Contents

Acknowledgements   vii

1 **Socially-committed programmes: exemplars
  and overview**   1
  Socially-committed programmes   1
  Exemplars of socially-committed programmes   5
  Issues and questions   20
  Parameters and perspectives   25

2 **The biography of commitment**   27
  Introduction   27
  Socialization to commitment   28
  A biographical approach   32
  Linear commitment   35
  Sectoral commitment   38
  Reactive commitment   45
  Flashpoint commitment   47
  Conclusion   49

3 **The discourse of commitment I: declaring
  one's intentions**   51
  Introduction   51
  'Unremarkable' intentions   54
  Inspirational representation   60
  Contestation   67

The participant's standing   70
Conclusion   74

4   **Educative action: epistemic status and
    psychological change**   76
    Introduction   76
    Epistemic status   76
    Psychological change   81
    Conclusion   100

5   **The discourse of commitment II: establishing
    legitimacy**   103
    Introduction   103
    Charismatic legitimacy   106
    Normative legitimacy   113
    Traditional legitimacy   117
    Rational legitimacy   123
    Conclusion   129

6   **The learning encounter: associative forms**   132
    Introduction   132
    Associative forms   134
    Membershipping   150
    Conclusion   162

7   **Coping with dysfunctional response**   164
    Introduction   164
    Interpreting dysfunctional response   166
    Reacting to dsyfunctional response   169
    Containing dysfunctional response   171
    Conclusion   179

8   **Conclusion**   182
    Introduction   182
    Human agency   183
    Structure   189
    Ideology   194

Bibliography   199

Acknowledgements

The issues relating to learning programmes with a social purpose which motivated this book arose during my editing of *Social Commitment and Adult Education*, a commemorative publication celebrating the adult education initiatives of Alfred O'Rahilly. Their exploration might never have taken the form of this book were it not for Jo Campling. Her positive and helpful advice when I approached her with the idea for the book at the publishing workshop she conducted at University College, Cork was invaluable. I also drew encouragement at this early stage from the support and expertise of Professor Peter Jarvis.

Credit for the production of the manuscript rests with Ms Fiona Murray. She saw the project through from audio tapes to camera-ready copy, and coped with countless drafts with good humour and efficiency. Peter Flynn gave technical advice and Patrick Commins, John Riordan and Declan Irvine helped with references and sources. Dr Jana Svecova, Charles University and the staff of the European Centre for Human Rights Education, Prague were welcoming at a critical stage. Throughout, the staff at Avebury were helpful and accommodating. I am grateful to the library staff of the following institutions for their assistance: UNESCO, Paris, Faculty of Education, Charles University, Prague, University of Surrey and University College, Cork.

I am happy to acknowledge a grant from the Arts Faculty Research Fund, University College, Cork which supported part of the research on which the analysis is based.

The book is dedicated to Eustás Ó Héideáin, O.P., who as Professor of Education at University College, Galway first gave me the opportunity to teach sociology. His unfailing humanity, trust and support of scholarship made my five years in Galway happy and exciting ones.

1   Socially-committed programmes: exemplars and overview

Socially-committed programmes

Programmes and people are the subject matter of this book: social programmes that are infused with a dedication to bringing about change through educative action and the people who, because of a personal conviction, initiate and enact them as well as those who are attracted to participate.

Purposeful interaction along these lines varies widely and is a good deal more commonplace and universal than might be imagined. It is not a minority or esoteric activity. Neither is it necessarily ideologically extreme or zealous. It doesn't have to involve institutions of the kind that are traditionally associated with changing people and society such as schools and colleges. Nor does it require a set of encounters that are pre-planned in terms of quantity, frequency and content. In other words, the experiences and political flavour routinely evoked by the mention of 'programmes', 'commitment', 'dedication' or 'conviction' need to be dissipated and set aside if the universality of this kind of collective experience is to be appreciated.

With a view to illuminating the variety and universality of socially-committed programmes a range of typifications of such social encounters is outlined below. Some well-known programmes have been purposely juxtaposed with those that may not be readily recognizable as educational efforts. These will vary in the nature of their objectives and strategies, their level of commitment, their social and cultural contexts, and their structuration and intensity. Both housed and unhoused educational programmes are represented. The personnel involved includes social workers, community activists, religious, health workers, feminists, pacifists, environmentalists, trade unionists, politicians, literacy workers, educators and parents. The political tone can indeed be of the left, and radically so; it can equally be right-wing, conservative or proclaim itself to be neutral.

The understanding of socially-committed programmes underpinning the analysis in this book is consciously wide-ranging and inclusive. Because of this it is especially necessary to establish some parameters lest the focus of the analysis becomes unduly blurred. If what distinguishes the socially-committed programmes considered in this book is capable of being reduced to a core indicator it must be the desire to bring about social change through educative action. From this focus further dissection and elaboration yields six characteristics. To be treated as a socially-committed programme a social encounter was required to exhibit the following characteristics: the social interaction needed to be *purposeful, relentless, patterned, educative, unequal* and *instrumental*.

- *Purposeful* interaction assumes some degree of intentionality, however subconscious, inadequately articulated or lacking in proclamation on the part of those who initiate and enact the encounter. It is to be set apart from incidental interaction and fortuitous change.
- This purposeful interaction should be *relentless* in the sense of being relatively unwavering in its objectives, and is to be distinguished from genuinely exploratory interaction in which the ends and not just the means are the object of experimentation, consideration or reflection.
- *Patterned* interaction doesn't necessarily imply good planning, coherence or meaningful sequence. It should, however, be recognizable as a systematic experience when considered over a reasonable time span.
- The intent of this patterned interaction should be *educative*. It should be aimed at lasting change in the individual. It is to be distinguished from collective action that is primarily designed to mobilize people as a social or political force with a view to bringing pressure on decision makers to change

some aspect of social policy.
- Unlike peer relationships or collaborative learning in their ideal form the interaction is *unequal*. Socially-committed programmes are initiated by some and experienced by others. It involves a context in which someone is educating, training, helping, developing, advizing, leading, facilitating and in which others, as individuals or as elements of a collective entity, are being educated, trained, helped etc.
- Interaction in the programme is considered to be *instrumental*. The educative action involved is not an end in itself. It is meant to contribute to the stability of an existing system, to its modification or to the emergence of some new social order.

Apart from problems of definition, and decisions as to what varieties of social interaction are to be considered, there are normative complications that need to be identified and made explicit. To describe a person or programme as committed is to confer on them an exalted position on the moral high ground. Commitment is normative: it is value-laden. It is indisputably 'good'. Contributing to this normative status is the activist orientation to life associated with commitment. It is the antithesis of passivity and acquiescence, of standing on the sidelines, indulging in armchair theorizing or reflecting in academic ivory towers. Commitment is sympathetic to the rallying cries of many famous advocates of social change. Of these, Marx's exhortation in his *Theses on Feuerbach* (in McLellan, 1977) that the 'philosophers have only interpreted the world in various ways; the point is, to change it' is probably the best known. There is also Freire's (1972, 1972a) encouragement to ordinary people, particularly the oppressed, to make rather than to live in history. Similarly, Blum (1971) contends that it is ordinary people 'with their ordinary practical notions sometimes aided by theories but usually in spite of them' who change society. 'Theorizing', he argues, 'is not designed to save worlds'.

Relatedly, commitment is associated with 'taking a stand' in opposition to some unsatisfactory state of social affairs. It implies a challenge, often requiring courage, sacrifice and personal compromise, to inequality or domination. The task in hand, the liberation of people or the erosion of disadvantage, may be of such a magnitude that the chance of success, particularly in any one person's lifetime, is realistically slight. This adds to the sense of sacrifice,

3

courage and of unflinching confrontation cogently captured in Merleau-Ponty's (1969) description of the French resistance fighters as 'taking sides against the probable'.

As frequently happens with valued-laden phenomena, the treatment of commitment as a concept and a practice is elliptical. Important questions aren't merely left unanswered; they remain unposed. Analysis is accordingly short-circuited and the cognitive comprehension of socially-committed programmes operates as a tightly-framed paradigm. A paradigm's regulatory power over the nature of enquiry is described by Kuhn (1962, p.37) as follows:

> One of the things a scientific community acquires with a paradigm is a criterion for choosing problems that, while the paradigm is taken for granted, can be assumed to have solutions. To a great extent these are the only problems the community will admit as scientific or encourage its members to undertake. Other problems, including many that had previously been standard, are rejected as metaphysical, as the concern of another discipline, or sometimes as just too problematic to be worth the time. A paradigm can, for that matter, even insulate the community from those socially important problems that are not reducible to the puzzle form, because they cannot be stated in terms of the conceptual and instrumental tools the paradigm supplies. Such problems can be a distraction.

In advancing an alternative conceptual framework, together with an associated vocabulary for the naming of experiences and processes, derived from the paradigm of participant subjectivity the book seeks to instigate the reflective procedures that are frequently guillotined in the conventional treatment of socially-committed programmes. In pursuing this objective it is likely that questions will be raised and confronted that might well be considered as 'distractions' by those who direct socially-committed programmes. The orientation of the analysis shouldn't, however, be interpreted as antagonistic to those who are often dedicated and altruistic people. On the contrary, it is hoped that they will benefit from the reflection that is encouraged and, by posing the type of questions that are recommended about themselves and their programmes, will expand their self-knowledge and understanding. Indeed, it is incumbent on those who operate with such influence over others, particularly within heavily-insulated paradigms, to be open to what they might be inclined to dismiss. The issues and questions a paradigm most desires to exclude, marginalize or dismiss can be an unerring guide to precisely the questions which those whose consciousness is guided by the paradigm ought to confront.

One of the reasons why the questions raised in the analysis are likely to be perceived by providers as discordant or threatening is that the perspective throughout is that of the 'client' of socially-committed programmes. Its focus are those who experience programmes which seek to change them and society. This book is in their interest in that it is concerned to give due attention to their needs, rights and, above all, their personal autonomy. This orientation of taking the side of the underdog has a long tradition in sociology. Yet, it can be an orientation that is discarded when social activists seek to work through others to bring about social change.

Exemplars of socially-committed programmes

An Irish workers' course

In 1946, University College, Cork in Ireland instituted the two-year part-time course leading to the Diploma in Social and Economic Science. Referred to locally as the 'workers' course', it was directed at members of local trade unions, in particular those who held positions of responsibility. This was the culmination of a series of educational initiatives, such as university extension lectures, tutorial classes and study circles, designed, according to one of the planners, Fr Jerome O'Leary, 'to make available in some small way the benefits of university education to the working classes of Cork' (quoted in Ó Murchú, 1989).

The driving force behind the inauguration of this diploma, and indeed much of the earlier initiatives as well, was the Registrar and later President of University College, Cork, Alfred O'Rahilly. He took a great personal satisfaction in conferring the diplomas on twenty-four workers in 1948. At this inaugural conferring he pointed out that it marked 'the first occasion, since the establishment of the college 100 years ago, that workers were allowed to attend a complete course here... I consider it a great honour and privilege to award the diploma to them today. I hope that many more will follow their example. The door is now open' (quoted in Ó Murchú, 1989). Many did indeed follow the example. The 'workers' course' spread throughout the province of Munster, the

5

catchment area of the university, and even towns that were little more than villages have at some stage provided a centre for them. Further programmes were developed for rural communities and for women. This model of university extra-mural provision for adults also became the prototype for the other Irish university colleges.

O'Rahilly was single-minded and assertive in his advancement of the education of workers. In this he was guided by a conviction about society and the individual formed by Roman Catholic social teaching of which the encyclical of Pope Pius XI, *Quadragesimo Anno*, in 1931 is representative. This proclaimed the freedom and dignity of the individual, the danger of statism and the need to cultivate intermediate associations between the individual and state in accordance with the principle of subsidiarity — that larger bodies shouldn't do what is best and more effectively done by lesser associations. Versions of existing groups such as trade unions, political parties, mutual aid societies and professional associations based on Roman Catholic social principles were recommended. O'Rahilly conceived of the diploma programmes as both facilitating the emergence of such associations as well as a training ground for their future leaders. In all of this, O'Rahilly was equally antagonistic to the evils of capitalism and socialism.

The conferring of these diplomas continues to be a key event in the life of small communities, widely reported and photographed, and there is scarcely a political party, cooperative society, community association and trade union or agricultural grouping that doesn't include a diplomate among its leadership.

The Antigonish movement in Canada

The Antigonish movement, based at the University of St Francis Xavier in Nova Scotia in Canada, was also imbued with Roman Catholic social principles. During its early phase in the 1920s and 1930s, its motivating forces were two priests, initially Fr Jimmy Tompkins and, later, Fr Moses Coady. They were responding to the social and economic problems of their catchment area, largely rural, disadvantaged and economically depressed. Like O'Rahilly, they rejected communism and condemned the excesses of capitalism. Coady, too, was a strong personality. The Antigonish movement located much of its activity in the community and its interventions were varied in content, format and appeal. It involved constant interpenetration between action and education. The lived economic situation of people was recognized as the source from which an individual's learning needs could be identified. Not that disadvantaged individuals were expected to know what their real needs were until their awareness and, in particular, their sense of place in the social and economic structures were activated. As Coady put it, 'a fish doesn't know he lives in water until he's taken out of it' (quoted in Lovett, 1980). Coady didn't believe in waiting for people to act, and used mass meetings to take the initiative by preaching his theories of community, grass roots action, cooperativism and the formation of alternative institutions. Study clubs or discussion groups drawing on local leaders and radio listening groups followed from the mass meetings, and these mobilized and directed action. The community extension department at the university supported these community-based activities with the preparation of study materials, leadership training programmes, conferences and short courses. When Coady died in 1959 the movement appears to have lost much of its momentum.

It is said that many of the economic problems which the Antigonish movement sought to confront still remain and that it may well have contributed to the lack of change by subduing radical political action. Nonetheless, Lovett (1980) concluded that 'it did succeed in engaging large numbers of workers in relevant education linked to social action with methods and techniques which even today would be regarded as too radical for many educational institutions'.

Highlander, Tennessee

Like O'Rahilly's workers' courses and the Antigonish movement, the Highlander folk school in Tennessee was founded, by Myles Horton, under the influence of religious principles. Though a contemporary of these Irish and Canadian programmes, having been established in the 1930s, Highlander was based on an explicit class analysis on society. It was committed to 'educating for a revolution that would basically change economic and political power relationships to the advantage of the poor and the powerless' (quoted in Lovett, 1980). As such it emerges as radical rather than reformist in political analysis and prescriptions for action. Horton's objective was to cultivate class consciousness among workers and an awareness of the ugliness of the class divisions of the social structure in which they were embedded. Horton's approach was even less institution-based than Antigonish. The Highlander strategy was to associate with social movements or situations involving workers and to offer support and assistance, facilitate discussions on strategy, and later to provide opportunities for more detailed analysis using experts at Highlander.

New needs and challenges emerged as new social movements were identified. During the 1950s and 1960s Highlander became involved with civil rights movements and the expansion of citizenship schools established to help illiterate negroes to pass the voting test. Having been suppressed by the state of Tennessee in 1961, it reorganized under its present name, Highlander Research and Educational Center Incorporated, which continues to provide a forum for discussion and a resource for educational methods and techniques to radical groups.

The Women's Education Centre, Southampton

The Women's Education Centre in Southampton was also radical and class conscious in its analysis of society but, as the name suggests, it dealt exclusively with women. Jane Thompson (1983, p.193), a founding figure of the centre and a lecturer in adult education at the local university, explains the rationale for its establishment together with the guiding philosophy of its activities.

> If women are to anticipate equality in a society in which our inequality is institutionalized both in public bodies and in private relationships which reflect patriarchal attitudes the need for a separate physical and symbolic space for women, in which we can learn from each other's experience, clarify our needs and our rights, confirm our allegiances and prepare for our possibilities, is of paramount importance.

Founded in 1981, the Women's Education Centre grew from such initiatives as Second Chance for Women. This programme was first offered in 1979 and was itself a reaction against what were perceived to be the inadequacies and inconsistencies (patronising, diluted knowledge, socially therapeutic, male presence) of the traditional liberal approach to the education of disadvantaged women such as single parents, prisoners' wives and public housing mothers of pre-school children. Second Chance for Women distanced itself from education of the '"low profile" variety which gets smuggled by stealth into community centres, mothers-and-toddlers groups and gatherings of women on housing estates — slipping in between the afternoon "cuppa" and the organization of the jumble sale—fearful of being seen to be serious' (pp. 151–152). Second Chance for Women aspired to offering 'serious education' to working-class women with a view to helping them collectively to develop a critical stance on what it was like to be female in society and what might be done to help them escape from the limitations imposed on women in a patriarchal society. The content and approach combined the introductory study of law, literature, sociology, politics and history presented through team teaching with interdisciplinary and student-selected project work—writers' workshops, oral history, radio workshops and media groups. Like Highlander, it attracted suspicion and criticism from some local sources such as councillors, education officers and ratepayers associations which typically raised 'fears about indoctrination and encouraging "over-robust attitudes to securing women's rights"' (pp. 183–184).

The Italian 150 hours scheme

In the Italian 150 hours scheme—the title refers to the amount of paid leave provided by employers in the early years—'serious' education took the form of, mainly, one-year part-time courses for adults returning to school to take the middle-school diploma but, also, university and literacy courses. The scheme was a response to the low rates of educational participation among the Italian working class, their lack of educational qualifications and high incidence of illiteracy. Negotiated between the engineering workers' joint union (the FLM), the employers and the Minister for Education, courses under the scheme were first offered in 1973. The organization of the bedrock 150 hour courses, those preparing students for the middle-school diploma, usually taken by students aged 14 or 15 years, varied between industries and areas. Typically, they now last 350 hours spread over the school year, giving students four hours per week on each of the four components of the course—Italian, science, history and a foreign language. Classes usually take place in middle schools at the end of the school day. Participation has also widened from the core engineering workers in the early years to include a greater representation from smaller firms, the public service, the unemployed and women.

The educational aims of the 150 hours scheme aspire beyond the acquisition of a formal qualification and include 'acquiring the indispensible instruments for knowledge and autonomous expression of one's thoughts' and 'being able to understand in a critical spirit one's personal experience of life and work within the overall historical frame of reference' (quoted in Yarnit, 1980a). In this, there is a conscious attempt to transcend the conventional school location and traditional educational content areas. Titmus (1981, p.211) tells us that 'magisterial instruction' is avoided and there is a concentration on the interdisciplinary approach, collective management of learning and group discussion in which the student's experience is the starting point. Tensions appear to remain among organizers, teachers and students between a collectivist orientation to social change and the individualist aspiration to acquire qualifications and further personal advancement. There is also a concern that the 150 hours scheme might become a 'workers' ghetto' isolated both from the 'real' educational system and the struggles of the working class.

The 'sunken middle class', Huddersfield

For the 34 families categorized in *Education and the Working Class* as 'sunken middle class' there was no doubt about the emphasis on the acquisition of educational credentials and individual social mobility. This was the largest sub-group in Jackson and Marsden's (1966) classic study of 88 former working-class pupils from Huddersfield, England who, untypically of their social background, successfully completed grammar schooling. Manual worker in economic position, the sunken middle class were so described by Jackson and Marsden because, in exploring how their 'whole style of living' (p.68) set them apart from traditional working-class families, it was discovered that some of them had owned businesses which for various reasons hadn't prospered and most had one middle-class grandparent. Repeatedly, this group adverted to themselves as the 'poor relations' within their kinship group and seemed more intent, having failed in business or come down in the world as they saw it, 'to reinvest their energies in the education of their children than in building up a new concern' (p.69). Seeing themselves as the submerged wings of middle-class families they retained many elements of middle-class lifestyle and revealed themselves as 'thrusting their way upward through free education' in the desire to 'educate their children out of their fallen condition and reclaim the social position of their parents and grandparents' (p.70). To this end, sunken middle-class parents encouraged their children to apply themselves to their studies, to adapt to grammar school values and to sever community links in favour of school-based associations and groups. The Priestly family epitomized this pattern. It had lost three separate businesses through economic recession and ill-health, but, apart from their native gifts, the Priestleys had 'ambition, contacts, knowledge' that enabled them to send all four children to grammar school and university. Despite having difficulty making the academic grade, this new generation 're-established the Priestleys as a middle-class family' (p.96).

Literacy programmes in Nicaragua and Ethiopia

Literacy programmes in third-world countries respond to the wide-spread and extensive problem of adult illiteracy which, despite optimistic predictions in the 1960s that it would be eradicated by the end of the century, has actually grown. The objectives of literacy campaigns are, however, very rarely confined to developing the skills of reading and writing. This is well illustrated in some of the programmes from Nicaragua and Ethiopia described by Alemayehu (1988).

The Nicaraguan national literacy crusade has been variously referred to as a 'war on ignorance', a 'cultural insurrection' and the 'second war of liberation'. There, a former Minister for Education stressed that literacy education is a means to an end rather than an end in itself.

> The attainment of literacy was not simply the gaining of an academic skill, but the empowerment of a people who became aware of their reality and gained the tools, reading and writing, to affect and determine their future. The Literacy Crusade was not a pedagogical undertaking with political effects; it was a political undertaking with pedagogical effects. It was a political mobilization with political goals (quoted in Alemayehu, 1988).

Similarly, in Ethiopia literacy education was considered to be inextricable from political and social change. A programme in which Alemayehu was personally involved had the character of a mass campaign about it. All university students and their teachers, together with about 60,000 senior secondary students, were mobilized, by the provisional military government of socialist Ethiopia, known as the Derju. The student tutors in turn were known as

'Children of the Derju' in the almost 400 districts throughout the country to which they were allocated. A million became literate but, as well as that, 158 new primary schools and 206 clinics were built and poor peasants were organized in associations and defence committees. Literacy campaigns have to be seen as a dimension of programmes which seek to mobilize action, effort and enthusiasm against such third-world evils as disease, famine, poverty and powerlessness.

The peace movement

As Hall (1988) points out, peace is a complex concept that varies in meaning according to the context in which people live. Fear of nuclear war, sectarian killing, the establishment of a homeland, colonial exploitation and despotic political leaders have in locations as disparate as Europe, the USA, the USSR, Northern Ireland, Palestine, Nicaragua, South Africa and Chile provided the stimulus for the emergence of the peace movement. The common denominator appears to be the desire to disseminate the conviction that disputes, however deeply rooted, can be resolved without recourse to violence. But the peace movement is more than a vision of a world without violence or armed struggles. Nor does it involve a quietist disposition to injustice, inequality or oppression. Its goal is the creation of a 'culture of peace':

> we must engender a reverence for life, love of life, we must enable ourselves and others to understand and act on the fact that social justice and human equity should go before economic profit. And the fact of our interdependence and global sisterhood and brotherhood needs to be stressed and supported (Hall, 1988).

The learning and personal change required by this 'culture of peace' occurs at various levels. Informing people about the existence of the peace movement, generating an awareness in relation to its concerns and objectives, and succeeding in convincing people that its anxieties are well grounded and its vision of the future worthwhile and realizable are essential prerequisites. Some may follow through from this level to participation in organizations committed to peace objectives that provide the full gamut of learning opportunities: experiential and participative learning derived from projects, campaigns and advocacy, informal learning through reading and lectures, and the formal learning of systematic educational programmes. But this may be to view the personal change aspired to by the peace movement unduly in terms of organizations, recruitment and participation. The mass learning (or relearning) goals of social movements range far beyond those who assume positions of leadership and activism, and extend to the general run of non-politicized citizens. This mass learning includes the facilitation of greater cultural understanding between people, appreciation of human rights and development issues, the dissemination of facts about the cost of military weapons and the cultivation of qualities of compromize, negotiation and co-operation.

The Australian anti-uranium movement

Another social movement, with affinities with the peace movement, is the environmental movement. Martin (1988) has traced the origins, aspirations, strategies and experiences of a national manifestation of that movement—the Australian anti-uranium movement. He identifies some of the forces which shaped the concerns of this movement from the early 1970s. External influences included Friends of the Earth. Locally, the trade union movement with its history of activism on social issues was involved from the beginning. Because uranium deposits were located far from urban centres in Australia it focused more on the global proliferation of nuclear weapons than on the anxieties of local residents.

Within the movement, particularly in its early days, the emphasis was on self-learning, a process that resulted in members becoming expert on topics in which they had no formal academic background. This was supported by an 'informal college' comprized of leading anti-uranium figures and which operated by the exchange of writings, national meetings, personal discussion and telephone calls. It covered both technical and political issues, and was directed towards the enhancement of the anti-uranium position in public debate and advocacy rather than academic inquiry.

Martin estimated, in the light of his own experience in this movement, that the role of social movement organizations is particularly vital in the early stages of a campaign if the concerns of the movement are to be widely perceived as issues and if education in the widest sense — disseminating information, developing arguments, questioning established truths and formulating alternatives — is to take place. He lists attempts by the uranium industry interests to curtail this process by means of smear campaigns, blocking tenure or promotion, or dismissal directed against the movement's spokespersons in public positions or with formal status, the very people who could give the movement's world-view standing and legitimacy. He equally acknowledges that 'knowledge' within the movement was frequently compromized in the interests of media attention and fear mongering, and subjected to the short-term needs of the movement. Environmental education within the formal educational system is faulted for the manner in which it is presented 'as a neutral subject cut off from political and economic controversy'. It is 'education for individual understanding, not education for social action'.

Thailand: immigration and social integration

Faced with an influx of Chinese immigrants, Thailand used its secondary school system to contribute to the assimilation of Chinese youth and to facilitate their integration into Thai society (Guskin and Guskin, 1970). The intention was to avoid social disharmony, a dilution of national consensus and the emergence of cultural and political pluralism. The schools' role was an ambitious one — to change the Chinese students' sense of national identity as well as their ethnic identity. What was being attempted was a process of resocialization of Chinese students which sough to detach them from the conception of themselves which had been formed during childhood and replace it with a conception of themselves as Thais.

In Thai schools the Chinese background of the students was almost totally ignored and discussion of Chinese culture was discouraged. All students were required to learn the Thai language and the use of Chinese was severely restricted. The role models available within the school were Thai: there were no adult Chinese role models in the institution and peer role models were less accessible since students who were successful in school were those who had adopted the Thai language, behaviour and identity. The wearing of uniform also helped to induce a sense of cohesiveness and common identity. The process of changing one's identity from Chinese to Thai was facilitated throughout by routine practices such as the withdrawal of rewards for previously desired behaviour, punishments and social disapproval. The Guskins describe the process as going through the stages of compliance, identification and internalization, at which point the 'Chinese student begins to feel Thai and eventually to think of

14

himself as Thai' (p.120).

Cuba and Tanzania: education for revolutionary change

Heyman (1974), on the other hand, describes the role of the formal educational system in revolutionary societies. In this he draws on the analysis of Paulston (1972) on cultural revitalization and educational change in Cuba and on the writings of Julius Nyerere (1968) in Tanzania. Both countries had as their objective the creation of a new society characterized by socialist principles and, correspondingly, the destruction of the old society. The school systems were given the responsibility of forming the new model of citizen who would facilitate the transition. Such a person would be a 'creative, productive worker, a fighter against injustice and exploitation, selfless, and motivated by revolutionary fervor, self-sacrificing for the group'. In Tanzania a fundamental reform of education followed from Nyerere's 'Arusha Declaration'. This programme was entitled 'Education for Self Reliance' and was meant to move schooling from its traditional colonial structure to a more egalitarian, productive and efficient system in tune with the requirements and values of a society that was both socialist and African. In this transition the different levels of the educational system were entrusted with related tasks. At primary level, schools were required to prepare pupils, not for examination success and secondary school entry, but rather for the type of farming life which the majority of them will lead. Beyond that level, secondary schooling and higher education, education had to be justified in terms of the contribution which those who benefited from it could make to the community. The old system led to the cultivation and rewarding of the individualistic instinct and the social valuing of personal material wealth. The new system would be assessed in terms of its relevance to the country's ideological needs — the promotion of community and egalitarianism and the elimination of elitism. As Nyerere put it, 'let our students be educated to be members and servants of the kind of just and egalitarian future to which this country aspires'.

The charismatic renewal movement: confronting secularism

The Catholic Pentecostal movement, latterly and more popularly referred to as charismatic renewal, sees itself as confronting the

15

forces of secularization in modern society, McGuire (1982) studied a number of Pentecostal groups in America in terms of their beliefs, practices and likely impact on society. In their early contact with a group, recruits are presented with an interpretation of social problems which suggests that Satan is responsible and that human beings themselves cannot fight such powerful forces. War, poverty, riots, social conflict, generation gap and exploitation are projected as a manifestation of a society that itself is rudderless, with no one directing its course and with technology and social change out of human control. The only solution is considered to be through the power of Jesus.

The effect is to develop among recruits a dissatisfaction and a lack of confidence in their existing world-view and to redefine it in terms of the Pentecostal ideology. Through interacting with existing members a process of resocialization commences which integrates recruits into the group's practices and ideology. Affective bonds within the group are important as the recruits come to identify with the group members and to withdraw from competing social relationships. The experience of conversion is usually marked in some symbolic way to indicate that a personal transformation has occurred. Speaking in tongues may act as a 'bridge-burning' event, as a symbol of abandonment of a former identity and meaning system. McGuire, however, interprets the practice of testimony or witnessing, in which experiences demonstrating God's power and revelation are shared with other member of the group, as the principal act of commitment and public abandonment for the Catholic Pentecostal. Witnessing also serves to confirm the belief system for existing members. With regard to its impact on society, McGuire concludes that while 'members can be personally strengthened against normative relativism' it is 'not likely to effect a reversal of pluralism by a re-establishment of a christian hegemony' (p.224).

Even this cursory scanning of efforts to effect social change through the medium of educative action reveals how the six conditions necessary for inclusion as socially-committed programmes can be fulfilled in a manner that is diverse in kind and degree. The brief descriptions of these programmes have been presented in such a way as to maintain a line of continuity in relation to some aspect of their objectives, justifications or strategies. And yet it is likely that organizers and participants from many of these programmes would have difficulty in recognizing that they have anything in common with one another. In fact, for some there could well be ideological objections to the company in which they find themselves. The programmes in this overview are presented as exemplars of socially-committed programmes. In outlining below the different forms which purposeful, relentless, patterned, educative, unequal and instrumental interaction can take we establish the identity and contours of the genus. We also isolate some of the sociological issues that arise and will be addressed in this book.

The purposeful character is most evident in those programmes which aim at specific change in relation to a particular aspect of society. This is true of the literacy schemes, the anti-uranium and the peace movement. What renders the intentionality particularly visible in such cases is their adversarial character. They operate in opposition to an aspect of technological development, existing states of affairs or of the human condition. In owing their origin to a desire to eradicate what are regarded as unacceptable, threatening or iniquitous social or human conditions, their purposeful nature is made all the more salient and recognizable. Programmes which prepare participants in a structured manner within established institutions to master particular bodies of knowledge with a view to meriting a named award or qualification are also readily seen apart from incidental or fortuitous learning. On the other hand, the sunken middle-class parents, though distinguishable because of their commitment to improving their families' socio-economic position through the education of their children, could easily go unremarked because they represent a special case of parenting rather than a set of experiences publicly named and planned.

Adversarial programmes, also, are most obviously relentless in their pursuit of whatever objectives they have set for themselves. By setting themselves against a particular social or human condition their unwavering orientation is crystallized. Since the task in hand is perceived to be so crucial and immediate, theorizing is regarded as, at best, a luxury, though, most likely, as a distraction from the singularity of purpose that is considered necessary if the offending situation is to be corrected. Utopian programmes overlap with adversarial programmes in that they both involve a protest against existing conditions and an aspiration towards a better social order. Utopian programmes, however, are relentless in their pursuit of comprehensive social reconstruction. They seek to create a new rather than an improved social order based on religious teaching, feminist principles, egalitarianism or environmentalism. Programmes that are dogmatic in legitimation and autocratic in teaching style also pursue static goals. Religious conversion is concerned in its procedures with the most effective strategy for winning the maximum number to its world-view and for guaranteeing orthodoxy of belief and action. Cultural and religious induction are equally concerned with the efficiency of their socialization procedures. Neither see any necessity to question the change they are seeking to bring about. While counter positions or the anxieties and doubts of participants may be entertained and incorporated into the programme, this will be with a view to making the learning experience more real and 'client-centered'. In such cases, any openness to doubts about the validity of the goals being pursued is a feature of the strategy of change rather than a manifestation of a diluted commitment.

It is easiest to recognize the patterned and educative nature of programmes where participants meet at a set time, for an agreed period of interaction, in the same location, to follow planned courses of study, under the direction of an established leader, with a view to submitting their learning to independent scrutiny. O'Rahilly's workers' courses are in this mould. There the intention was to provide access to established educational institutions for those who had experienced educational disadvantage in their youth. The 150 hours scheme and the literacy campaigns deviate in their own ways from this conventional mould in the manner in which they vary the designation of appropriate content, the cultivation of motivation and the organization of learning. Nonetheless, what emerges is by way of variation rather than disruption of patterned educative action. Even those programmes of change considered in this overview which seem far removed from mainstream educational institutions can be seen to incorporate some of the generic features of educational activity: a notion of ultimate goals, short-term objectives, learning strategies, motivational techniques, resources and evaluation. This is the case with the diffuse organization of personal learning which we have seen to be associated with the selected examples of environmental and peace movements. There we find auto-didactic, experiential and therapeutic learning styles, resources that include protests, debates, campaigns and marches, and self- and peer-evaluation.

Some of the contexts of the socially-committed programmes surveyed above have a structural inequality built into their relationships. Where there are parental or teaching roles involved this is most evident. Disparities of position, age, experience, and knowledge are the basis on which differentials of power are justified in such instances. Those who know transfer knowledge to those who don't, those who have reached adulthood initiate others, the experienced guide and advise the inexperienced. In such instances the unequal nature of the relationship — some designated to teach, initiate, guide and direct, others to be taught, initiated, guided and directed — is culturally unremarkable to the participants. The transaction is perceived to be in the best interest of those who occupy the subordinate positions. Those with power are expected to be using it to serve the needs of whoever has been entrusted to them. Of course, even within the most conventional versions of these roles this provides only the crudest of sketches of the complexities involved. And it is certainly possible to point to parenting styles, child-centered education and adult-to-adult learning encounters in which such disparities of power are less pronounced, and where the flow of learning and change is not so obviously one-sided. Many involved in socially-committed programmes would contend that their encounters are open, free-flowing and democratic and embody nothing of the disparities of power which characterise more conventional learning relationships. This contention may well be ideological. The empowerment aspirations of literacy programmes, the harmony evoked by environmentalism, the compromize of peace education and the collaborative ideals of emancipatory action lie uneasily with even a hint of inequality among those involved. And, yet, wherever there is a commitment to change society through educative action the qualities of single-mindedness, leadership, resourcefulness and perseverance are likely to be such among the initiators that, even on the basis of personal attributes alone, they will find themselves with more control over the participants than they can immediately recognize.

All of these examples of socially-committed programmes considered have a broader agenda of objectives beyond the immediate change they are structured to cultivate among the participants. In this sense they are instrumental — they are a means to an end. This takes a number of forms and is evident in their focus, orientation, objectives, clientele and approaches to social change. While all involved individualistic learning in that they seek to assist in the acquisition of educational qualifications, reading and writing skills, personal attributes and a wider range of knowledge, this is not their terminal objective. The qualifications, knowledge, skills and personal development are for a purpose beyond the benefit and enhancement of the individual involved. At its narrowest, this took the form of families improving their socio-economic position; at its broadest it encompassed the principles by which humanity at large resolves its disagreements and regulates its technological development. With such social ends in view, some programmes build a collective emphasis into their educative strategy: group projects, workshops, team teaching, collaborative learning, and the sharing of experience. Others rely on the knock-on impact of individualistic change — by way of improvement, ripple-effect, change agent, redirection — on the organizations, communities, classes or families to which those who experience change belong. The instrumental character of programmes can also be differentiated in terms of their target groups. Those who are designated as the object of educative action may include humanity at large, as with the activities of social movements, a sub-group within society such as women, a particular class, or a community. Finally, the intention may be, on the one hand, to alter society in certain of its dimensions or, on the other, to fundamentally reform it.

Issues and questions

Having established the identity of the social interaction which we are seeking to analyse and isolated and exemplified its defining characteristics, it is now necessary to anticipate the issues, of a broadly sociological nature, which arise in relation to these programmes and which are to form the subject matter of this book. In all, there are three categories of issues — individualist, structuralist and ideological — that need to be confronted. These arise organically from socially-committed programmes in that any of the participants who might care to consider their experiences in seeking to influence others or in being the object of such attempts should be capable of recognizing their significance. They should emerge in the light of reflection on lived experience. They are also particularistic manifestations of universal concerns within the social sciences. These concerns range widely and involve much that is contested and controversial within social theory.

There is a pronounced emphasis on the individual in socially-committed programmes. They emerge as people-driven and people-centered. One is struck by the strength of personality and conviction demonstrated by those who initiate and lead socially-committed programmes. They display an urgency in their single-minded pursuit of their desire to change society. Underpinning this conviction and single-mindedness is an obvious confidence in the capacity of individuals to change society. Individual action, its scope, influence and limitations, immediately presents itself as an issue. Since the contribution of human agency to social change is disputed in social theory there is a vast corpus of theoretical analysis that can be brought to bear on this issue. In this sense, the exploration of the role of individual action within socially-committed programmes has a contribution, way beyond its immediate context, to make to the explication of these sociological concerns. And if individual action has any significance in this regard it also represents an invitation to those who work with others to change society to consider how their biographies, theories, values and world-views pervade their practice.

Structuralism is the counter position to the centrality of individual action in sociological theory. In positing the dominance of structure in explaining social change, individuals are relegated to a circumscribed status. In some versions of structural theory they can emerge as puppet-like, as mere epiphenomena of underlying forces which shape their behaviour. Individuals are variously perceived to be conditioned, impelled by or reflective of such forces as language, thought-forms, psychological orientations, and recurring and patterned interaction. If change occurs it is mediated through them and not caused by them. Are the strong personalities who lead, and the participants who are presented as central in socially-committed programmes, little more than mediators — conduits through which the influence of structural forces realize themselves in the shaping of social life? Are they deluded in assuming that they are free agents seeking to direct the future shape of humanity and of the world by means of educative action among their fellow human beings? Are they, despite their leadership and initiative, as entrapped as those whom they commit themselves to redeeming, improving, empowering, emancipating or liberating?

Such is the nature of socially-committed programmes that the classic educational question as to what knowledge is of most worth has been resolved. The learning which a programme seeks to facilitate is predicated on the social change which constitutes the ultimate objective of its educative action. This is frequently associated with a lack of reflexivity in relation to the task in hand. The concern is with strategy — how to change people and society — rather than with establishing the legitimacy of the programme's objectives. And, yet, objectives aren't always as they immediately seem. Some programmes such as literacy schemes are recognizable by the skills which they seek their participants to master. But literacy programmes in developing countries embody a wider agenda of objectives — health, community development, agricultural improvement, political action — beyond the cultivation of reading and writing skills. Is there a possibility of entrapment whereby participants find themselves involved in learning experiences which fundamentally differ from what initially attracted them to the programme? And are the strategies of personal formation such that the autonomy of the participants is threatened or compromized? Unproblematic, taken-for-granted knowledge, an absence of reflection, entrapment and personal autonomy all arise in considering the relationship between ideology, consciousness and social action. Some versions of ideology define it in terms of false consciousness, as an understanding of one's social situation which confirms one's subordinate position and strengthens and legitimizes established power structures. In this view, ideology is identified with misrecognition, delusion and unscientific knowledge. Exploitation is implied as is the centrality of consciousness-raising in any efforts at intervention. Even the most benign interpretations of ideology see it as the socially-interested meanings attached to phenomena. This involves the proposition that consciousness about reality is influenced by one's social situation together with the suggestion that ideology acts to the benefit and advantage of some and not of others. Socially-committed programmes pursuing contradictory world-views nonetheless regard themselves as transmitting true and valid understandings of society. They are equally confident about their special vantage point on society. Accordingly, the same set of learning experiences can be regarded as exploitation or entrapment by some and liberation, empowerment and emancipation by others. Clearly, there is much about socially-committed programmes that needs to be ideologically interrogated.

These three sets of issues — individualist, structuralist, and ideological — are not discrete groupings but rather represent different perspectives on the same or similar experiences. Their strength lies in what they define as problematic, in the questions they ask and in the categories of analysis they bring to bear on socially-committed programmes. In pursuing the analysis with these issues in mind, six key questions about seeking to change people in a socially-committed way are posed.

- How do people come to be committed to the active pursuit of a particular kind of change? What are the origins of personal conviction, be it in relation to religion, politics, the economy, gender, language or the environment, and what are the forces that translate these convictions into an activist commitment to change people and society in the direction of desired ends? Are there psychological predispositions to commitment? What is the significance of parental orientation and educational experience? What contribution do the diffuse socializing encounters of lived experience make? And is there a role to be found for flashpoints in one's biography which represent a turning point in politicization such that one is impelled in a particular ideological direction?
- How visible is the underpinning logic of the motivation to bring about change? Are the intentions of the programme declared? Are participants aware of the guiding philosophy of the encounters involved? Assumptions of neutrality often disguise ideology. Professionalism can obscure power, interest and the ability to define the needs of others. Some statements of intent can be at such a level of generality that they are useless in prescribing or evaluating action. And even where the objectives are made explicit, participants aren't always equally placed to fully appreciate their implications.
- What is the epistemic status of the desired change, the substance of which can range across religious, political and social dogma, leadership skills, self-awareness and a host of personality characteristics? How can the differentation of this substance be conceptualized in such a way as to draw attention to the kinds of claims that are made for the desired change and for the implications that follows for the psychological modification of participants? And what conditions of socialization are required by such diverse varieties of epistemic and psychological formation?
- How is the legitimacy of the programme established? To be credible a programme must establish the authority of its agents and the validity of its world-view, and continue to maintain this status as long as it seeks to influence people. What kinds of appeals are used — legal authority, expertise,

truthfulness etc. — and do they vary in the light of the epistemic character of a programme? In justifying their agents and their activities, what demands do programmes make on participants in terms of affective engagement, suspension of rationality and the ceding to others of the entitlement to identify one's needs?

- What is the associative character of the learning encounters that feature in the programme? How are participants required to relate to one another in a manner that acknowledges shared interests, facilitates bonding or encourages disengagement from others? Is there an exhortation to mobilize and engage in social action? What mechanisms are used by programmes to manage the transition of participants from one associative status to another?
- How is dysfunctional response from participants coped with? In what manner are expressions of doubt, disbelief, rejection, role distance or incapacity interpreted? Are they accorded credibility, confronted as threats or dismissed as irritants? How might dysfunctional response be contained in such a manner as to reduce its subversive effect on the programme's activities and objectives?

These six questions relating to socially-committed programmes are (with apologies to Pirandello) in search of an answer. To this end, Chapters 2 through 7 address those questions in turn. In the light of this, the conclusion returns us to the issues of human agency, structural forces and ideology which allow us to raise the autonomy and empowerment of participants as topics worthy of the concern of those who initiate and enact socially-committed programmes.

As if to underscore the point made earlier in this chapter about the guillotining of questions of this nature in the treatment of socially-committed programmes, Charters and Hilton's (1989) authoritative comparative study of adult education excluded them as meaningful issues. This was a study of eight 'landmark' adult education programmes in a wide range of developed countries 'significant in and of themselves', but of such an order of magnitude and generalizability that they deserve a wider knowledge and understanding. A specific protocol was followed in the analysis of each programme. This included the identification of needs, mission and objectives, historical background, cultural considerations, principal players/facilitators, operational aspects and evaluation, influence and impact. The perspective of the client, considered individually or as a target group, was at best submerged, at worst ignored. None of the six questions posed above figure in the protocol.

Parameters and perspectives

Before we commence on the exploration of these questions a number of brief observations, in some cases involving the heightening and affirming of earlier emphases and disclaimers, need to be made relating to the parameters and perspectives of the analysis.

Firstly, the study is focused on programmes directed at adults. However, attempts to use the formation of younger people as a mechanism of social change are introduced, largely to make a telling point, where they provide apt, evocative or clear examples of a specific process or phenomenon important in adult-centered socially-committed learning programmes.

Secondly, within a sociological framework the method of inquiry is qualitative. It seeks to be humanistic, naturalistic, non-intrusive and interpretive rather than experimental, positivistic and predictive (see Walker, 1985).

Thirdly, the perspective of the client is central. Olsson, usually credited with being the father of the Swedish study circle movement, coined the expression 'for the people, through the people' (Rubenson, 1989). The aspiration of this study is to reclaim the participant's subjectivity as a focus of moral concern rather than as an object to be acted upon or acted through.

Fourthly, it isn't the desire of the study to arbitrate on the validity of the objectives of the socially-committed programmes isolated for attention or on the credibility of their ideological presuppositions. Gurvitch's (1971, pp. 10–11) warning has been heeded:

> the sociologist of knowledge must never pose the problem of validity and value of signs, symbols, concepts, ideas and judgments that he meets in the social reality being studied. He must only ascertain the effect of their presence, combination and effective function ... To deduce an epistemology from the sociology of knowledge would be as ill-fated as to link the fate of the sociology of knowledge to a particular philosophical position.

This is a crucial disclaimer given the nature of the analysis that follows. Gurvitch advises sociologists to remain modest and renounce inordinate pretension. It is hoped that such a disposition pervades the inquiry.

2   The biography of commitment

Introduction

What are the origins of personal conviction, be it in relation to religion, politics, the economy, gender, language or the environment? And what are the forces that translate these convictions into an activist commitment to change people and, through them, society in the direction of desired ends? Is there such a psychological propensity as a predisposition to commitment irrespective of its social focus or ideological character, or is commitment context-specific, a response that is evoked by the nature of a particular issue? What is the significance of parental and family orientation? Is there an independent educational influence in terms of general school ethos or specific programmes or personnel? Is lived experience, with its diffuse and unsystematic socializing encounters, the key to explaining the extent to which people seek to 'create history' as opposed to being content to 'live in history'? And what is the role of 'flashpoints' — experiences, events and conflicts in one's biography which represent a turning point in insight, reflection or politicization such that one is impelled in a particular ideological direction?

If there was a possibility of reducing such committed activism to a set of distinct behavioural and ideological specifications the approach to answering these questions could more easily be mapped out. From the overview of typifications of socially-committed programmes, however, we have seen that such commitment is to be found in the service of the full spectrum of ideological positions, involving material and transcendental realms, and ranging from broad world-views to relatively small-scale social adjustment, realignment or equilibrium. Moreover, our concern is with programmes which use educative action as a means of achieving such objectives. The social phenomenon under consideration, therefore, is both specialized, in its focus on learning, and diverse, in the range and ideology of its content. There is, therefore, no single recognized body of research or even research tradition that can be drawn upon to situate and explain the origins of whatever contexts, roles or predispositions which distinguish those who take the initiative, show leadership or participate in directing socially-committed programmes. What Rejai and Phillips (1983, p.38) had to say in their study of the personality of revolutionary leaders is likely to be also true of this more diversified commitment, and for similar reasons. 'No single motivation or dynamic is sufficient to explain the formation of all revolutionary personalities', they argue. Yet, the mix of forces is unlikely to be unpatterned and endlessly and randomly variant. The experiences, agencies, dispositions that are likely to be worthy of attention, together with the dynamics of their interaction, must first be identified. Later, in adopting a biographical approach, an attempt will be made to construct a typology of commitment in terms of the sources and dynamics of its formation over the lifespan. In advancing this analysis it will be necessary to look at the formation of commitment as a general orientation and at the dispositions and skills which are likely to be associated with it, and not exclusively at the formation of those who would use educative action as a means of changing the social order.

Socialization to commitment

Since the questions we have posed in relation to the formation of commitment are essentially political ones, in that they deal with relations of power, the control of material and symbolic resources and the direction a society takes, the answers must first be sought in the study of political socialization in its wider interpretation. Following Greenstein, a narrow understanding of political socialization refers to 'the deliberate inculcation of political information, values and practices by instructional agents who have been formally charged with this responsibility'; at the broader level it can be taken to mean 'all political learning, formal and informal, deliberate and unplanned, in every stage of the life cycle, including not only explicitly political learning but also nominally non-political learning, of politically-relevant personality characteristics' (quoted in O'Sullivan, 1973). It should be immediately obvious that such a broad definition extends political socialization almost to the limits of general socialization. Literacy, analytical and critical skills, a facility for compromize or an inclination for confrontation, and capacities for empathy, loyalty or leadership can all merit inclusion. This shouldn't surprize since families, communities and schools are political systems in microcosm, and the type of learning that routinely occurs in these settings is likely to activate skills and dispositions which are relevant in the broader political arenas.

This wide-ranging interpretation of political socialization is appropriate in the designation of the dispositions, skills, agencies and dynamics which need to be considered in attempting to understand the formation of the committed person. It incorporates predictable issues such as the formation of one's orientation towards political forms. For some, this orientation realizes itself in a capacity to engage in explicit political debate. Political ideologies are embraced or rejected. Parties, groupings and movements are joined or supported. Personal positions are justified, be they in relation to the role of the state, the freedom of individuals, the distribution of resources or the allocation of ownership and power. For others, political orientation operates at a more affective level. Emotions, loyalties or hostilities are evoked. The slogans of a political ideology may be a sufficient stimulus to excitement. Or, as the poet Jerry Murphy (1993) tersely illustrates in a poem entitled Headgear of the Tribe, referring to Northern Ireland, symbols can be equally effective.

> Brits on the pavement
> ice on the wind,
> my mother is knitting
> my first balaclava.

But this interpretation also encourages us to think beyond formal political institutions and ideologies and address the central element in the political dimension of everyday life—power to influence others, determine the nature of social relationships and shape the future of society. This results in the consideration of many types of formation — religious, family advancement, environmentalist — which would not routinely be labelled as political but which, upon inspection, incorporate the processes of power. The fact that such power processes can deploy coercive and instrumental controls which are readily transparent, as well as normative and symbolic controls that are more opaque, not alone adds to the complexity of the political dimension of social relationships but it also results in variations in its visibility to participants in a social encounter. The operation of power can frequently go unremarked in relationships between people, in families, social movements and organizations, and participants vary in their inclination and alertness in recognizing its existence. Desiring, seeking out, establishing and maintaining power are recurring processes in the biographies of those who wish to regulate the development of others and reshape society or some aspect of it.

As well as alerting us to the operation of power throughout society and the importance of understanding how a need for power is linked to commitment, the wider interpretation of political socialization also focuses attention on the personality traits and social skills which are associated with commitment in an individual's make up. Those who display singular attachment to a particular social objective, to the extent that they invest considerable time and energy in its pursuit, in some cases risking personal, economic or physical hardship, are unlikely to be introverted, indecisive, reflective, socially and politically cynical, or lacking in self-confidence or assertiveness. Activist, goal-directed, relentless in their definitions of reality, truth and justice, they are likely to be the antithesis of the caution, fallibility and doubt exemplified in the following caricature of the intellectual in Umberto Eco's (1980) *The Name of the Rose*:

'But then. . . ' I ventured to remark, 'you are still far from the solution. . . '
'I am very close to one', William said, 'but I don't know which.'
'Therefore you don't have a single answer to your questions?'
'Adso, if I did I would teach theology in Paris.'
'In Paris do they always have the true answer?'
'Never,' William said, 'but they are very sure of their errors.'
'And you,' I said with childish impertinence, 'never commit errors?'
'Often,' he answered. 'But instead of conceiving only one, I imagine many, so I become the slave of none' (p.306).

In the wider view, also, since political socialization is something that occurs in a variety of social settings—family, playground, school, church, mass-media, voluntary associations—there is a need to assess the contribution made by such agencies or occasions of socialization to the formation of the committed person. This is less a question of quantifying the significance of each agency, even if that were possible and desirable. What is required is the qualitative evaluation of the type of formation peculiar to the family, school, mass-media etc. For instance, are broad orientations more likely to be formed in the home, more specific objectives in voluntary associations and a range of relevant skills and dispositions in the school? Are distinct experiences provided by different agents and are some types of people more amenable to particular agents? What Almond and Verba (1963, p.270) have to say about the possibility of understanding the formation of general political attitudes is also valid for our awareness of the cultivation of commitment: 'clearly many types of experience can affect basic political attitudes and the experiences can come at a variety of times... If political attitudes are not simply derived from one source, we can at least attempt to find what sources appear most significant and for what sorts of people, and what combinations of experiences are most closely associated with particular types of political attitudes'.

The aspirations to prediction in this quotation from Almond and Verba are as ambitious as I would wish to be in understanding the formation of commitment. There is the assumption of 'lawfulness' in the socialization process while at the same time there is an implicit distancing from a deterministic stance on what the end product of any particular combination of socializing experiences might be. Commitment doesn't just happen to develop. It is assumed that there is an order in human development that lies beyond the comprehension of the individual. Reliance on the explicit beliefs and intentions of individuals is considered to be insufficient to explain 'regularities in the antecedents and consequences of their actions' (McPherson and Raab, 1988, p.22). But, neither is it in keeping with the nature of human beings or the complexity of social processes to assume that all that is required to predict adult behaviour is a 'synchronization of development' (Merelman, 1972) in research on socialization.

A biographical approach

Traditionally, socialization has been defined as the preparation for the successful performance of adult roles, with the adequacy of one's performance in occupational, family, civic and social spheres constituting the ultimate test of socialization (Clausen, 1968). Society was seen as imposing itself on this process in numerous ways, particularly by establishing norms in relation to physical, cognitive, emotional and social development (Inkeles, 1969). Psychologists such as Havighurst (1953, p.2) sought to identify the tasks that need to be mastered at various critical stages in the cumulative process of socialization towards adulthood if 'unhappiness in the individual, disapproval by society and difficulties with later tasks' were to be avoided. A number of writers have criticized the one-sidedness of this approach, arguing that it incorporated an unduly passive view of the socializee. Danziger (1971, p.14), in his review of socialization research, contends that 'socialization is usually thought of as something that happens to or is done to the individual — the focus is not on the active shaping of his life by the individual but on the plasticity and passivity of the individual in the face of social influences'. Wrong's article 'The oversocialized conception of man' (1961) appears as a seminal source of resistance to the image of the person as someone who is completely moulded by society. Having reacted against such abstractions as economic, political, sexual or libidinal, and religious man, it would be ironic, he argued, if sociology were to contribute to the reification of yet another abstraction, that of 'socialized man'. Wrong was to be repeatedly quoted over the years, particularly as theoretical innovations within sociology conceived of the person as an active and creative participant in social life.

Theoretically, socialization has been inextricably linked with the debate in sociology relating to the structural-functional perspective and its alternatives. Durkheim (1956), with whom this perspective is classically identified, defined the school's function as the 'methodical socialization of the young generation' (p.71). For him, society, which is larger than the sum of people who go to make it up, constrains and directs the behaviour of individuals.

> When I perform my duties as a brother, a husband or a citizen and carry out the commitments I have entered into, I fulfil obligations which are defined in law and custom and which are external to myself

and my actions...The system of signs that I employ to express my thoughts, the monetary system I use to pay my debts, the credit instruments I utilise in my commercial relationships, the practices I follow in my profession etc. — all function independently of the use I make of them (Durkheim, 1982, pp. 50–51).

As well as positing the independent existence of society, a consensus was said to prevail in relation to basic values. Socialization contributed to social cohesion and stability through the integration of children and young people into the world of adult roles. Criticism of Durkheim's legacy in the study of personal development refers to its passive view of the socializee, peripheral consideration of social change, celebration of the status quo, and its failure to acknowledge the reality of differentiation or conflict in society. In consequence, socialization as a concept is frequently identified with conservative ideologies.

Of the theoretical perspectives which emerged in a turning away from structural functionalism, phenomenological and symbolic interactionist perspectives are most relevant to the study of socialization. Central to the phenomenological approach is the thesis that such everyday realities as concepts, roles, and institutions are socially constructed, i.e. they are human products created by people. Phenomenological sociology is a sociology of subjective meaning, and in its application to socialization theory and research the effect has been to establish the socializee as subject as well as object (Dreitzel, 1973). Symbolic interactionism is concerned with the manner in which meanings for gestures, social positions, behaviour etc. are transmitted and negotiated in social interaction. It contends that it is by means of such processes that individuals are 'linked to, shaped by and in turn create, social structure' (Denzin, 1971). In contrast to structuralism, phenomenology and symbolic interactionism stress the active participation in socialization of the individual.

In warning against the oversocialized concept of the person Wrong was drawing attention to the limitations of the structural interpretation of human formation in terms of its stress on the forces of society and their uncontested shaping of the individual. Yet, since all actors operate within inherited cultures, linguistic systems, families and peer groups there is an equal danger of adopting an autonomous, voluntaristic understanding of the actor in a social situation as someone who is free to reinterpret and change society. For Archer (1989, p.x), the problem of structure and agency is not just a theoretical issue in the understanding of society or a technical complication in the analysis of social action. It is 'the most pressing social problem of the human condition'. This is because, she argues, 'it is part and parcel of daily experience to feel both free and enchained, capable of shaping our own future and yet confronted by towering, seemingly-impersonal, constraints'. She draws the following implications for personal action:

> Those whose reflection leads them to reject the grandiose delusion of being puppet-masters but also to resist the supine conclusion that they are mere marionettes then have the same task of reconciling this experiential ambivalence, and must do so if their moral choice is not to become inert or their 'political' action ineffectual.

The *zeitgeist* of one's time is important. Sometimes, an era stresses individuality and the power of human agency, at other times the conditioning and constraining of individuals. Post-war existentialism with its emphasis on individual freedom, responsibility for one's actions and self-creation can be contrasted with Foucault's thesis on 'the death of man': 'to all those who still wish to talk about man... to all those who wish to take him as their starting point... who refuse to think without immediately thinking that it is man who is thinking, to all those warped and twisted forms of reflection we can answer only with a philosophical laugh' (Foucault, 1973, pp. 342–343).

By adopting a biographical perspective on the formation of commitment it is possible to take a holistic approach to socialization. This has a number of desirable features and seems to be particularly appropriate to the study of commitment. The behaviours isolated for attention are grounded in their social context where they are best understood in terms of their antecedents, full range of social forces and their consequences. Since the chronology is lifespan, it is possible to observe regularities and recurring patterns over a lengthy period of development. The experience of the participant is recognized with due attention to willfulness, motivation and contestation. The classical positivist ambition 'to known in order to predict in order to control' is of lesser concern than the desire to understand the processes involved in all their complexity, irregularity and contradiction. It is quite likely, for instance, that those who display commitment through action and participation in programmes are the exceptions to whatever predictions might be extracted from less rounded analyses. Not all those who are well placed in terms of personality traits, skills and dispositions commit themselves to influencing others and changing society. Not all those who so commit themselves are fully or adequately prepared for the task. Above all, the biographical approach is accommodating towards the influence of both social structure and human agency, and allows the realities of restraint and freedom, limitation and potential, inertia and energy, passivity and action to be juxtaposed in the light of lived experience throughout the lifespan.

Linear commitment

It is possible to discern a linear pattern of socialization in the biographies of some activists. Their commitment can be traced back to the values of their parents, the environment of influences which they created for them, as well as to more self-selected socializing experiences. This influence can be general or specific. Parents may cultivate general dispositions of a liberal, conservative and atheistic or religious orientation. Or, families may be single-minded in their attachment to a specific cause.

Where such parents have available to them a sufficiently wide range of school types they can choose a school ethos supportive of their value orientations. Such an ethos will be reflected, where possible, in the curriculum, the role models, the extra-curricular activities and in the hidden curriculum of social learning, implicit meanings and valued or excluded orientations. Clearly, school-based enhancement of family socialization is more likely to occur at the level of general rather than specific dispositions. Where this confluence of socialization occurs during the formative years it can result in a stable and set realm of values, meanings and people constituting one's social and ideological world. By the time the young person experiences a more open environment, and is exposed to contrary values and role models, their invalidity and negative status will have been established and rationalized. Indeed, such competing influences may well serve to confirm the validity of one's formation. Most likely, socializing experiences into adulthood will be shaped through self-selection in the choice of friends, mass-media consumption and voluntary associations.

It is important to incorporate the distinction between geno-typic continuity, phenotypic continuity and complete continuity (Kagan, 1969) in tracing the linear formation of the committed person.

Genotypic continuity exists when the underlying psychological processes remain stable but the form of the behaviour changes. Rokeach (1960), in his work on dogmatism, on the notion of the open and closed mind, draws attention to the fact that authoritarianism and intolerance are not just to be found among fascists, anti-semitics and members of the Ku Klux Klan. He points out that dogmatism can be observed among individuals ranging from left to right, among those who are religious and anti-religious and in the academic and business worlds. For Rokeach, the closed-minded individual has a dogmatic way of making sense of belief systems irrespective of their content, is rigid in opinion and belief, and is authoritarian and intolerant towards those who hold contra-dictory beliefs. Such a person may at one time be attracted to a right-wing organization because of its authoritarian structure; at another time, the appeal of religious conviction and certainty may lead to the pursuance of goals ranging from social rescue to the radical liberation of disadvantaged people.

With phenotypic continuity the behaviour remains stable but it is in response to a varying set of motives or needs. Behaviour can be maintained for long periods of time by social reward and punishment despite significant shifts in underlying psychological characteristics. Likewise, one motive may initiate a particular pattern of behaviour but a different motive may maintain it. The active participation in a social movement committed to a particular ideology may result from the experience of family-based socialization into social and political belief; involvement may persist, despite a waning of personal conviction about the guiding ideology of the movement, due to social attachments, solidarity needs and personal loyalty. Throughout, there may be no obvious break in participation or enthusiasm.

Complete continuity is said to occur when both psychological processes and overt behaviour are stable over time. Kagan estimates that this type of stability is most likely to occur after puberty when the pace of change in the basic components of personality is slowing down since 'the motives for group acceptance and mastery have become established and the desire to match behaviour to internalized standards is usually strong by early adolescence. With complete continuity the regulatory power of role expectations and the impulsion of psychological characteristics proceed evenly and in tandem.

In Andrews' (1991) study of sustained commitment throughout the life-cycle, *Lifetimes of Commitment*, fifteen British socialist activists were interviewed at a time when they ranged between the ages of seventy and ninety. Two of these, Walter Gregory, author of *The Shallow Grave: A Memoir of the Spanish Civil War*, and communist Rose Kerrigan approximate, in Andrews' (1991, pp. 79–81) description of their ideological formation, to a linear pattern of political socialization.

Walter Gregory's first political activity was, as a ten year old, pushing Labour Party pamphlets through neighbours' letter-boxes. Born in 1912 into a working-class, trade unionist background his family experienced chronic economic hardship. His father was to suffer long-term unemployment as a result of being blacklisted because of his strong trade unionism. The Workers' Educational Association provided for his more formal political education and he subsequently participated in groupings such as the National Unemployed Workers' Movement, the No More War Movement and the Communist Party. Having fought with the International Brigade in the Spanish Civil War he became very active in trade union affairs. In retirement he travelled widely speaking on behalf of the International Brigade Association.

Born to working-class, socialist parents in Glasgow in 1903, Rose Kerrigan also experienced extreme economic hardship as a child. Her father lost his job because he was regarded as too outspoken. She participated in the Glasgow Rent Strike, encouraging her neighbours to take part, at the age of twelve. Having left school at the age of fourteen, she attended a socialist Sunday School. She met her husband through a socialist group to which she belonged. They were both members of the Communist Party, he becoming one of the leaders. There were political visits to Russia and support for the Spanish republican cause. At the time of interview, Rose acted on the chair of her local pensioners' rights group and was also active in CND.

Both of these accounts suggest complete continuity in political formation, engagement and activism whereby psychological orientations and social roles mutually reinforce one another to maintain a political consistency throughout the lifespan. In fact, Andrews' overview of the biographies of her fifteen respondents and the manner of their 'growing into socialism' provides a perceptive description of linear socialization to commitment:

> Development in the lives of the respondents has not been marked by a radical reorganization of their belief systems. They have not 'outgrown', but grown into the very principles which they endorsed as young adults. The development in their lives, thus, can be best described as change within constancy; their growth can be charted by an examination of the ways in which their political concepts have become more complex through years of experience (p.174).

When linear socialization is at its most effective the tenets of one's world-view can assume a hegemonic status and be perceived to constitute the limits of normality and common sense. Those who don't share this world-view are likely to be judged to be ill-informed, deluded, narrow, and regarded as either opponents or suitable subjects for conversion or rehabilitation.

Sectoral commitment

Commitment can also be experienced in terms of sectoral socialization. This occurs when a particular agency of socialization is responsible in a special way for the commitment. The contribution of other agents is at most non-contradictory. The family is particularly well placed to exercize a lasting influence on a person's formation. This is because of the extent of the contact, almost exclusive during the early years, the high emotional intensity of the relationships involved, and the right of parents to regulate the experiences of their children. Among the various formative agencies to be considered under sectoral commitment, the family is an obvious starting point and has accordingly received the greatest attention in any attempts to explain the origins of a great diversity of adult dispositions and behaviours. As Langton (1969, pp. 22–23) concluded in his review of research on political socialization, 'political loyalty, patriotism, national heroes and devils are all seen as developing early in life', and 'there is little doubt that parents have a profound impact on the formation of certain political orientations'.

The most explicit statement of the formative power of family influences comes from the 'national character' research tradition. Kardiner (1945), an influential representative of this tradition, argued that most of the institutions of a society are a reflection of the national personality type produced by characteristic patterns of child-rearing. If you wish to change society, he argued, you should change its child-rearing practices. Explaining political culture in terms of national character, and its formation through the experiences of children within the family, has proved to be attractive, and a considerable amount of research exists in many countries. The acceptance of authoritarianism in political cultures such as Germany is said to derive from the emphasis on authority in German families, and respect for and unquestioning dispositions towards parents and others in positions of authority. American families, on the other hand, are said to be more receptive to the democratic participation of children in family discussions and decision making (Almond and Verba, 1963). In France, Belgium and the Netherlands a distrust in politicians and a feeling that political activity is ineffectual has been attributed to parents who regulate their children's social contacts and who closely control their emotional development. The fact that this pattern was stronger in France and Belgium than in the Netherlands may contribute to the negative political attitudes allegedly found among French and Belgium adults (Langton, 1969, p.25).

Should it be possible to establish a predisposition to commitment in terms of personal traits, it is likely to be derived from individual needs and orientations originating within the family. Rejai and Phillips (1983), in their analysis of the personality traits of over a hundred revolutionary leaders throughout history and across different political systems, isolated such dispositions as vanity, egotism, narcissism, nationalism as well as a sense of justice, mission, relative deprivation and status inconsistency. They identify two essential personal characteristics — a mental set that propels them towards revolutionary action and a set of verbal and organizational skills which help them to perform the task. They point out, however, that the emergence of revolutionary leaders is due to both dispositional and contextual factors. Their approach to explanation, 'combines trait theories of leadership with situational theories' (p.40).

Mead's (1934) symbolic interactionist approach provides a more integrated perspective on personal formation. In Mead's analysis of the processes of socialization he draws attention to the role of significant others in the formation of one's personal identity. Significant others are those with whom children have most contact in the early years, those who provide for their physical needs and those who supply the emotional supports of affection and security. In most cases these are parents, siblings and the immediate kin of the child.

Mead describes how it is in relation to these significant others that the child initially learns to adopt the attitude of the other, taking on their verbal, facial or emotional responses to a particular action or event even to the point of acting out the response in the form of a skit or cameo. Later, as this process becomes more substantial and routinized, the child can be seen to take the role of the other. A crucial point is reached when the significant others assume the status of representatives of more universal expectations, obligations and morals which in turn are internalized as standards derived from the wider society. Mead resolves the problems of voluntarism, subjectivity and determinism by distinguishing between the *I* and the *Me*. The *Me* refers to the socially-formed dimension of the person, what has been internalized in interaction with significant others. The *I* is reflected in impulsive and spontaneous behaviour and represents the personal awareness of one's own sense of self.

In explaining the formation of identity, Mead attributes a central role to parents and others who have access to children during the early years. Berger and Berger (1976, p.69) put it well in their commentary on Mead's theory of socialization by using the image of internal conversations:

> Internalization not only controls the individual but opens up the world for him ... only by internalizing the voices of others can we speak to ourselves. If no one had significantly addressed us from outside, there would be a silence within ourselves as well. It is only through others that we can come to discover ourselves. Even more specifically, it is only through significant others that we can develop a significant relationship to ourselves. This, among other reasons, is why it is so important to choose one's parents with some care.

Furthermore, the meanings and messages from the significant others control the individual, not alone in the act of personal formation or opening up the world, but by doing so within parameters which are themselves regulatory: the world is comprehended and interpreted in the light of the organizing principles and meanings of the significant others.

If we are to rely on the results of empirical research, it is rare for educational institutions to exercize an independent influence on individual development in areas other than cognitive achievement and attainment in curricular-related bodies of knowledge and skill. This runs counter to a confidence in the school as a crucial agent of socialization to be found among those with a concern for personal and social improvement or with an attachment to ideologies. This confidence is reflected in the history of conflict over the control of education among political, linguistic, racial and religious groups, as well as in the existence of a wide range of interest groups advocating specific additions to the content of school curricula. Morrison and McIntyre (1971, p.174), in their review of research, conclude that 'there is virtually no evidence of a primary independent effect arising from education and most of the educational studies indicate that such effects as arise do so from individuals being in educational communities rather than from processes of school or further learning'.

Research across many countries has established an association between educational level and political behaviour and orientations (O'Sullivan, 1973). Almond and Verba (1963), for instance, in their five nations study reported that the more educated individual

- had more political information and a wider range of opinions on political subjects, and was most likely to follow politics and election campaigns;
- was more likely to engage in political discussion, and with a wider range of people;
- was more aware of the impact of government and was more likely to feel capable of influencing government;
- and was more likely to participate in organizations, and to express confidence in other people's trustworthiness and helpfulness.

The problem is how to isolate the impact of the school as distinct from home and social-class influences in explaining this association. Studies of the influence of civics courses have not been positive. The contribution of participation in school roles and extra-curricular activities is likely to be in relation to the cultivation of social trust and interpersonal and leadership skills. In shaping political orientations, ethos, social climate and tradition, particularly in third-level institutions, have emerged as the most likely independent educational influence (O'Sullivan, 1973).

Theorists who conceive of the role of schooling as social control see its contribution largely in terms of functional integration and legitimation. Some even consider the school to be particularly well placed for this task because of compulsory attendance and its public misrecognition as a neutral institution. Much of this is said to be achieved by means of the hidden curriculum of implicit meanings and social learning and adaptations relating to personality, merit and the individualization of educational success and failure. But its contribution is nonetheless considered to be a supportive one propping up the system of rewards and power that exists in society rather than having the capacity to direct change through personal formation.

The juxtaposition of the family and extra-family agents, as influences on personal formation, is provided in the biographies of George Bernard Shaw and Simone de Beauvoir in a manner that suggests the distinctive potential of particular sectors of socialization in the cultivation and orientation of commitment.

The philosophy of George Bernard Shaw, inveterate campaigner and supporter of diverse causes ranging from socialism and women's rights to hygienic dress, has been traced to his 'lost childhood' by his biographer Michael Holroyd (1988, p.19).

Shaw himself recalled that he had a 'devil of a childhood ... rich only in dreams, frightful and loveless in realities'. According to Holroyd, Shaw was unable to confront this bleakness directly. He coped with it by adopting his 'criticism of life', the technique through which 'he turned lack of love inside out and, by attracting from the world some of the attention he had been denied by his mother, conjured optimism out of deprivation' (p.17). He claimed, for instance, that he learned of the need for independence and self-sufficiency from the experience of uncaring parents. Such was the mutual disappointment of his parents that he suffered no illusions about family life. A lack of attention to his formal education left him with 'very little to unlearn', particularly in relation to moral and religious formation.

> He strove to bring the world into harmony with his lonely nature... his vision was complete in all but substance: he could see everything but touch little. For what he had done was not (as he claimed) to change dreaming into reality, but to replace the first loveless reality with one dream and then another (pp. 19–20).

Shaw was unable to entertain feelings of sadness or to engage in grieving. But Holroyd traced his fear of poverty and his campaigns against it to a death anxiety, and 'any sediment of apprehension was done away with a hygienic campaign against earth burial' (p.22).

The controversalist and campaigner, who in a letter to H.G. Wells in 1917 asserted that 'we must reform society before we can reform ourselves... personal righteousness is impossible in an unrighteous environment', found substance for his dreams in diverse sources ranging over books, groupings, ideologies, personalities and personal experience of social evils.

An experience that was said to have dominated his early years was the sight of the Dublin slums to which his nurse would bring him when she visited the tenements of her friends. Shaw recalled: 'I saw it and smelt it and loathed it'. According to Holroyd, 'Shaw's lifelong hatred of poverty was born of these lonely days of slumming. Poverty became a crime responsible not only for prostitution, but lovelessness' (p.27).

The London that Shaw moved to in 1876 is described by Holroyd as a 'City of Revelation' with its 'philosophical ruins' and 'pedants and prophets' including agnostics, atheists, anarchists, reformers of dress and diet, feminists and philanthropists (p.124). Having read *Das Kapital* in its french translation he described it as a turning point in his career, 'the only book that ever turned me upside down'.

> Marx was a revelation ... He opened my eyes to the facts of history and civilization, gave me an entirely fresh conception of the universe, provided me with a purpose and a mission in life.
> It achieved the greatest feat of which a book is capable—that of changing the minds of the people who read it (p.130).

Another publication, *Why are the Many Poor?*, introduced him to the Fabian Society, a group he considered to be appealing to the middle-class intelligentsia, 'my own class in fact' (p.131).

Dr Gustave Jaeger, who advocated woolen clothing on health grounds to facilitate 'the disposal of poisons in the body through the exhalations of the skin' (pp. 159–160), replaced the Svengali-like Vandeleur Lee, the music teacher who dazzled Shaw when he came to live with the Shaw family.

If Holroyd's interpretation is valid, Shaw's espousal of causes can be attributed to psychological needs formed in his early years. The underlying psychological impulsions—the search for love, managing anxieties, coping with reality—developed within the family with the effect that Shaw needed causes. With Shaw, a propensity to attach oneself to causes seemed to feature in his psychological make-up, and this orientation has been attributed to early experience within the family. This may well be the unique sectoral contribution of the family to the formation of commitment, with later influences accounting for the nature of the causes and campaigns through which psychological orientations are given a public realization and an ideological substance.

In her authoritative biography of Simone de Beauvoir, the author of the seminal feminist study *The Second Sex*, and the campaigner for a host of liberal and emancipatory causes, Deirdre Bair (1991) describes how her association with a student group 'resulted in the cementing of the most important friendship she made at the Sorbonne, the one which determined the outcome of the rest of her life' (p.127).

This group, including Jean-Paul Sartre, Paul Nisan and Rene Maheu, remained aloof from the general student body which they used as the target for their satire and derision. They confirmed their identity through the use of private nicknames and coded speech. They set themselves apart from the system by their selective attendance at lectures, and from the social mores by their libertarian lifestyle. According to Bair, de Beauvoir was 'fascinated by the bravery of their indifference to convention' and longed to be a member of their clique 'because it was the most authentic behaviour she had ever seen' (p.127).

Alongside their distinctive reputation was de Beauvoir's record of academic achievement which, despite her youth and sex, had involved accelerated progress and exceptional marks. Following a period of positioning, standoffishness and strategic moves, de Beauvoir was introduced to the group through an acquaintance who had weak links with it.

Maheu gave her the lasting nickname *Castor*, meaning the beaver, because of her prodigious work habits, following her efforts to persuade him to adopt a more serious attitude to his studies. Association with the group also involved setting her distance from others, such as the 'Holy Willies', a group at the École Normale Supérieure mocked because of their excessive piety and respect for priests.

Following a phase at the fringe of the group, she became more fully integrated into it and formed her lifelong association with

Sartre. She described their intellectual relationship of over fifty years as follows:

> Sartre was philosophically more creative than I, and it is in this respect that he had a great influence on me, because I didn't have a personal philosophy. I was interested in philosophical ideas and Sartre was creative and I quickly fell under the sway of his philosophy (quoted in Bair, 1991, p.144).

As Bair points out, de Beauvoir's repeated declaration that Sartre's intellect was superior to her own 'caused consternation and anger in equal parts among those who study her life and work', and that 'this is probably because she frequently describes herself in ways which would make it seem that she never had a thought or idea that was not first given to her by Sartre' (p.143). Sartre himself spoke of an equal rapport in which they mutually assisted in the shaping of each other's ideas.

What is beyond doubt is the impact on de Beauvoir's subsequent trajectory of ideas, political positions and relationships of integration into this distinctive group during her student days in her early twenties at the Sorbonne. But what equally needs to be acknowledged, and this complements the mix of forces in Shaw's formation, is that de Beauvoir came to the group from a background that included an influential atheistic father who encouraged her to take pride in her mind and who formed the basis for her ideal of an intellectual relationship, and at a time when she was searching for a personal philosophy.

Reactive commitment

For a variety of reasons, individuals can react against events, experiences or persons within their biographies to such an extent that they actively set themselves against whatever they consider to epitomize the target of their reaction. This response is frequently premised on a reevaluation of some aspect of their biography. As a result of a reassessment of a person, ideology or relationship the values and energies of the individual are redirected. This can occur in the light of learning which facilitates reflection and encourages a distancing from some earlier experience. Where this is associated with a sense of disillusionment, misguidance or betrayal the reaction is usually more assertive and strident. It can also be occasioned by the experience of inequality or discrimination either personally suffered or observed. In reactive commitment change usually occurs undramatically, the reassessment and response involving a slow awakening.

Reactive commitment can be as muted as the orientation of parents in *Education and the Working Class* who saw their careers retarded by the absence of qualifications, who believed they didn't belong in the social milieu in which circumstances had located them, and who felt their families had not achieved their rightful social standing. Where former priests or religious experience disillusionment the reaction against religious bodies, their distinctive strategies of formation and even the interpersonal relationships involved, can be quite bitter and confrontational. Revolutionaries and social and political activists can react similarly. In some cases, too, drawing on C.Wright Mills' (1970) distinction, private anguish, such as family conflict, abuse, alcoholism or drug addiction, can be reconstructed as a political issue resulting in lobbying, campaigning, advocacy, and in the activation of social movements and initiatives.

This latter variety of reactive commitment has been most comprehensively recorded and is well-represented in the biographies of social activists.

In her biographically-derived novel, *Mercy*, Andrea Dworkin (1992), the uncompromising campaigner against pornography and the sexual exploitation of women, has the central character, Andrea, utter the following at the age of nine years:

> I wasn't raped until I was almost ten which is pretty good it seems when I ask around... (p.5).

Later, at the age of twenty-seven she threatens:

> One day the women will burn down Time Square; I've seen it in my mind; I know; it's in flames. The women will come out of their houses from all over and they will riot and they will burn it down, raze it to the ground, it will be bare cement; and we will execute the pimps. No woman will ever be hurt there again; ever; again; it is a simple fact (p.328).

Erin Pizzey's (1978) response to her childhood and early family life, characterized by neglectful and unloving parents and a quarrelsome relationship between her aggressive father and a self-obsessed mother, found a more tangible form in the establishment of the Chiswick Women's Aid.

> I do realise that what happened to my mother created a need in me to give shelter to women and children and that gradually as I saw more and more men like my father my anger turned to compassion. One way of looking at my father's value as a human being is that as a result of his behaviour there is now refuge, not only in England but across the world...So what began as a destructive course in my life was changed into something creative and good (p.116).

The lived experience of rural poverty, with its associated evils of ill-health, family break-up, limited opportunity and social rejection, is a recurring point of reference in the radical social philosophy of Dr Noel Browne, a controversial Irish Minister for Health and an unrelenting critic of the conservatism of Irish society. In *Against the Tide* (1986) he recalls how his widowed mother, recognizing her terminal illness, sought to provide for her seven young children in the absence of state and kinship support. In desperation, she decided to take them to her eldest daughter, Eileen, in England, selling all their belongings to pay their fares.

> My mother had saved us just in time; within days of our arrival she lay in a coma ... The final humiliation of this proud, brave Mayo country girl still awaited her; she was buried in an unknown pauper's grave in London because Eileen could not afford anything better for the mother she so dearly loved (p.37).

Family disintegration followed and, for some members, the work-house, exploitation and early death.

As these instances would seem to indicate, reactive commitment has a context-specific origin. Those affected are likely to be attached to a cause rather than causes.

Flashpoint commitment

In *Satori in Paris*, Jack Kerouac (1967) tells of how ten days in Paris changed the pattern of his life. As he searched for the origin of his Breton name he experienced a *satori*, the Japanese word for 'sudden awakening' or 'sudden illumination'. It is when an abrupt and blinding arousal of this kind results in an attachment to a cause that flashpoint commitment is recognizable.

Paul's conversion on the road to Damascus must rank as the best-known example of flashpoint commitment. In many senses it also serves as the paradigm of a flashpoint experience and its influence on a person's orientation in life. The experience was dramatic and the effect immediate. There was a total immersion of the person with an intense emotional investment. It resulted in a comprehensive change of world-view and a total redirection of life course and career for the person involved.

Andrews (1991, p.123) tells of how one of her respondents, a CND campaigner, environmentalist and one-time communist party official, came to reevaluate his comfortable and unquestioned life situation. She quotes his own description of his political awakening as

> a real conversion ... you suddenly see the world in a different perspective, the world becomes much more luminous and exciting and comprehensible and involving and significant and you feel that you have a sort of function in the world, as distinct from being a little dry leaf that is blown around by the wind.

In Gogol's story, 'The Overcoat', a poor copying clerk Akakey Akakeivitch, the regular butt of jibes, insults and jokes, is the unlikely source of a flashpoint that results in a reinterpretation of life for a colleague.

> Only when the jokes were too unbearable, when they jolted his arm and prevented him from going on with his work, he would bring out: 'Leave me alone! Why do you insult me?' and there was something strange in the words and in the voice in which they were uttered. There was a note in it of something that roused compassion, so that one young man, new to the office, who, following the example of the rest, had allowed himself to mock at him, suddenly stopped as though cut to the heart, and from that day forth, everything was as it were changed and appeared in a different light to him. Some unnatural force seemed to thrust him away from the companions with whom he had become acquainted, accepting them as well-bred, polished people. And long afterwards, at moments of the greatest gaiety, the figure of the humble little clerk with a bald patch on his head rose before him... And the poor young man hid his face in his hands, and many times afterwards in his life he shuddered, seeing how much inhumanity there is in man, how much savage brutality lies hidden under refined, cultured politeness, and my God! even in a man whom the world accepts as a gentleman and a man of honour (quoted in O'Connor, 1963, pp. 15–16).

The key components of a flashpoint are graphically represented in this passage. The reassessment was unexpected and sudden. The instigation, 'something strange in the words and in the voice', was inexplicable. The occasion had previously involved a relatively stabilized set of social arrangements and relationships. The defining feature of the nature of the change involved is captured in the half-sentence 'and from that day forth, everything was as it were changed and appeared in a different light to him'. The effect persisted throughout the life cycle resulting in a greater depth of personal analysis and a reassessment of the significance of material and symbolic power — 'savage brutality... hidden under refined cultured politeness... and... (in) a man of honour'.

All of these patterns of coming to commitment — linear, sectoral, reactive and flashpoint — are in evidence in studies of contemporary and earlier initiators of adult learning programmes (Charters and Hilton, 1989; Jarvis, 1991; Long, 1991), those who would have explicitly conceived their programmes to advance a particular kind of social change, though the biographical detail given in these studies isn't sufficiently extensive to allow for their illumination in the manner required in this chapter.

Conclusion

This chapter has sought to come to some understanding of those who pursue social objectives by means of educative action. The strategy of seeking to restructure society by means of changing individuals, however, isn't addressed by any distinctive research tradition, such is the diversity of the ideologies represented and the specialized nature of the strategy for social change. Since what all of the agents deploying such a strategy, be it in relation to material, social, cultural, economic, political or spiritual spheres, have in common is a desire to take control over the direction of society and to orchestrate human resources to this end, political socialization in its wider interpretation seemed to be the most relevant common formative experience. This revealed the need for power and the personal attributes and skills of those who initiate and lead socially-committed programmes, together with the contribution to their formation attributable to the various agencies of socialization, as fruitful topics for advancing our understanding of committed education.

In using the biographical approach to the exploration of these topics four patterns of coming to commitment — linear, sectoral, reactive and flashpoint — were identified. Each of these patterns of formation leave their own distinctive mark on the individuals who experience them and have implications for their degree of self-awareness, engagement, rationality, affectivity, and confidence in relation to their commitment and educative action. Such is the encompassing nature of linear commitment that what other real-ities and world-views exist for those who experience it are prone to be ones targeted for correction, conversion and disestablish-ment. Self-doubt and moral dilemmas are likely to be minimal. Sectoral commitment originating in the family can also be quite pervasive where dispositions and needs formed during the early years propel the individual. Where these psychological orienta-tions persist into adulthood and realize themselves in behaviours that are socially rewarding, the individual can experience a degree of genotypic/phenotypic equilibrium that is similar in its effects to linear socialization. Reactive commitment is more measured and considered, and those who come to a cause in this manner remain more vulnerable to vicissitudes in attachment, security of world-view and faith. One suspects that, because of its impulsive origins, volatility would characterize flashpoint commitment, and that those who become so suddenly and blindingly engaged could disengage with equal haste and unpredictability. Where there are mavericks attached to social causes or movements their engage-ment (and disengagement) can usefully be explored in terms of flashpoint experiences.

Depending on their patterns of coming to commitment, there-fore, the initiators and agents of socially-committed programmes will vary in their approach to the task of educative action and to the participants attracted to their programmes. It is to the processes of this educative action and the experience of the participants that the analysis now turns.

3   The discourse of commitment I: declaring one's intentions

Introduction

The charge of indoctrination that is commonly raised against programmes of study which seek either overtly or covertly to win the hearts and minds of people to a particular creed or ideology is approached by Hogan (1990) in a novel manner. Intellect, he points out, is never cultivated in a neutral fashion; learning of any kind always brings our beliefs and attitudes into play, and all the more powerfully when we are unaware of it. He acknowledges that many of those who accept that learning cannot be neutral infer from this that indoctrination cannot be avoided, and then go on to argue for a curriculum that can be defended by appeal to a distinguished tradition, to a prevailing wisdom or to the strength of a particular ideological position. However, he contends that 'the inference that indoctrination cannot be avoided is an invalid one to draw from the sound premise that no learning can be neutral in its effects on sensibility and character'. He illuminates this point by reference to the analogy of courtship.

> There is a kind of courtship which declares its intentions openly, which recoils from the forcing of a suit, which has the courage to face difficulties as they arise, which prizes both frankness and the dignity of personal privacy, which seeks to escape the indolence of the habitual, and which draws its special character from the delights, disappointments and surprises of mutual discovery. We are well

aware however that there is another, perhaps more common kind of courtship, where considerations of a more politic kind are to the fore, and where all of the above are secondary to securing the prize, or perhaps more accurately, the imagined prize.

This analogy of courtship is a useful starting point for the analysis of those involved in socially-committed programmes. It commences with the engaging of the participants' attention. But it doesn't end there. It recognizes an ongoing relationship involving a sense of attachment and emotional involvement. It implies integrity. Throughout, there is the obligation on those who invite participation — those who advance the suit — to declare their intentions and to continue to do so as the relationship evolves and develops.

Habermas' theory of communicative action helps us to develop the imagery of the courtship. Habermas is concerned with the illocutionary force of a communicative act, that is with its ability to create the interpersonal relations intended by the speaker.

> The essential presupposition for the success of a speech act is that the speaker enter into a specific *engagement*, so that the hearer can rely on him. An utterance can 'count' as a promise, assertion, request or question if and only if the speaker makes an offer which, insofar as the hearer accepts it, he is ready 'to make good' — the speaker has to 'engage himself', that is to indicate that in certain situations he will draw the consequences for action' (quoted in McCarthy, 1988, p.284).

Habermas goes on to consider the source of the hearer's reliance on the speaker's declaration of intent. He contends that the questions of validity raised in the communication have a cognitive character and are open to testing and refutation. Habermas identifies four different kinds of validity claims, mutual recognition of which provides the basis for consensus, in communicative interaction. These relate to comprehension, truthfulness, trustworthiness and appropriateness. McCarthy (1988, p.288–289) usefully illuminates these by considering them as four different dimensions in which communication can break down.

- At its most basic level, where the comprehensibility of an utterance is questioned, communication breaks down unless the misunderstanding is clarified as, for instance, through paraphrasing, explication or expansion.

- The truthfulness of the communication might be questioned. Sometimes this can be resolved by reference to experience, information or recognized authorities. But it can also generate argument and counterargument or lead to a breaking off of communication.
- Consensus can also be endangered where the intentions of one of the parties involved is questioned. Where there are accusations of deceit, fabrication or pretence, if communication is to continue on a consensual basis good faith must be restored in the ongoing interaction.
- Finally, consensus is disrupted if the entitlement of one of the parties involved to communicate as they do is questioned by reference to their status or role, or to established relationships and values.

Where these four validity claims are met and disruption doesn't occur there is a meeting of minds, an interaction involving mutual comprehension, shared knowledge, reciprocal trust and interpersonal accord.

As Habermas himself appears to acknowledge, living up to these standards is not an easy or straightforward task. One cannot readily assume that those who initiate or lead programmes are capable of fully knowing and articulating what their social objectives and intentions for the participants are. Their pursuit of social change and personal learning may be relentless, but achieving a balanced and even exposition of the detail of these objectives is a good deal more illusive than is commonly assumed. As we have seen in Chapter 2, where attachment to a programme results from linear formation or from coordinating sectoral influences it can be difficult to achieve a sense of perspective on one's world-view. Those who come blindingly, through flashpoint commitment, to a cause may similarly experience impediments in rationalizing their attachment and specifying their intentions. More problematically, one needs to consider the impact of the social dynamics of goal-setting within a programme which can operate independently of the plans of those who initiated the programme in the first instance. Certain objectives may appear to be so obvious as not to require specification. Yet, the taken-for-granted ideals of one era may be regarded as highly questionable in another. Unspecific notions of goodness are often at such a level of generality that they are useless in prescribing or evaluating action. Explicit objectives have the merit of making public the purpose of the encounter and inviting contestation, but this in turns raises questions of comprehension, knowledge, voluntarism, power and false consciousness on the part of the participants.

'Unremarkable' intentions

The systematic elaboration of objectives is not a common feature of adult learning programmes, as Charters and Hilton's (1989) review of landmark adult education programmes seems to confirm. They found it common for providers to believe that the needs being responded to were 'self-evident' and 'a necessity', that their programme's response could be 'taken as axiomatic', and that they were entitled to proceed with confidence as a matter of urgency (p.164). Accordingly, programmes tended to be represented 'in very broad, highly generalized, and not infrequently, quite lofty terms' (p.166). This tendency is expanded on below in relation to four varieties of educative action with very diverse social objectives — literacy schemes, democratization programmes, community education and socio-cultural animation.

Literacy programmes

The objectives of a literacy programme may appear to be unremarkable. The skills of reading and writing could be said to scarcely require elaboration. A programme which seeks to cultivate such skills might well be regarded by the organizers as transparent in its objectives. Students attracted to the programme would be expected to know what the intentions of the organizers were. Indeed, the organizers could well argue that to lay undue stress on the objectives of reading and writing would be not alone redundant and a waste of valuable time, but also a distraction from the urgent task in hand. It might even serve to demoralize and further stigmatize the participants who come to learn rather than to be preached at. Ideology or social change appear remote since the learning objectives are instrumental and individualized.

Frank C. Laubach, the founder of the Each One/Teach One method of literacy teaching, would have adopted such a view of literacy programmes. Laubach is said to have developed, along with his associates, literacy materials in over a hundred countries and three hundred and twelve languages. He was the author of more than forty books and is credited with teaching sixty to a hundred million people to read. Laubach was a practitioner rather than one who theorized about adult literacy. For Laubach, such theorizing constituted an unnecessary distraction, even an irritant. Given that for him the objective was clear-cut and unproblematic, his writings were designed to publicize his programmes and win support and funding. He rarely participated in academic conferences on adult education or literacy. His assumption, that there was little to be said in relation to objectives, is captured in Inglis' (1990) description of one academic conference which he did attend with his son Robert, a symposium on illiteracy organized by the Harvard Educational Review in 1970.

> Brought together with other well-known figures from the world of literacy to discuss 'Illiteracy in American', it was only towards the end of the symposium that father and son made a contribution. The other participants had been discussing in detail the relationship between been illiterate and being able to think, act, communicate and live in and change one's world, when Laubach suddenly intervened: 'could we all come down out of the clouds again'. Literacy, he insisted, was about helping people to get a job, earn a living and to escape from hunger and misery. Avoiding entering any abstract theoretical debate, Laubach described a campaign in which he was engaged with Chinese migrant workers in San Francisco helping them to train as janitors. His son, Robert, shared his disgust with the emphasis in the symposium on 'the theory of thinking and all that kind of stuff' and the absence of discussion about practical programmes and objectives to deal with illiteracy.

Yet, literacy programmes vary in their objectives, and the intentions of those who organize and run them can be ideologically and functionally diverse. Shor (1986, pp. 189–190), for instance, distinguishes between the following varieties of literacy:

- Basic literacy: the rudimentary skills of decoding a printed passage and of encoding spoken words into a written language;
- Functional literacy: the ability to cope with political, legal, commercial, occupational and social demands in daily life, such as voting, making tax returns, applying for work, signing leases and contracts, and following printed instructions;

- Higher order literacy: the ability to be self-directive in relation to literacy-based projects, to do unsupervized research, to look up information in books, catalogues and retrieval systems;
- Cultural literacy: the ability to speak, read, write and make references within the elite idiom in the light of its prescriptions for standard speech, correct usage and appropriate accent;
- Critical literacy: recognition of and the ability to use one's critical and creative resources with a view to freeing one's self from the dominant ideology, from a worship of upper-class speech and official information, and from mechanical training and basic literacy.

There is a world of difference in the assumptions relating to the learner, society, social change and the role of literacy workers between programmes which seek to cultivate basic literacy and those which are committed to critical literacy. It seems highly unlikely that the tensions represented by these differences in prescription and assumption relating to adult literacy would be absent from Laubach's programmes. Inglis (1990), for instance, points out that although none of the literacy primers produced by Laubach had any direct reference to christian beliefs and concepts, there are constant references to his evangelical christian interests in his other writings on literacy. In fact, Laubach seemed to be of the view that literacy was essential for good christian missionary work. He is credited with the following assertion in relation to literacy: 'we missionaries have worked out a technique which we are convinced presents the christian church with the best opening in two thousand years to go and make disciples in all nations' (quoted in Inglis, 1990). Laubach was also convinced that the best way to keep the world free from communism and the threat of nuclear war was through literacy work. He saw strong connections between being hungry, being functionally illiterate and becoming communist. He tried to convince the United States Congress and Senate that rather than spending millions of dollars on arms it would be far more effective to spend the money on literacy campaigns. Inglis doubts that Laubach was the anti-communist that he made himself out to be, particularly towards the end of his life.

It is probable that Laubach beat the communist drum, which was certainly popular in the States in the 1950s, primarily as a means of drawing attention to illiteracy. Laubach was a skilled public orator who knew how to play to his audience. The bait with which he caught their attention was the threat of Communist world domination. Once he had them hooked he hauled them into his own net of passionate interest — literacy.

His final statement on communism and American capitalism was prefaced with the following observation: 'what I honestly think but I dare not tell the public'. And all of this was from someone who asserted that theorizing about adult literacy was unnecessary, that what he was doing was obvious, and that no useful purpose was to be served by dissecting the aims and objectives of literacy programmes.

Democratization movements

Like literacy, democracy and democratization can appear obvious as programme objectives. Bron-Wojciechowska and Bron (1990) have analysed the contribution of adult education programmes to the development of democracy in Europe. They identified a range of providers with different, and often contradictory, social objectives but which nonetheless appealed to the ideals of democracy and democratization. These included national movements, political and social reform groups, cultural and scientific associations, all of which sought to use adult education as a means of achieving their ends. Also represented were emerging industrial workers' movements and, later, political parties, which saw adult education as a strategy to gain political and economic power, and individual employers and their associations as well as charity organizations who required a literate, but passive, workforce. The ideologies and social projects of these providers yielded the following objectives for adult learning programmes:

- The awakening, preservation and/or the development of national consciousness — in Czech and Polish lands, and in Denmark since the 1930s;
- The liberation of the underprivileged — socialist workers' movements since the 1920s in France, and later in Germany, Austria, Poland and the Czech lands;
- The development of national unity — in Polish lands before gaining independence, Germany after World War I and

Czechoslovakia after Independence;
- Providing opportunities for the meaningful use of leisure time— Weimar Republic, conservative organizations in Poland and France;
- The organization of social networks—Sweden and Denmark.

Programmes in pursuit of these objectives, all in the proclaimed interest of democracy and democratization, sought to train activists, cultivate a moral responsibility for political events, revive spiritual life, encourage self-education, train the peasantry, facilitate local participation, develop good citizens, and raise educational standards.

Community education

Many writers have pointed to the uncontestable appeal of the concept of community and to the manner in which community education as a theory and a practice has inherited this virtuous and worthy image. In his typology of social and educational activities in disadvantaged areas, which can claim inclusion under the broad umbrella of community education, Lovett (1989) has identified five varieties.

- Community organization. This involves concentrating on the effective coordination and delivery of a wide variety of educational resources with a view to meeting local needs and interests. Outreach workers draw on existing networks in working-class communities to increase participation in adult learning programmes. A limitation of this approach is that while it can be very successful in encouraging working-class adults to participate in education it can leave the position of the general community unresolved.
- Community development. An effort is made to educate the institutions and organizations providing services and resources for working-class communities. The emphasis is on cooperation, coordination and improved understanding at local level.
- Community action. Local people are assisted in setting up their own alternative social and economic structures—cooperatives, credit unions, resource centres, etc.

- Cultural action. This stresses the need to engage working-class communities in a process of discussion and dialogue about their culture and way of life. It emphasizes the need for reflection on their values, roles and world-views with the intention of relating them to wider social, economic and political structures.
- Social action. This involves more structured and systematic education and is suspicious of the view that community action of itself is a learning process. It involves educators identifying themselves with the local community and its members, acting in solidarity with them and taking action on their behalf.

These varieties of community education range from reformist to radical in ideology, vary in their definition of what is to be accepted as education and learning, and conflict in their identification of the origins of the problems they are seeking to correct.

Socio-cultural animation

Titmus (1981) points to a similar openness in interpretation in his discussion of informal adult learning initiatives at local level in France. There the term 'popular education' was replaced in general and official usage by 'socio-cultural animation'. But what this expression means and what the change signified isn't clear: 'one of the difficulties in arriving at a clear notion of its sense derives from the fact that *animation* in French, like community in English, has become a cosmetic word. It automatically evokes a favourable response when applied to any activity, whether it is appropriate or not'(p.140). Socio-cultural animation initially denoted a process, later a technique to be used to achieve this process, and subsequently the field in which these activities take place. The process involved stimulating communication between people with a view to social action for the ultimate purpose of transforming individuals and society for the better. The technique involved learning by mutual interaction in which the animator acts as a catalyst, as a non-directive stimulant and resource person. Titmus points out that it still has to be explained why popular education, the field in which socio-cultural animation takes place, should have taken on the name of the process. Since 'the change of name has brought about no significant alteration in the nature and extent of the field of action, nor in the organizations that operate within it, nor in its structures, except possibly for the devolution of responsibility from central to local government', he concludes that 'perhaps the most plausible explanations are tactical and political' (p.141).

The tactical uses of the process of naming (and renaming), labelling and communication in representing a programme's activities and intentions are not confined to the development of socio-cultural animation in France and are distinguishable in the other varieties of educative action considered above—literacy schemes, democratization movements and community education. A characteristic tactical use of discourse in a programme's self-presentation is evident where it functions to inspire rather than describe.

Inspirational representation

The inspirational representation of a socially-committed programme has little to do with communicating to participants or potential participants its social purpose or intentions for individual learning. Its functions range across legitimation, celebration and integration. This helps to explain the appeal of concepts like literacy, community, social animation — 'euphonious appellations' in W.C. Fields' usage. What Brookfield (1983, p.60) says of community can apply more generally in discourse of this nature:

> the word 'community' is one which has the power to inspire a reverential suspension of critical judgement in the minds of adult educators, social workers and those within the caring and health professions. It is as if in invoking this term adult educators thereby imbue their practice with a humanistic concern and an almost self-righteous compassion which pre-empts any considered analysis of its central features. The term functions, therefore, as a premature ultimate; that is, as a word possessing such emotional potency that its invocation immediately precludes further debate.

A feature of this inspirational discourse is its use of slogans — 'each one/teach one'; 'make history'; 'everyone a teacher'; 'the personal is political'; 'think globally, act locally'. These should not be dismissed as 'mere slogans' (Komisar and McClellan, 1961); nor should they be 'rationally scorned as "vague"' (Rozycki, 1987). Komisar and McClellan (1961) stress the role of slogans in appealing to as wide a constituency as possible and in cutting across ideological cleavages and considered positions: 'for slogan systems do not die from explicit rejection but through lack of attention... When the general slogans in the system fail to capture the imagination, no longer command loyalty, and creative disciples fade away, the system dies'. Slogans are grounded in appeals of a high moral loading which are considered self-evident, beyond dispute and not demanding justification to anyone educationally, economically or socially alert. Because of their uncontentious appeal many diverse viewpoints are capable of being attracted.

Operationally, unspecific discourse is a means of managing conflict arising from the actual goals of a programme. Perrow (1979) has distinguished between public and actual goals. Actual goals are said to exist only when specific operations by which they are pursued within the programme can be identified. When public goals are translated into actual goals, tensions usually arise since maximizing the attainment of one is likely to minimize the attainment of another. As Rozycki (1987) contends, 'public goals formulations straddle the conflict of operational goals'. In this way they serve the ideological function of obscuring whatever goals are sacrificed in a particular situation, mindful of the possibility that they may need to be given greater advantage and prominence, and accordingly greater publicity, on another occasion.

> 'Vague' policy helps to manage such dilemmas. Good policy is 'vague' for the reason that treaties and contracts are vague: it is unwise theoretically to predecide possible conflicts before they arise, especially if they represent the struggle of good against good.

The dynamics of representation

An understanding of the processes by which public goals emerge from programmes as statements of ideology and intent, and the dynamics by which they arise as a means of resolving tensions within a programme as to what its priorities should be, can be gained by considering the research on goal conflict and displacement in formal educational institutions. The general observation by sociologists that goal tension and conflict can be extensive in nature and degree within organizations has been confirmed in studies of schools.

The operating goals of a school may differ from the original stated goals of the kind to be found in a school's charter or in a founder's declaration of a school's philosophy. Slow evolution, the impact of personalities, changing circumstances or most subtle processes of goal displacement can change the focus of a school over time. And this goal-modification can coexist with a relatively static public discourse on the goals of the school.

School personnel have also been found to differ among themselves in their priorities. Non-teaching personnel such as guidance teachers/counsellors, social workers, chaplains and managers may be less likely than classroom teachers to stress the need for order and discipline. Those with a special responsibility for the personal development of pupils — guidance teachers, counsellors, physical educationalists — may feel that the academic goals of the school are over-emphasized. Similarly, religious teachers may feel that the spiritual formation of pupils is under-played. The principal may be more inclined to view pupil behaviour and progress in terms of its implications for the prestige and reputation of the school. The differing orientations of those involved in the same programme are vividly portrayed by the pupil who described his experience of a sex education course as follows: 'the Reverend told us (why) not to do it, the doctor told us how not to do it and the head told us where not to do it'(Schofield, 1968, p.89). These examples highlight the varying priorities that can be attached to instrumental goals, expressive goals and maintenance goals within a school.

Teachers and pupils may also differ in their orientations. Pupils intending to leave school early may be concerned with devising strategies for avoiding the demands of schooling as long as it continues to be compulsory, while teachers may be under administrative, professional and parental pressure to maintain order and discipline and work towards standardized examination goals, at the very least.

The degree of structural lag has also been found to be relevant. This was defined by Corwin (1967) as 'an inconsistency throughout the organization due to the fact that the sub-parts change at different rates'. Structural lag fragments the school's formative processes. According as new demands are made on the school they may be adopted in some features of the school and ignored or rejected in other areas. This can result in both emergent and traditional goals being supported by different elements within the school. For instance, civic courses designed to train pupils for life in a democracy may well provide relevant information, but the ability and motivation necessary may be hindered in their development by certain features of the school's organization and authority system which deny pupils the opportunity of participating in a democratic manner in the making of decisions which affect them. Teachers can also find that their attitudes lag behind organizational innovations, as Barker-Lunn's (1970) extensive study of streaming in British primary schools demonstrated.

Another source of variation stems from the fact that pupils can be differentiated in the pursuance of educational goals. The allocation of pupils to different types of courses is an obvious formal example. Informally within the class one would need to consider the ideas that teachers have about different pupil needs, be they in relation to social class, gender, race or personality. Fundamental to this process are the assumptions of educators as to what constitutes suitable knowledge and learning experiences for different school types, school social compositions and individual categories of pupils.

The extent of these tensions, and the strategies employed to manage them, will influence the manner in which a programme publicly represents itself. Silverman (1970, p.9), in his discussion on organizational goals, concludes that 'it seems doubtful whether it is legitimate to conceive of an organization as having a goal except where there is an on-going consensus between the members of the organization about the purpose of their interaction'. This poses the question as to what constitutes consensus within an organization. Mohr (1973) has defined consensus as 'explicit or tacit agreement among those concerned that a certain behaviour will under the circumstances be followed, notwithstanding the possibility that some might prefer other available alternatives'. Organizational intent, he suggested, ought to be an aggregated characteristic based on unanimity though not necessarily involving 'enthusiasm, spontaneous selection, top priority or exclusive agreement'. One well-known study by Strauss *et al* (1964, p.14–15) in a hospital setting developed the concept of hospitals 'as grounded upon minimal bases of consensus, which one might term, after traditional political science practice, "concord"'. Concord was considered to include 'those bedrock agreements about the most generally accepted goals of the organization'. One important consequence of this was that it was to leave 'vast areas of responsible behaviour uncovered by pertinent rules', thus creating the need in these unruled areas of action for agreements to be made by personnel. Internally, this generated a considerable amount of important activities characterized by such terms as politicking, persuading, bargaining and negotiating. In such situations, public discourse contributes to the management of tensions surrounding the goals of an organization by stating goals in the most general and non-prescriptive terms and so distracting attention from the internal dynamics of goal setting.

Similar tensions can be identified in programmes of a socially-committed nature operating apart from the formal system of schooling, and these in turn generate their own forces which influence the manner in which the programmes are publicly represented.

Organization and ideology

How general these tensions and forces among the socially-committed programmes being considered in this book will be, and the effect on their public discourse of intent, will be influenced by the nature of their organization and ideology.

Because of the diversity of these programmes it is difficult to find a model which adequately represents their characteristic organizational and ideological features. Some programmes are relatively simple in organization in that they involve small numbers, a limited set of roles and tasks, little differentiation, simple authority structures and an *ad hoc* existence. Others embody more complex organization. Programmes can also be differentiated between in their degree of bureaucratization — the extent to which they mirror Weber's 'ideal type' of bureaucratic organization. Indicators of bureaucracy include a set of distinct roles, with defined tasks and duties and a circumscribed area of competence, arranged hierarchically with written procedures, and incorporating rational decision-making.

Weick's (1976) distinction between 'loosely-coupled' and 'tight coupling' systems seems to have a particular application in the understanding of socially-committed programmes. In consideration of the degree of clarity of their goals, their social and formative techniques, supply of participants, personalist and affective ethos, coordination of sub-systems and their monitoring and evaluative strategies, socially-committed programmes can most generally be described as loosely-coupled. A sense of structure and pattern is apparent without the order and rationality of the bureaucratic model. Probability and possibility replace predictability in estimating their internal relationships. As Tyler (1988, p.88) puts it, loose coupling is 'neither a humanistic catch-cry nor a radical label, but rather an attempt to provide an alternative to the "hyper-rational" model albeit within a systems framework'. Weick pointed out that the more loose the coupling within a system the more symbolic integration becomes necessary to maintain cohesiveness and solidarity and a sense of membership. A common rhetoric and imagery is required. Tyler's (1988, p.89) interpretation of this has implications for a programme's public discourse: 'the reciprocal relationship between the strength of coupling and the symbolic field of control... brings us to consider more broadly conceived attempts to move the sociology of organization away from structure into that of culture'. This shift of focus from structure to culture can draw attention to the manner in which the public representation of a programme will be shaped by its symbolic requirements. To criticize the discourse of a programme because it fails to illuminate in an explicit and detailed manner its processes and world-view is to fail to understand the function of discourse within a loosely-coupled system and to ignore its cultural realm. A crucial function of discourse in socially-committed programmes is the dissemination of its terminology, definitions and images, the cultivation of allegiance, and the integration of its participants and sub-systems. Its weak descriptive power shouldn't be interpreted as evasion. Where socially-committed programmes are loosely coupled their discourse is likely to be symbolic rather than expositional.

In considering the ideology of a socially-committed programme the degree to which it exhibits utopian characteristics is important for discourse. Kumar (1991) identifies four characteristics of the utopian vision — harmony, desire, hope and design. These are derived respectively from archetypal varieties of the ideal society: the golden age, a time of simplicity and sufficiency, involving a harmonious relationship between people and nature; the age of paradise, a land of exuberance and plenty; millenarianism, with its belief that a new era characterized by peace is at hand; and the ideal city or perfect commonwealth. Of their nature, utopian programmes are guided by a vision of an ideal society, unattainable but nonetheless on the margins of possibility. Kumar (1991, p.3) concludes that utopia's value 'lies not in its relation to present practice but in its relation to a possible future. Its "practical" use is to overstep the immediate reality to depict a condition whose clear desirability draws us on, like a magnet'. He illustrates this by reference to H.G. Wells' *A Modern Utopia*.

Our business here is to be Utopian, to make vivid and credible if we can, first this facet and then that, of an imaginary whole and happy world. Our deliberate intention is to be not, indeed, impossible, but most distinctly impracticable, by every scale that reaches only between today and tomorrow.

Utopian discourse, accordingly, seeks to stir the imagination, broaden horizons, disrupt complacency and raise hopes of a better life.

The impediments experienced by utopian programmes in seeking to adequately represent their processes and objectives are evident in Corson's (1986) study of holistic change in the form of the reorganization of further education in Tasmania. Drawing on Popper's (1961) critique of social planning, he points to the problem of controlling the course of utopian programmes: 'the greater the changes attempted by the utopianist, the greater will be their unintended, uncontrollable and severe repercussions upon the values, aims and sensitivities of the participants in the planned reconstruction'. Corson grounds these impediments to the control and representation of utopian programmes in relation to Popper's epistemology, to his contention that all knowledge is the product of conjecture, contestation and refutation. The theoretical force of a programme, according to this premise, depends on how open it is to refutation. This requires that in its formulation it is reasonably unambiguous, and that its evolution and stages of development are anticipated. Where a policy underpinning a programme 'is not a refutable theory in the sense of being testable against experience, or which alternatively does not provide integral stages of development that are each themselves susceptible to testing', it is a 'holistic or utopian policy and is in principle beyond the rational control of its authors'. Corson relates the failure of the programme for change to the limitations of its discourse: 'the policy failed because its merits and potentials could not be communicated to participants, nor to other influential persons, in such a way as to produce genuine commitment to its success'.

The application of Popper's epistemology has a more general relevance beyond the critique of utopian discourse. The extent to which the intentions of socially-committed programmes are capable of contestation is an important element in the maintenance of authentic communication between providers and participants. If for whatever reasons — conflict resolution, symbolic integration or the disruption of complacency — ambiguities surround the public declaration of a programme's objectives in a manner that invites moral assent, as targets for refutation they become blurred, mobile and morally out-of-range. To attempt to refute what is imprecise or to appear to diminish inspiration is to disrupt communication. The existence of contestation in relation to a programme's intentions, and the degree to which this is facilitated by the self-representation of the programme, is an important indicator of how well the conditions of clarity, openness and reciprocal initiation exist in the communicative relationship between providers and participants.

Contestation

Accounts may exist which dispute the official statement of intent and description of the nature and character of socially-committed programmes. These competing views often come from those who have personal experience of a programme and who, in some instances, may have themselves been the most committed of participants or providers. Some women who participate in feminist programmes experience them as anti-man or unduly radical. Environmental programmes have been criticized for giving a low priority to the creation of employment. Peace education may be said to generate acquiescence and passivity. Such views are likely to lead to a disenchantment with a programme and subsequently to dropping out. Those who hold views of this nature are unlikely to be given prominence in a programme's publicity. Such individuals and viewpoints are usually invisible.

Sometimes, disenchantment can be such that it leads to a single-minded desire to 'expose' the programme involved. This is most likely to occur where the level of emotional investment is greatest and where there is a holistic engagement of its participants by the programme. Revolutionary movements, apocalyptic-type associations, religious groups and, in particular, cults and sects are examples of programmes which have generated through disillusioned and, frequently, embittered former members a counter discourse of intent. The programmes of religious formation within the Roman Catholic Church provide a clear example. In its declaration on religious freedom, promulgated on behalf of the Second Vatican Council in 1965, it is proclaimed that, in spreading religious faith and in introducing religious practices, everyone ought at all time to refrain from any manner of action which might seem to carry a hint of coercion or of a kind of persuasion that would be dishonourable or unworthy, especially when dealing with poor or uneducated people. Such a manner of action would have to be considered an abuse on one's own right and a violation of the right of others (in Abbott, 1966, p.682).

Clarke (1985, p.198), however, disputes this statement of objective and practice in religious formation and interprets it as religious and moral indoctrination of young children. He points out that young children acquire their religious belief at an age when they are unlikely to understand even the terminology of religious formation: 'five-year olds casually discuss on heaven and hell, of God and the afterlife, in roughly the same way in which they talk of Santa Claus or the tooth fairy'. Clarke concluded that 'if the church thinks it reprehensible to take advantage of the uneducated and to persuade them of beliefs to which their ignorance exposes them, why does it not take a similar view of the indoctrination of children at an age when they could scarcely to said to "freely" adopt religious beliefs?'

And, yet, Hull (1992) in his analysis of religious education in a pluralist society draws on Habermas' distinction between the descriptive disciplines, the interpretative disciplines and the emancipatory disciplines to argue that, alongside Marx's economics and Freudian psychoanalysis, religious education can be identified 'as one of the emancipatory disciplines within the critical social sciences, one whose goal is human freedom'.

If this juxtaposition of 'coercion' and 'human freedom' in identifying the intent of similar socially-committed programmes seems confusing it pales by comparison with the disputation surrounding the ideals, intentions, practices, principles and transparency of Opus Dei, an organization within the Roman Catholic Church, particularly when this involves former and current members of the organization (Walsh, 1989).

Contestation surrounding the true character of a particular religion is more systematically represented in Wallis' (1976) study of scientology, *The Road to Total Freedom*. The Church of Scientology, founded by Ron Hubbard, is categorized by Wallis as a manipulationist movement, in that through its theories and techniques it claims to supply the individual with a means of personal improvement. While these techniques may ultimately aspire to the freeing of man's spiritual nature, the literature of the movement concentrates on more immediate objectives. Personal improvement is envisaged in terms of the amelioration of psychosomatic ills and psychological disabilities, coping with loneliness or lack of success, or as a means of improving one's competence and efficiency. Wallis contends that 'no radical challenge is offered to prevailing values. Rather means, held to surpass any other means available, are provided for achieving these culturally valued ends' (p.245). He describes communication within the movement as relatively impersonal, its relationships role-articulated and its organization bureaucratic. Yet, in an appendix to the study, J.L. Simmons, a sociologist and a member of the Church of Scientology, disputes this characterization asserting that he 'cannot take Wallis' work seriously' (p.269), and describes it as unscientific, selective and based on the experience of dissenting members. Much of this contestation comes to light in the study because Wallis, fearing litigation and from a concern for the rights of the subjects of his research, made his manuscript available to the Church of Scientology, itemized the subsequent modifications made and included Simmons' response which had been commissioned by the Church.

Programmes operating under the ambit of formally-organized bodies with bureaucratic characteristics, such as the Roman Catholic Church, will have available to them clearly established structures for identifying their goals and also for disseminating them. In the case of the Roman Catholic Church, the centralized nature of these processes means that in terms of official goals, at least, there is likely to be unanimity. This can be contrasted with the Protestant Churches, where individual interpretation is given greater prominence, while it is likely to have more in common with programmes derived from charismatic leaders or texts. The existence of formal statements — written constitutions, visions of the future, for instance — by which the declaration of intent of the programme is made public increases the likelihood of a counter discourse emerging. The more specific, definitive, permanent and accessible is the official discourse, the more counter discourse is likely to be generated, and the more multiple accounts of the programme's reality (Greenfield, 1978) are made available to potential participants for consideration.

The participant's standing

The status of the participants and their relationship to those who are organizing or enacting the educative programme which is seeking to change them can influence the likelihood of objectives and intentions being announced and communicated.

The voluntary nature of adult learning programmes is usually adverted to as an explanation for the absence of detailed or sustained exposition of the goals of such programmes. The publicizing of courses together with the title and brief description of course content will be considered sufficient. Adults can be said to be aware of what they are enrolling for. Where social movements are involved as initiators or sponsors it is assumed that their objectives are easily inferred from their ideologies by adults who are under no compulsion to participate.

On the other hand, where participants are inferior in age, education, knowledge or awareness to those who might be expected to explain the object of the encounter, it could be argued that explanations of intent would not be fully understood and, accordingly, would be redundant. Parents' plans for their children's development is an obvious example. It could be equally a feature of programmes with a social rescue, social reform or emancipatory intent since in such cases an assumption of the rationale for the programme's existence would be the misrecognition, delusion and false consciousness of the targeted participants in relation to their true social condition. The story of the university extra-mural lecturer in England who, in discussing their learning needs with a group of young farmers, interpreted their expressed concerns about farming techniques, book-keeping and agricultural legislation to mean that what they were really looking for were lectures on the history of the British monarchy may not be entirely apocryphal. In an open letter to Workers' Educational Association tutors, Raymond Williams gave the following advice: 'in adult education the class meets before the session and decides the syllabus with its tutor. This was sometimes a formality, sometimes a combination of skillful persuasion and briefing but, often enough, a genuine participation of the definition of educational means' (quoted in McIlroy, 1990). Moses Coady of Antigonish is reported to have said of his early approaches to local inhabitants, 'when I started in adult education work twenty years ago, not five per cent of the people I talked to understood what was meant by production, economic, natural resources, proletariat, exploitation, or any such words, but now they all know — people catch on fast' (quoted in Lovett, 1980).

Even though few providers of socially-committed programmes would deny that the unambiguous specification of objectives is difficult to achieve, and that participants can often as a result find themselves involved in programmes which aren't quite what they had intended, the implications of this for individual rights and personal freedom are rarely pursued. This is most obviously the case where adults are involved since it is assumed that they are free to withdraw if their learning needs aren't being met. Thompson (1983, p.185) expresses it as follows:

> inevitably in a course like Second Chance these issues are controversial, and unlike the 'hidden political curriculum' of most adult education provision, they are more explicit. We have not lost a spattering of students each year by default or because it was raining or because their lift did not arrive or because they had decided to try pottery instead, but because they knew the implications of what they were learning from us and from each other and it proved objectionable to them ... In the end, as adults our students will make up their own minds.

Even where socially-committed programmes involve open access and freedom of choice it is wrong to assume that participation represents a knowledge of the programme's intent and, much less, assent to its objectives. People participate in programmes for many reasons often using programmes for purposes for which they were never intended. Research on the self-declared reasons for adults participating in voluntary learning abounds with examples of how diverse participant motivation can be and of the variety of the needs which they hope will be responded to in a learning programme. These include the desire to know, to reach personal, social or religious goals, to escape, to take part in an activity and to comply with formal requirements (Burgess, 1971). A programme with the most exalted of social aims — the protection of the environment, the cultivation of harmonious relationships between nations, races and religions, the liberation of the oppressed and disadvantaged, the empowerment of the politically marginalized — can attract participants with the most narrow, mundane and individualized motivations. An Irish programme that had been represented for over thirty years in terms of altruism, cooperativism, nation building and the cultivation of balanced social and economic advancement was found to attract participants primarily because of their desire to be mentally stimulated, to be introduced to a wider range of ideas, to develop self confidence in their learning abilities and to learn more about the individual subjects on the programme. Collective and social objectives were given very low priority in their declared motivation for attending (O'Sullivan, 1989). Research of this nature calls into question the rationalist interpretation of participation in learning programmes which assumes the congruence between the formally-stated objectives of a programme and the participants' consciously-articulated learning intentions. Participants are often motivated by a series of affective, relational and emotional needs which may indeed be satisfied by the programme but which have little to do with its public representation, and may be understood only in an intuitive or impressionistic manner, if at all.

The related voluntaristic interpretation of adult participation must also be circumscribed. People do not select from an infinite choice of programmes. Social, economic and personal circumstances influence participation, nudging some and impelling others. The assumption that in participating in socially-committed programmes people are necessarily taking control of their lives, and using the programme's learning opportunities to move forward according to some personal developmental or social reform plan which they formulated, is not supported by the findings of research on participation in adult learning. In his review of the research on the motivation of participants in adult education, Courtney (1992, p.153) makes the 'rarely observed' point that

> people may undertake formal programs of learning due to a lack of clear goals, and not because of them, or a desire to obtain goals within the new environment and not because they already have them ... It ought not to surprize us if people arrive at stages of their lives when former goals can no longer sustain them.

Even where refutations and alternative accounts of a programme's processes and objectives are available in the form of counter-discourse these restrictions of self-awareness, reflection, motivation and circumstance also apply. Nonetheless, where counter-discourse exists and is available to potential participants it is much less likely that a programme's official statement of intent will be accepted as taken-for-granted and unproblematic by anyone caring to consider or inspect it. The crucial consideration where alternative accounts are available is the capacity of potential participants to juxtapose, analyse, contrast and interrogate the competing accounts. This capacity cannot be taken for granted despite the fact that generally in society, particularly where the aspiration is to democratic decision-making, assumptions are made about the discursive abilities of those of adult years. This tension between political power and political capacity is cogently captured by Paul Valery: 'politics was, at first, the art of preventing people from interfering in matters that concerned them. To this, in later times, was added the art of compelling people to decide matters which they did not understand' (quoted in du Preez, 1982).

But this is only to ask if potential participants in socially-committed programmes really understand what such programmes entail, and if they are capable of balancing competing accounts where these are available. There is, however, Lukes' (1974, p.24) 'third face' of power to be considered. This has its basis in 'false consciousness' which relates to the distinction between an individual's subjective and real interests. To experience 'false consciousness' is to fail to recognize one's true interests and, in consequence, to be an acquiescing participant in one's own exploitation for the benefit of others. Where individuals' perceptions of their learning requirements and the benefits to be derived from a particular programme are 'false or manipulated' and at variance with their real needs, the conflict between their interests and those of the providers of the programme involved remain at a latent level. The contradiction may be obvious to neither party. For Lukes, this 'third face' of power is the 'supreme and most insidious exercise of power' since it involves the shaping of individuals' 'perceptions, cognitions and performances' in such a way that they then operate in a manner that violates their own real interests. In failing to recognize their real interests individuals are depowered, and this can occur while maintaining the illusion of autonomy as they freely move in and out of socially-committed programmes.

This consideration of rationality, voluntarism and power in relation to the discourse of socially-committed programmes returns the analysis to the issue of the communicative relationship between provider and participant and the context in which this discourse occurs. Habermas' 'ideal speech situation' provides us with a set of precepts which should guide the organization of communication in such contexts (McCarthy, 1988, pp. 306–310). An overriding principle is that there should be a 'symmetrical distribution of chances to select and employ speech-acts. . . . and effective equality of opportunity in the assumption of dialogue roles'. Certain requirements follow from this principle. Participants must have the same chance to initiate and perpetuate conversation, to refute or question so that nothing in the communication is exempt from examination. Communication should proceed on the basis of the strength of an argument without distorting constraints, be they open domination or self-deception. Participants should be free to express their feelings, emotions and intentions, and interpersonal transparency should prevail in the relationship. It is obvious that these conditions are rarely, if ever, achieved in reality. It represents an ideal but, according to McCarthy, with Habermas it is more than a critical standard for assessing real life. He quotes Habermas: 'the ideal speech situation is neither an empirical phenomenon nor a mere construct, but rather an unavoidable supposition reciprocally made in discourse', and comments 'the ideal speech situation is not just an idea spun from thought and placed critically over against a deficient reality, for it is a supposition that must be made if argumentation is not to lose its sense'

Conclusion

In engaging the minds, emotions and time of participants through socially-committed programmes a fundamental point of contact is represented by knowledge: the communication of the formative processes and social objectives which characterize the programme. It seems a reasonable requirement that those whom a programme aspires to influence ought to be clear in their understanding of its intentions for their personal change and its designs for the society which they inhabit. Yet, as we have seen in this chapter, the conditions set by the application of a number of standards in this regard can be difficult to achieve. In considering the discourse of intent of socially-committed programmes we found many threats to the self-declaration of the courtship, to the meeting of minds required in communicative consensus and to the symmetry in dialogue, disputation and power of the 'ideal speech situation'. These impediments to communication derive largely from the character and function of the representational discourse of socially-committed programmes. They have to do with the need to recruit participants, the generation of allegiance and cohesiveness among those involved, and with mechanisms for coping with goal conflict and tension. There is little to be added to our understanding by attributing these threats to the evasiveness or deceit of the providers of socially-committed programmes. The source is more likely to be the structural imperatives of loosely-coupled systems and utopian ideologies.

To find fault with the precision of self-representation in socially–committed programmes is to assume that appropriate conceptual schemes and vocabularies are available to more completely and explicitly communicate the intentions of the providers to potential participants. Some possibilities for the conceptualizing and naming of the designs of socially-committed programmes for the personal formation of participants follow in Chapter 4. This will be a linking chapter setting out pivotal conceptual tools. Retrospectively, as a foil to this chapter, it describes how the substance of personal change is capable of differentiation in a manner that could usefully inform the declaration of a programme's intentions. By way of anticipation, it distinguishes between the kinds of psychological change that are required, and invites consideration in later chapters of the appropriate strategies of legitimation, forms of association and management of dysfunctional response where the different varieties of substantive change are intended.

4   Educative action: epistemic status and psychological change

Introduction

Socially-committed programmes seek to change participants in qualitatively disparate ways. A basic consideration in this regard is the substantive form of the personal change involved. Such personal change takes many forms — being better informed about an issue, mastering a skill or body of knowledge, developing a greater tolerance towards religious or social groups, attachment and commitment to a cause or movement, altering one's identity, or changing one's world-view. All of these changes, in turn, can occur in relation to a particular content — mastery across the full range of human knowledge; technical, social and cognitive skills; and the wide spectrum of world religions and ideologies. I use epistemic status to refer to these variations in the substance of the personal change which socially-committed programmes seek to achieve.

Epistemic status

Epistemology is the study of knowledge, its forms and their validity. In addressing the question of the epistemic status of the substance of personal formation within socially-committed programmes the range of inquiry is more truncated. Four questions are being posed:

- Can the substance of the personal change be differentiated in terms of its immediate purpose?
- What is its cosmic function?
- In relation to what criteria are its claims to truth determined?
- Is it distinguishable as a particular type within the general field of knowledge?

These questions are heuristic devices. They allow the substance of personal change to be internally differentiated with a view to demonstrating the complex variety of intentions for personal change to be found across the range of socially-committed programmes. They also facilitate a consideration of the psychological character of learning appropriate to each epistemic variety. The epistemic status of the desired change, be it in relation to information; self-awareness, assertiveness and sensitivity; leadership skills; or religious, social or political dogma, together with its psychological character have implications in turn for the extent to which the totality of the person is engaged, for the basis of its legitimation and for the associative character of the interaction, as well as for more immediate formative strategies of socially-committed programmes.

A common distinction with regard to the immediate purpose of knowledge is outlined by Hirst (1974, p.57).

- 'Knowledge with a direct object' refers to the direct awareness, recognition and naming of people, places and things.
- 'Knowledge that' refers to propositional knowledge, expressing what is the case or uttering a true statement.
- 'Knowledge how' includes procedural knowledge, knowing how or when to do certain things.

Habermas extends this question of the function of knowledge to a more cosmic plane in his theory of cognitive interests. These cognitive interests, or interests that guide knowledge, are orientations or strategies that shape and direct the different modes of inquiry. He distinguishes between technical, practical and emancipatory orientations which are reflected in the empirical – analytical sciences, the historical-hermeneutical sciences and the critical-oriented sciences, respectively (McCarthy, 1988, pp. 53–56).

- Technical interest refers to the most basic of survival needs, the desire to domesticate nature. This ranges from the necessity of forging the basis of an existence from nature in terms of food and shelter, includes craft and technical skills, and culminates in modern technology. It is derived from a concern to understand, predict and control the workings of the natural environment.
- Practical interest is derived from a desire to establish and further reciprocal understanding in the relationships between people, and seeks to enhance communication and a mutuality in world-views.
- Emancipatory interest is rooted in a concern to free people from imposition, ideologies, self-imposed limitations and dependencies.

According to Habermas these orientations towards technical control, mutual understanding and emancipation are perspectives in terms of which reality is comprehended. They are not 'influences on cognition that have to be eliminated for the sake of the objectivity of knowledge; rather they themselves determine the aspect under which reality can be objectified and thus made accessible to experience in the first place' (quoted in McCarthy, 1988, p.58). For Habermas, cognitive interests are deep-rooted anthropological orientations.

According to Hirst (1974, p.84) the domain of human knowledge is capable of being differentiated 'into a number of logically distinct "forms", none of which is ultimately reducible in character to any of the others'. For Hirst (1974, p.85), a fundamental distinction between these forms of knowledge is the 'criteria for truth in terms of which they are assessed'. He distinguishes between seven areas of knowledge each of which embodies a distinctive type of test for its objective claims.

- The truths of formal logic and mathematics where the deductibility within an axiom system is their particular test of truth.
- The physical sciences are concerned with truths that in the final analysis stand or fall on the basis of the test of observation by the senses.

- Interpersonal experience and knowledge refers to our awareness and understanding of our own and other people's minds. Unlike the physical sciences, it is 'knowledge without observation'. According to Hirst, the irreducibility of objective judgements in this area to other types of test can be most readily seen in judgements of our own states of mind.
- Moral judgement, the objectivity of which is the subject of long-standing dispute, is considered by Hirst to have a serious claim to independent status because of its irreducibility to other forms of knowledge.
- Aesthetic experience, for similar reasons, is considered as a separate form of knowledge.
- Religious knowledge involves claims that are also irreducible. Irrespective of whether or not they have an objective basis, according to Hirst they cannot be simply dismissed.
- Philosophical understanding involves distinctive second-order tests of objectivity.

Finally, with regard to particular types of knowledge within the general field of knowing we draw on Phenix's (1964) realms of meaning. Phenix bases his scheme on the assertion that 'six fundamental patterns of meaning emerge from the analysis of the possible distinctive modes of human understanding' (p.6). He labels these as symbolics, empirics, esthetics, synnoetics, ethics and synoptics.

- Symbolics includes ordinary language, mathematics and various types of symbolic forms such as gestures and rituals. These meanings are contained in arbitrary symbolic structures created as instruments for the expression and communication of any meaning whatsoever. In one respect these symbolic systems constitute the most fundamental of all the realms of meaning in that they must be employed to express the meanings in each of the other realms.
- Empirics comprizes the sciences or the physical world, of living things and of humanity. These sciences provide actual descriptions, generalizations and theoretical explanations which are based on observation and experimentation in the world of matter, life, mind and society.

- Esthetics contains the various arts such as music, visual arts, movement and literature. Meanings in this realm are concerned with the contemplative consideration of particular phenomena as idea-generated objectifications.
- Synnoetics refers to personal or relational knowledge and is concrete, direct and existential. It can apply to other persons, to oneself or even to things. It is derived from the Greek σεννοια (*synnoia*), meaning meditative thought.
- Ethics refers to moral meanings which prescribe obligation. It has to do with personal conduct that is based on free, deliberate and responsible decisions.
- Synoptics refers to meanings that are integrative and includes areas such as history, which recreates the past, religion, which is concerned with ultimate meanings, and philosophy, which provides clarification, evaluation and co-ordination of all the other realms of meaning through conceptual analysis and interpretation (Phenix, 1964, pp. 6–7).

Phenix claims that these provide 'the foundations for all the meanings that enter into human experience' in that they 'cover the pure and archetypal kinds of meaning that determine the quality of every humanly-significant experience' (p.8).

Differentiated in the light of these questions on purpose, cosmic function, truth criteria and forms of meaning, the substance of personal change is revealed as an epistemically-diverse experience. This is a pivoted variable in socially-committed programmes that has crucial implications for various aspects of their functioning. In later chapters it will be seen to be significant for a programme's legitimatory basis, its associative character and its interpretation of dissent and doubt. Here we consider the imperatives that follow for the psychological character of personal change and for the formative strategies adopted within a programme. The available space, however, forces a selectivity: the examples of epistemic intent considered are not comprehensive and are meant to be illustrative of the possibilities for drawing out the consequences of the full range of epistemic change in all its diversity.

There is a world of difference between 'knowledge how', procedural knowledge, and 'knowledge that', propositional knowledge, such that it invites comparison with the instruction/education distinction in the analysis of learning. Habermas' emancipatory interest requires personal change that touches an individual in a deep, experiential and comprehensive manner. Contrasted with technical interest, which focuses on the domestication of the natural environment, it embodies a persuasive direction for action in relation to one's personal life and career. The transmission of religious truths requires a suspension of the truth criteria of the physical sciences. Like aesthetic experience, and to a lesser extent moral judgement, it involves immersion in an inter-subjective community where characteristic verities are imbued from the status of first principles because of revelation, inherited tradition or trust. Phenix (1964, p.8), himself, recognizes the special position of symbolics and synoptics within the realms of meaning. Symbolics are the necessary means of expressing all meanings and, therefore, encompass the entire range of meanings. Because of their integrated character, synoptics 'gather up' all other meanings. To seek symbolic or synoptic change is to desire to alter the manner in which an individual understands, names, orders and interprets reality across all its physical, social and transcendental dimensions. To maximize these epistemically-diverse forms of change, a programme will need to aspire to psychologically appropriate personal change. This is a structural imperative, derived from the epistemic character of the substance of change, if a programme is to achieve its objectives.

Psychological change

In pursuing this structural link between content and process in socially-committed programmes, between the substance of change and the psychological processes of personal formation which are demanded by epistemically-varied forms of change, three types of personal change can be distinguished between. These are segmental change, which touches no more than a particular aspect of an individual's personality; role/identity change, which prepares an individual for performance within, and possible identity with, a social position; and interpretive change, where a redefinition of one's personal reality is involved. Procedural knowledge and technically-motivated knowledge are the clearest examples where segmental change is adequate. The other extreme, interpretive change, is essential if the transmission of emancipatory-motivated knowledge, religious knowledge and synoptics are to be successful. Propositional knowledge, and even scientific and axiomatic knowledge as well as empirics, are deceptive. They appear on the surface to demand no more than an addition to one's stock of knowledge; in fact, they can often involve induction into distinctive roles and interpretations of reality. Role change can operate to different epistemic levels: the direct awareness and naming of people — 'knowledge with a direct object' — practically-motivated knowledge, moral knowledge, synnoetics, aesthetic experience and ethics. Symbolics is perhaps the most deceptive of all, and for the same reason that Phenix himself draws attention to: it is fundamental to and has the potential to shape all the other realms of meaning.

Segmental change

Segmental change involves the alteration of no more than a particular facet of an individual's make-up. Socially-committed programmes rarely confine themselves to segmental change in their participants, either because such limited change is inadequate as a motor for their social objectives or because what is projected as segmental change is often deceptive, in reality involving more comprehensive personal change. The former point can be illustrated in relation to trait change, the latter by means of a consideration of the Manpower Services Commission's (MSC) project of economic rejuvenation in England.

Trait change is concerned with those personality dispositions which are relatively stable across social contexts and positions. It can be seen as the sociological interpretation of certain surface dimensions of personality, deriving its organizing concepts from the psychometric approach to the study of personality. Bromley (1977, p.230) explains that a 'person's personality is defined by the consistencies and regularities running through the behaviour episodes making up his life-history or some major phase of his life-history'. He distinguishes between the psychodynamic and the psychometric approach to the study of personality. The psychodynamic approach focuses on individuals' relationships with their environments and, using clinical case study methods in the main, concerns itself with, for instance, the causes and consequences of anxiety, guilt or depression. The psychometric approach has tended to concentrate on the study of traits which Bromley defines as 'stable psychophysiological dispositions within the person inclining him to react in "characteristic" ways in given situations' (p.230). Traits would include such dispositions as confidence, timidity, aggressiveness and sociability.

According to Brim (1968), in his review of research on the topic, 'the most important, most difficult question about adult socialization is how much change can take place in adult personality'. While recognizing the complicated interaction of such variables as heredity, environment and specific context, the relative stability of many aspects of personality is suggested by research (Kimmel, 1974). Yet, in relation to the trait dimension of personality there are some noteworthy indications of variation over time and in relation to such specific experiences and phases of life as marriage, parenthood and occupation. Vincent's (1964) study of personality change during marriage identified changes in such traits as dominance and self-acceptance. He also found that those who marry early show the greatest subsequent change. While parent-child interaction has most often been studied in relation to childhood learning it can also be seen as a source of personal change for the parent. Responding to the needs and demands of a young child can, according to Brim (1968), require 'unselfishness, control of aggression, mature handling of numerous mild frustrations and adaptation to an interrupted work schedule and interrupted leisure'. Indeed, case studies of parents convicted of child abuse suggest that such parents have failed to make these adaptations (Kempe and Kempe, 1978). In discussing the impact of occupation on personality, Moore (1969) has used the French phrase *déformation professionelle* to refer to the possible distortion in character deriving from occupational experiences, and argues that in social situations outside the workplace popular occupational stereotypes such as the didactic teacher, the argumentative lawyer and the fussy accountant may have some validity. A theoretical interpretation of trait change is provided by the Marxist correspondence theory which sees the social relations of production influencing the personality traits elicited and confirmed in other social institutions.

Few people are unfamiliar with individual examples of modified personality traits, and frequently these do indeed centre around the social experiences of family and work. Reviews of research on personality change during adulthood support the conviction that change does occur (Neugarten, 1963). However, doubts about the persistence of trait change, its phenotypic rather than genotypic nature and its location within specific environments raise questions as to its adequacy as a means of facilitating and motivating the kind of action demanded by the social objectives of socially-committed programmes.

The MSC was established in 1974 in England, following a review of the 1964 Industrial Training Act, for the purpose of restructuring and rationalizing the existing training and employment-related services of the Department of Employment. This has been interpreted as a response to 'fundamental problems encountered by capitalism in crisis' in the analysis by the Centre for Contemporary Cultural Studies (1981, p.228) of schooling in post-war England, *Unpopular Education*. This analysis charts a litany of social and economic instabilities which were translated in official discourse within the state, industrial and commercial sectors to take the form of individual inadequacies, particularly among young adults about to enter the labour market. These included an absence of 'good' work attitudes, an insufficient supply of technical competencies, and inordinate expectations and aspirations. Anxieties about the employability of young people were such that the MSC soon extended its ambit to include the adequacy and relevance of all the educational and training experiences of young people before and after entry to the labour force.

The advocacy of segmental change — procedural knowledge, 'knowledge how' — labelled as 'skill' was a central prop in what became a national programme of reconstruction. A more skilled labour force was said to be required because of changes in automation, technology and scientific applications. As *Unpopular Education* points out, this notion of skill remained unexamined and uncriticized: 'It functioned as a sign which combined impressively neutral references to technique with some thoroughly positive moral connotations. Who could gainsay the value of "skill" especially if the immediate point of reference was medicine, the conquest of space or the magic of the computer' (p.145). As the discourse evolved, 'skill' expanded in meaning and range to encompass a scale of formation comprehensively in excess of segmental change. Social and life skills came to be included, as did the capacity to face the risks involved in economic change and growth, flexibility in work expectations and practices, adaptability and mobility. These were projected as though they were 'purely technical concomitants of production divorced from broader issues of economic and social organization' (p.145).

This analysis of the MSC in *Unpopular Education* makes the point that formation which poses as no more than segmental change is often more comprehensive in its designs than is immediately apparent. Relevant to this consideration of skill formation as segmental change, and to the analysis of role/identity change that follows, is Althusser's (1971) analysis of the processes of formation involved in the reproduction of labour power. In learning 'techniques and knowledge', he argues, a person also learns the 'rules' of good behaviour. These include 'the attitude that should be observed by every agent in the division of labour, according to the job he is "destined" for: rules of morality, civic and professional conscience, which actually means rules of respect for the socio-technical division of labour, and ultimately the rules of the order established by class domination'. In short, 'know-how' is transmitted 'in forms which ensure subjection to the ruling ideology'.

As a synthesis of the limitations of *authentic* segmental change, even when both trait and skill dimensions are involved and where the intervention begins early in life, the US 'War on Poverty' during the Johnson/Kennedy administration in the 1960s is illustrative. The expectation was that people could, in President Johnson's words, be 'educated out of poverty'. A multitude of specially-designed programmes at pre-school, elementary and high school levels sought to boost self-confidence, raise educational and occupational aspirations and improve social, linguistic and cognitive skills. Despite the short-term nature of many of the social and cognitive gains, it would appear that some qualified successes were recorded in improving the life chances of individual pupils (Natriello, McDill and Pallas, 1990). But, as has been frequently pointed out in criticisms of programmes which rely on individual change as a means of solving social problems (Alcock, 1987), structural factors in the reproduction of poverty — lack of opportunity, discrimination, financial want — were given insufficient attention in this 'War on Poverty'. Poverty is most fundamentally a social rather than an individual problem. Yet, poverty-eradication programmes which rely on segmental change are premised on explanations of poverty in terms of individual inadequacies rather than structural inequalities.

Role/identity change

Role/identity change refers to the personal change relevant to a social position. Role change involves an alteration of an individual's capacity to perform with competence in a designated position. Identity change requires internalization and exclusion: one 'becomes' the role concurrently as one distances oneself from contradictory roles. While the distinction between role change and identity change is to be found in the difference between social competence and self-definition it is nonetheless a qualitative distinction that can be overstated in the interpretation of personal change.

This relationship between role and identity change, between social competence and self-definition, emerges in changing approaches to the induction of immigrant groups on the part of their host society. Potentially a source of cultural diffusion and political instability, the conventional approach up to recent times was to work towards identity change among immigrant groups. The Thai policy towards immigrant Chinese, outlined in the overview of exemplars of socially-committed programmes, sought such an identity change, and utilized its educational system to encourage and facilitate the Chinese in assuming a Thai identity. This was in the tradition of programmes such as the Frontier College in Canada, founded at the turn of the century in response to the massive influx of immigrant labour for the mining and timber industries, and for railway and highway construction. Here also the objective was one of assimilation, the Canadianization of the immigrant workers in terms of the indigenous language, customs, principles and political ideologies (Morrison, 1989). Up to 1980 a similar approach was adopted in Holland to immigration resulting from the decolonization of Indonesia, Surinam and the Dutch Antilles (Vocking, 1988). The official policy was to integrate and adapt the immigrant to Dutch society. By means of 'information on Dutch laws, regulations, institutions and customs, the ethnic groups were to be better equipped to make their way in society and to fit into it'. Following the ratification of the Bill on Minorities in 1984, however, as well as equality of participation in Dutch society, freedom to live according to one's own culture were stated as policy principles. Courses in their own language and culture were to be provided for the 'new compatriots' in adult learning programmes which were no longer 'geared to foreigners adapting to a majority, but to mutual acceptance and equality of co-existence'. It would appear that identity change was replaced as a programme objective by role change, as a result of which immigrants would be able to fulfil the requirements of Dutch citizenship without disengaging from their native identities. In reality, the nature of the change was likely to have been a good deal more fluid and blurred. The extent to which a person experienced identity rather than role change in such a situation would depend on their degree of immersion in the role of Dutch citizen and its cultural congruence with their native identity.

While identity is fundamental to one's sense of selfhood and cultural location, and far-reaching in its implications for group affiliation and social action, role change can also be quite pervasive in its effect on the individual, as Brim's (1966) analysis of socialization throughout the life-cycle suggests.

Brim has attempted to outline some probable changes in the content of socialization as the individual progresses from childhood to adulthood. Central to his analysis is the process of role socialization which he regards as the most important aspect of personal change during the adult years. He identifies the three things individuals require to perform satisfactorily in a role: they must know what is expected of them (knowledge), they must be able to meet these requirements (ability), and they must desire to produce the behaviour (motivation). Each of these requirements is, in turn, extended by distinguishing between its behavioural and value dimensions, thus yielding the following typology:

	Behaviour	Values
Knowledge	A	B
Ability	C	D
Motivation	E	F

Cells A and B indicate that the individual knows what behaviour is expected and what the end or object of this behaviour is; C and D indicate the capability to carry out the behaviour and to hold supportive values, while E and F suggest motivation to behave appropriately and to pursue the socially-desired objectives.

Brim's scheme can be usefully extended by reference to a number of other concepts from role theory and the sociology of knowledge. The vertical axis of the scheme is retained and the horizontal axis is extended to incorporate three dimensions — instrumental, status and legitimation. This produces the following modified typology:

	Instrumental	Status	Legitimation
Knowledge	A	B	C
Ability	D	E	F
Motivation	G	H	I

The first two dimensions of role—instrumental and status aspects—serve to differentiate within Brim's 'behaviour' component. They refer to different sides of role behaviour, instrumental aspects referring to the fundamental distinguishing behaviour, the *sine qua non* of a role, with status aspects referring to the associated social presentation of self. This distinction is adapted from Parsons' (1961) discussion of the functions of schooling. Legitimation, which replaces 'values', refers to the justification of role behaviour, its prescription as the 'natural' or correct arrangement by appeals to perceptions of 'how things are' in society, as well as to held standards of what is correct, appropriate or ideal.

This multi-dimensional representation of the potential of role change can be most strikingly illuminated by taking the example of an apparently neutral and unremarkably-routine role, that of bank official.

- Cell A: Knowing the job description, be it manager, cashier, foreign exchange etc.
- Cell B: Knowing the style of grooming, dress, demeanour, recreation, residential location, social and political activity expected.
- Cell C: Knowing the justificatory rhetoric of banking, 'service to the community and industry' etc.
- Cell D: Ability to meet the requirements of the job description, e.g. to supervize staff, relate to customers, control finance.
- Cell E: Ability, in relation to social skills, cultural knowledge and financial resources, to meet the status requirements of the role.
- Cell F: Ability to accept the justification of the work, e.g. acceptance of free enterprize, free from inhibiting scruples about the role of banking in social and economic life.
- Cell G: Motivation to meet the requirements of the job description, e.g. interest, personal satisfaction, salary, working conditions, prestige.
- Cell H: Motivation to meet the status requirements of the position, e.g. interest in the prescribed cultural pursuits, styles of dress etc.
- Cell I: Motivation to accept the legitimation of the role behaviour, e.g. competitive, achievement-oriented, profit-maximizing dispositions.

In using Brim's typology it needs to be kept in mind that it can result in the content of role/identity change being treated as static and unproblematic. Not alone do role definitions change over time but role theorists have also produced an extensive body of research on instances of role conflict where definitions of appropriate role behaviour vary according to the individual or group making the definition. Nonetheless, what Brim's conceptualization highlights is that performing with competence in a social position clearly requires much more than know-how. Role change routinely involves an epistemically-varied substance: practical, moral and even aesthetic levels are suggested by Brim's scheme. Put another way, this indicates that role change has the capacity to influence individuals in a manner that is epistemically-diverse and of a high order. But this is dependent on certain conditions of learning being met, some of which are reasonably straightforward, others being more difficult to establish.

Knowing about the instrumental, status and legitimation dimensions of a role is fundamental, and any attempt at role change needs to cater for it. Yet, surprizingly, many examples of unsatisfactory role performance can be traced to inadequate knowledge about the requirements of the role. Some social positions create particular problems because of the diffuse nature of their role expectations or became they have been subjected to considerable social change. People-centered occupations, unlike object-processing occupations, also defy specific role definition. Whatever problems of definition may be associated with the instrumental component of role behaviour, it possesses little of the implicit and frequently concealed characteristics of status requirements. The status component of role is very much in the nature of a hidden agenda to be learned by informal means rather than through orientation courses, specific instruction or documentation. Gaining access to this hidden agenda is frequently facilitated by means of anticipatory socialization through reference-group identification, in which individuals adopt the orientations of the group to which they aspire but do not, as yet, belong (Merton, 1968). While knowing how a particular role is legitimated isn't necessary for successful role performance, an unfamiliarity with the justificatory rhetoric of a position may indicate a less than total commitment to the role. In cases where total immersion in a role is necessary, as, for instance, in political, ideological or religious spheres, special strategies are likely to be required to ensure that the legitimation of the new role is well known. These strategies will be more appropriately considered in relation to interpretive change.

To know what is expected by way of instrumental or status behaviour and to be familiar with its underpinning legitimation is, of course, no guarantee that a role will be effectively performed. An appropriate stock of knowledge, range of abilities and dispositions is essential, and provision must be made for their transmission. Not infrequently, such provision also encompasses status and legitimatory elements of role ability. It has been said of more traditional teacher training programmes that, as well as cultivating classroom strategies and justifying the role of the teacher by reference to various philosophies of education and aspects of human psychology, they also socialized teachers, by means of their narrow boarding-school type regime, to the conservative and restrictive status dimensions of teaching (Deem, 1978). Some writers have argued that this attention to status and legitimatory dimensions of personal change in teacher training programmes was motivated by the centrality of the teacher in transmitting a society's ideologies and in confirming existing power and economic relations within the social structure (Grace, 1978).

Motivation is much less a feature of socialization in adult life than in childhood. It is assumed that adults who volunteer for programmes involving role change are predisposed to perform the target roles. Socialization is accordingly seen to be a matter of communicating the requirements of a role and developing appropriate capacities and knowledge. This is only partly due to the voluntary nature of many adult roles which makes self-selection possible. In many cases, self-selection is supported by programme selection. More fundamentally, adult socialization relies on the formation of drives, needs and perceptions of reality during childhood which constitute a reserve of motivation. What motivational socialization exists in adult life tends to be more specific than in childhood and concerned with overt behaviour. The existence of dispositions supportive of the legitimation of this behaviour — self-esteem, social power needs, altruism, fear of punishment or loss — is assumed and appealed to rather than made the object of socialization. In only certain cases — where appropriate dispositions and needs cannot be taken for granted or are known to be suspect — do programmes need to concern themselves directly with legitimatory motivation.

A programme that appears to have effectively fulfilled these conditions for successful role/identity change is to be found in the strategies for the induction of Chinese youth adopted by the Thai school system. The following features of the programme have been abstracted by Guskin and Guskin (1970) as contributing to its success, and they argue that these might be said to be key elements for any effective programme of role/identity change:

- Desocialization. The Chinese students are disengaged from Chinese culture, language and traditions.
- Specification of role requirements. The Thai teachers and schools clearly specify the full range of behaviours expected of the Thai role.
- Atmosphere. The school provides a warm, supportive and concerned atmosphere.
- Language. The language of the Chinese students is developed to the point where it facilitates interaction with the desired role models.
- Performance. The Chinese students seem to understand the new role requirements and there is a high incidence of compliance.
- Social interaction. There are considerable opportunities for interaction with Thai students and teachers.
- Formal change agent. The teacher's role is formalized as an agent of role/identity change by means of instruction and role-modelling.
- Peers. Fellow students, in particular successfully-socialized older Chinese students, provide support and reinforce the pressures for change.
- Power. The teachers have the power to regulate student behaviour and to induce the desired role performance.
- Rewards. As well as the immediate rewards provided by the school, Thai society provides long-term rewards for assimilated Chinese.

This Thai programme of personal change is a benign version of the extreme processes of resocialization recorded in closed and, particularly, in carceral settings — prisons, mental hospitals, barracks, military academies, religious seminaries, communes — in which there is a disengagement from one's imported identity, and a new set of values and patterns of behaviour are established in the socially and culturally insulated setting. Goffman (1968) provides a number of descriptions of personal change in closed settings, but Bettelheim's (1986) account of personality change in Nazi concentration camps is the most strikingly vivid. He describes how details of previous lifestyles became blurred as imported identities were destabilized in the closed and physically-threatening camp settings. The camp guards, vested with the ultimate power of life and death, became the role models for the reconstructed personalities which were reflected even in changed clothing, leisure habits and speech. Obviously, these are extreme examples involving cultural invasiveness and physical oppression, but they nonetheless illuminate a repertoire of conditions of socialization that must be established in any programme which aspires to epistemically-significant transmission through role/identity change.

Interpretive change

In sociology the significance of subjective reality is a feature of a number of well-known traditions. Weber's (1978) concept *Verstehen* alerted sociologists to the need to take primary account of the subjectively-intended meaning of an act. In arguing that if we define something as real it can become real in its consequences, W.I. Thomas (1923) was to highlight the impact of the definition of a situation, however idiosyncratic it may appear, on the actor's behaviour. Schutz focused, *inter alia*, on the structure and functioning of the mental constructs — the typifications and relevance systems — embodied in the social world (Wagner, 1973). In *The Social Construction of Reality*, Berger and Luckmann (1973) attempted a reformulation of socialization theory in terms of these traditions. They regard socialization after childhood as the internalization of institutional sub-worlds, their extent and character being determined by the division of labour in society and by the associated social distribution of knowledge. These sub-worlds, internalized in secondary socialization, they point out, 'are generally partial realities in contrast to the "base-world" acquired in primary socialization, yet they, too, are more or less cohesive realities, characterized by normative and affective as well as cognitive components' (p.158). Furthermore, they require a legitimatory mechanism usually incorporating ritual and material symbols.

A variety of phrases in everyday use, e.g. 'to see the light', 'put a different slant on things', 'come around to our way of seeing things', 'get a different perspective on life' attests to a popular awareness of how interpretations of social reality can be open to change. While such interpretations can vary in coverage — a specific act or group, or the totality of reality in its political, religious or aesthetic dimensions — they relate to an epistemic level that is more encompassing and comprehensive than segmental or role/identity change.

Segmental change touches an individual in a limited way. Role/identity change prepares for performance in a social position, with the possibility of personal immersion in the position to the point of identification with it. Interpretive change involves a change of consciousness about reality — about the physical world and its phenomena, about people and their psychological nature, about society and its processes and requirements, and about the less accessible transcendental and spiritual realms. It is essential where the epistemic intent in emancipatory. But, if we exclude formal logic and mathematics, the successful transmission of any of the other epistemic types considered — Hirst's forms of knowledge with their varying truth criteria and Phenix's realms of meaning — is unlikely to occur without some element of interpretive change being experienced by the learners. Since even 'knowledge that' incorporates a particular perspective on reality, modification of a person's propositional knowledge itself represents interpretive change. It can reasonably be argued that any successful socially-committed programme will incorporate, at least, some dimension of interpretive change.

In adult education by far the most comprehensive and best known example of interpretive change is to be found in the programmes devized and advocated by Paulo Freire based on his work on adult literary and rural development in Brazil and Chile. Jarvis (1991a) sees Freire's thinking as having been developed in the same religious and cultural milieu as Acao Popular, a middle-class, radical intellectual movement which developed in Brazil in 1961. Described as para-Christian but with strong theological links with Roman Catholicism, in particular through the medium of the papal encyclical *Mater et Magistra* of Pope John XXIII, Acao Popular was committed to the humanization of the world by means of critical reflection on one's position in the historical process. A fundamental tenet in Freire's thinking relates to the relationship between people and their world: 'There is no history without men and no history for men, there is only history *of* men, made by men and (as Marx pointed out) in turn making them' (1972a, p.101).

In Freire's view the transformation of reality is an historical task, a task to be undertaken by people, but since consciousness of the world is conditioned by one's social context, which in turn conditions attitudes and ways of dealing with reality, it is necessary to develop in people a consciousness that is less and less false. 'Conscientization' — a process by which people develop a critical consciousness, expose myths and ideologies enslaving them, and act according to their own new awareness — is recommended by Freire as the means by which they can attain their rightful position in the historical process. In *Cultural Action for Freedom* (1972) Freire explains how his adult literacy schemes embodied the process of conscientization, and in *Pedagogy of the Oppressed* (1972a) he expands on the more general implications of the use of conscientization in adult education. Freire argues against what he refers to as the 'banking approach' to education because of the manner in which it 'regulates the way the world "enters into" the students' (1972a, p.49) and makes them more passive and adaptable. As an alternative, he suggests 'problem-posing' education in which teacher and students, their roles considerably blurred, analyse in dialogue their social, economic and political context. It is anticipated that by this method students will develop their power to perceive critically the way they exist, and come to see the world as an historical reality susceptible to change. But, this can only be achieved by respecting the students' world-view as a reflection of their situation and by engaging in dialogue about this view and that of the teacher. Any attempt to impose the teacher's interpretation of reality, no matter how well-intentioned, is considered to constitute 'cultural invasion'. For Freire, since knowledge is political, there is no such thing as a neutral education: education either controls or liberates and problem-posing education is 'a task for radicals' (1972a, p.19), and any attempt to prevent it is an act of violence.

In *Pedagogy in Process* (1978, p.24) Freire expands on this pivotal objective of his programme, cultivating the capacity and disposition to interpret and reinterpret one's world, in relation to his literacy campaign in Guinea-Bissau. The act of learning to read and write, in this view, is a creative act that involves a critical comprehension of reality.

> The knowledge of earlier knowledge, gained by the learners as a result of analyzing praxis in its social context, opens to them the possibility

of new knowledge. The new knowledge going far beyond the limits of earlier knowledge, reveals the reason for being behind the facts, thus demythologizing the false interpretations of these same facts. And so, there is now no more separation between thought-language and objective reality. The reading of a text now demands a 'reading' within the social context to which it refers.

Giroux (1979) has referred to this interpretive objective of Freire as the capacity 'to perform a critical reading of reality so that they can act on that reality'.

In recent decades many of these themes have become a feature of sociological theorizing on education: the social distribution of knowledge and its social control function (Young, 1971), Bourdieu and Passeron's (1977) description of the imposition of meanings by power groups in society as cultural violence, and the restraints and possibilities that are available to the dominated in confronting ideology (Apple, 1979; Giroux, 1983).

In developed countries a number of programmes relating to community development and emancipation in its various forms take sustenance and inspiration from Freire's writings. The linking of adult change with community development takes many forms, not all of which involve interpretive change. It is when adult education takes a more active part in the identification and formulation of a community's needs that interpretive change, in its various dimensions, becomes a possibility. Adult education may be *available* to communities seeking to define and respond to local problems or as Lovett (1975), quoting liberally and sympathetically from Freire, appears to propose, adult education can assume a more active advocating role, encouraging analysis and discussion, highlighting local needs and facilitating a local response, be it in relation to youth centres, play schemes or social problems. Related to this, though on a broader front, Mezirow (1978) has discussed the role of adult education in 'perspective transformation'. This form of personal change in adult life pertains to 'meaning perspectives', defined as 'the cultural and psychological assumptions that have influenced the way we pattern our lives'. Mezirow elaborates as follows:

A meaning perspective is an integrated psychological structure with dimensions of thought, feeling and will. What one wants to learn, his readiness to learn, the problems he chooses to act upon, his receptivity to attempts to inform or communicate with him, the sources of legitimation he requires before he will try out new ideas, his conception of what is bad and good and his determination to persevere in taking individual and collective action—all depend upon his meaning perspective.

Meaning perspectives are not merely ways of viewing reality. They also involve proposals as to how one should live one's life, and involve decision-making and action. Maturity is viewed as movement towards meaning perspectives that are more universal, that clarify the social and cultural forces impinging on people and that give them a sense of direction in life. Not surprizingly, Mezirow sees Freire's conscientization programmes as valuable examples of perspective transformation.

For Mezirow, 'there is no higher priority in adult education than to develop its potentialities for perspective transformation', and he mentions women's consciousness-raising groups and re-entry programmes, designed by more than three hundred colleges and universities for women returning to college or work, as relevant examples in the United States.

Both of these conceptions of interpretive change—consciousness-raising and perspective transformation—have generated much debate and a considerable literature. The applicability of Freire's ideas and programmes in developed countries, accusations concerning his respect for his students' viewpoints, and the adequacy of Mezirow's conceptualizations for a theory of adult learning are among the central issues from this debate which will be raised in later chapters.

We now turn to an analysis of some dimensions of interpretive change and to a specification of the learning conditions that must be met for the different kinds of interpretive change to be successful.

A prime consideration in the study of interpretive change is the degree to which the interpretation coincides with the mainstream definition of the world, that is the extent to which it represents institutionalized reality. Definitions of reality can be variously treated by society as 'error', 'unquestionable', or 'what everyone knows'. Society has changed considerably in the range and nature of its institutionalized realities. In a pluralist world there is much less that can be taken for granted or dismissed as error. Whereas Pascal could at one time observe that what was truth on one side of the Pyrenees was error on the other, religions are now inclined to be seen as alternative ways of viewing reality. Recognized as such they are expected to be adhered to by choice rather than officially arbitrated on. No so, however, in the case of the rights of minorities, for instance. To define slavery as improper or unjust in ancient times would have been highly idiosyncratic; at the time of the abolition debate alternative positions may well have been recognized, particularly by non-participants, as points of view; whereas, in modern times, to regard slavery as part of the natural ordering of people would be considered dangerously abnormal. The extent to which institutionalized realities are replacing one another in society is too wide as issue to explore here, apart from noting that the kinds of learning programmes being considered in this book are likely to add their own force to these processes. But, consider, as an example of alternating realities, how religious interpretation might be regarded as deviant in highly-secularized societies or as politically threatening in communist regimes.

Related to the degree of institutionalization is the importance attached by society to the interpretation. Some interpretations relating to the position of the family and the nature of the political order may be given constitutional or legal status. Others, pertaining to the distribution of status and material resources, the role of the mother in child rearing, or extended education may be deemed important for the well-being of society. And, apart from the interpretations which guide and sustain social interaction but remain within the private sphere, there is a multitude of such highly-institutionalized interpretations as language use, deviations from which are not considered critical for society.

The pervasiveness of the interpretation is a third dimension that needs to be considered. Is the interpretation one that pertains to a relatively closed set of phenomena, or does it have far-reaching implications for one's behaviour?

Finally, there is the extent to which the interpretation is identified with a distinct group in society, the degree to which the interpretation can be said to represent institutionalized reality for a particular group and is recognized by the group as such. While there are many interpretive sub-worlds, not all who inhabit them share a consciousness of kind. It is unlikely, for instance, that young children recognize the boundary and membership of the fantasy world of children's stories, magic and folk-heroes in the way that members of a religious sect identify the interpretive implications of membership and non-membership.

Change in relation to such highly-institutionalized realities as explanations of natural phenomena, systems of government and the distribution of rewards, punishments and scarce resources — more a feature of childhood and adolescence — finds its clearest example in adult life during experiences of political and social change, either because of migration to a contrasting political system or because of political upheaval in one's indigenous society.

The programmes of the European Centre for Human Rights Education (1992) in Prague recognize the challenges in attempting to change highly-institutionalized realities throughout post-communist Czechoslovakian society. Studies of popular perceptions of the extent of inequality, opportunity and universalism, and of the operation of meritocracy and achievement principles, suggest that these understandings are still rather vague, largely because the legacy of socialist ideology continues to affect the manner in which distributive justice is conceptualized (Mateju and Rehakova, 1992). The European Centre for Human Rights Education is aware that what is involved in implementing international norms of human rights must be pursued in relation to structures of thinking as they pertain to hierarchies of economic, social, political and civic rights.

The success of these attempts at interpretive change will depend very much on the degree to which resocialization is required. Unlike secondary socialization, which expands on primary socialization and draws on its internalizations, resocialization involves a process of unlearning and disengagement as the person enters new worlds. For Berger and Luckmann (1973, p.182), 'the reality base for resocialization is the present, for secondary socialization the past'. This is because with resocialization 'the past is re-interpreted to conform to the present reality, with the tendency to retroject into the past various elements that were subjectively unavailable at the time', whereas in secondary socialization 'the present is interpreted so as to stand in a continuous relationship with the past, with the tendency to minimize such transformations as have actually taken place'. While ostensively what appears to be involved in the programmes of the European Centre for Human Rights Education is resocialization — the abrupt replacement of communistic with democratic interpretive schemes — there is a view that change along these lines, or at least the conditions which support it, have already been a feature of the biographies of Czechoslovakian citizens. Muller (1991) draws specifically on Berger and Luckmann to argue that what has been experienced in Czechoslovakia is a gradual erosion of the symbolic universe through which communist institutions maintained their control over popular consciousness. He contends that as 'the memory of the generation which connected its individual biography with the victory of ideals of communism' became weak, the power of the old institutional order was blurred and it lost its support in everyday-life consciousness. If Muller's interpretation is correct, then the dissemination of a democratic world-view may be more socially evolutionary and individually progressive than the European Centre for Human Rights Education assumes. There may be a social and biographical past with its legacy of institutionalized realities, however covert, hesitant or dissident in their time, which can now be used as a reality base for the interpretive change its programmes are seeking to enact.

Similar considerations arise with programmes which seek to alter less obviously-political realities of an ecological or feminist character, since in these cases also, though on a limited scale, the degree of continuity in highly-institutionalized realities is at issue.

Interpretive change during the adult years, as has been pointed out, is most likely to involve induction into sub-worlds. To be successful this requires the existence of 'plausibility structures', the social base and social processes through which the sub-world establishes and maintains its view of reality (see Berger and Luckmann, 1973, pp. 166–182). These plausibility structures serve to reduce any doubts individuals might have concerning the new view of reality to which they have been introduced. Contact with those who do not share this new definition of reality — associates, friends, even family — may need to be curtailed or severed. If contact persists, the abrasion of world-views will need to be avoided, immunity to counter definitions of reality cultivated, or rituals developed for disparaging the bearers of these competing realities. At times of crisis, be it for individuals or collectively, these mechanisms may need to become more intense, explicit or extreme. Crisis maintenance is required to offset a serious threat to an individual's loyalty to the reality of the sub-world, or because of a more general threat to the plausibility of the sub-world from more institutionalized realities.

The more pervasive the interpretive change the more the socialization process assumes some characteristics of the parent-child relationship. The child is said to be socialized in a context of affectivity and power-disparity, whereas adult socialization is generally seen to be less emotionally-charged and less power-based. When interpretive change assumes comprehensive dimensions, as in political or religious conversion, or brain-washing in prisoner-of-war camps, figures of normative power, such as charismatic religious or political leaders, or coercive power such as jailers, and a considerable investment of feeling and sentiment are more likely to be involved. The existence of group support for a particular interpretation renders the process all the more explicit and recognizable. Social categories such as tenant farmers, women, ethnic groups and oppressed minorities existed long before their members began to recognize that they shared a common set of deprivations which could, at least, be ameliorated by interpretive socialization to a recognition of the exploitative nature of their condition and to an awareness of the possibilities for action. This process of 'consciousness raising' can be found in such social movements as the Land League in nineteenth-century Ireland (Lee, 1973), and is familiar to modern society in the context of black awareness, civil rights and feminist movements. Religious and political initiation and conversion are examples of interpretive socialization that is both pervasive and group-based and can be formally organized for the interpretive induction of new members.

Conclusion

The epistemic intent of a socially-committed programme is pivotal. So much hinges on the substance of its educative action that its epistemic status can be said to establish a number of imperatives for the manner in which it operates and organizes itself in seeking to achieve its objectives. Space has allowed for no more than a setting out of the basis for a conceptual framework in this regard and the drawing of indicative implications for psychological change and formative strategies. In no sense does the present exploration exhaust the possibilities for analysis that follow from a differentiation of the substance of personal change along the lines of purpose, cosmic function, truth criteria and forms of meaning. Relatedly, this conceptual organization of epistemic status itself invites elaboration, refinement and integration.

Yet, even allowing for the heuristic nature of the conceptualization of epistemic status, and the selectivity in establishing interconnections between epistemic intent, psychological change and formative strategies, it should be clear that to act to alter the consciousness of individuals is to set in motion a series of processes that are essential if the modification is to have any reasonable hope of success. Psychologically, procedural knowledge or technically-motivated knowledge may demand no more than segmental change in participants, an addition to their stock of knowledge or repertoire of skills, a modification of some aspect of their personality, all of which may be specific to a particular domain or setting. It is unlikely that this level of epistemic and psychological change would be adequate to precipitate any more than the most restricted forms of social change. To seek social change of any significance by means of educative action is to commit oneself to deeper and more pervasive psychological change among the participants.

Practical and emancipatory orientations, furthering mutuality in human understanding and freeing people from ideologies, respectively, recur in socially-committed programmes and make greater demands on the psyche. Both require some degree of role/identity and interpretive change. An emancipatory orientation in interpreting the world and establishing its objectivity involves disengagement from competing interpretations and the adoption of world-views that are so pervasive as to require a severing of links with representatives of these competing realities.

In the light of differences in the truth criteria they employ to objectify themselves, forms of knowledge will need to ensure that appropriate legitimatory strategies are in place if they are to be accepted as valid. Where the intention is to alter a person's aesthetic awareness, the educative action will need to mobilize feelings, perceptions and evaluations in such a way that the modification arises, at least in appearance, from the contemplative action of the participants. Such educative action needs to resolve the tension between the pursuit of its objectives and allowing participants to experience self-direction in whatever change occurs. Since they are premised on a vision of a new or adjusted social order many socially-committed programmes will embody a synoptic orientation. They incorporate a coordinated, integrated and valued interpretation of society that requires processes of induction to a sharing of such a drawing together of reality. The deceptive 'knowledge with a direct object' is anything but unproblematic in focusing attention on, delineating and labelling aspects of reality. Symbolic change is fundamental in that it refers to the means of expressing all forms of substantive change and can be used by participants to signal engagement and assent. As well as furthering interpretive change, the modification of participants' instruments of communication and the altering of the categories through which they represent the world operates also to regulate doubt or dissent within a programme.

In signalling the focus of this chapter I described it as a linking exercize, pointing to the possibilities its conceptual analysis of epistemic and psychological change provided for a more precise declaration of a programme's intentions, as well as anticipating the imperatives that follow for the organization of successful socially-committed programmes. We now turn to such an imperative — the establishment of the legitimacy of a programme's substance and agents.

5 The discourse of commitment II: establishing legitimacy

Introduction

To be accepted as legitimate is to achieve a taken-for-granted, natural or proper status within a particular circle of people. It results in the justification of authority, the making acceptable of the requirement that people act in accordance with the prescriptions of others, and the validity of the definition of reality underpinning these prescriptions. Where authority can be freely accepted or rejected, legitimacy is essential. Legitimacy confers rights and reduces contestation and resistance. But even where power is maintained through coercion, no system or individual can survive as an authority for very long unless some degree of acceptability is achieved.

In declaring its intentions — its design for personal formation and social change — a socially-committed programme is simply responding to the request that it outlines its learning objectives and world-view. It is being asked to represent itself in an open, comprehensible and explicit fashion so that those who might consider becoming involved, where they have a choice, can know what intentions the programme has for them and for society.

In establishing legitimacy a programme is being asked on what basis it can presume to influence people and society. Its right to operate as a programme of personal and social change is being held up for consideration. To be credible a programme must establish the authority of its agents and the validity of its world-view, and continue to maintain this status as long as it seeks to influence people. Where legitimacy is in doubt it dissipates commitment. For this reason when a programme's discourse operates to establish legitimacy it is directed not just at the participants but also at those who plan and enact it. The discourse of legitimacy has a self-confirming character about it: it is addressing itself as well as its audience.

The *locus classicus* of the sociological phenomena involved is Weber's discussion of power, authority and legitimacy. Weber's (1964, p.152) most relevant definitions, however, are framed in terms of the interaction of individuals. Thus, power (macht) is 'the probability that one actor within a social relationship will be in a position to carry out his own will despite resistance'. Imperative control (herrschaft), usually identified with authority, is 'the probability that a command with a given specific content will be obeyed by a given group of persons'. Weber points to the sources of motivation of actors to display obedience to commands: personal advantage, affective motives, custom, solidarity. But, he argues, no system of authority limits itself to such appeals as a basis for guaranteeing its continuance. In addition, 'every such system attempts to establish and to cultivate the belief in its legitimacy' (p.325). In raising the question of legitimacy, Weber extends it to a consideration of systems as well as individuals which is more in keeping with the application of the concept to the total operation of socially-committed programmes.

Weber (1964, p.328) distinguishes between three 'pure' types of legitimacy. These are 'ideal types' in the sense of being abstractions and are unlikely to be found in their pure form in real life. The validity of legitimacy claims can be based on rational, traditional or charismatic grounds.

- Rational: based on 'a belief in the "legality" of patterns of normative rules and the right of those elevated to authority under such rules to issue commands'.
- Traditional: 'resting on an established belief in the sanctity of immemorial traditions and the legitimacy of the status of those exercizing authority under them'.
- Charismatic: derived from 'devotion to the specific and exceptional sanctity, heroism or exemplary character of an

individual person, and of the normative patterns or order revealed or ordained by him'.

As well as acknowledging their 'ideal type' nature, Weber also asserted that it was not part of his thinking to expect that 'the whole of concrete historical reality can be exhausted' (p.329) within his conceptual scheme. Etzioni (1964), in his application of Weber's concepts to the study of organizations, drew attention to how crucial it was to realize 'the nature of the power increment which legitimacy bestows', an observation that has become a truism in studies of the functioning of educational institutions as agents of social control, cultural transmission/imposition and status and economic role allocation (Bourdieu and Passeron, 1977). Without legitimacy, as he points out, subjects are more likely to experience alienation from a programme and, because conformity is due to a variety of ulterior motives, participants are less likely to show initiative, be forthcoming and generally to display an openness to its goals and activities. Where a programme succeeds in establishing its legitimacy to participants its impact will be deeper and more effective. Participants are inclined to internalize the programme's culture, so that even where its power is weakened or where participants are removed from the scrutiny of its agents, its impact on their behaviour is more likely to persist. All of this seems particularly appropriate where programmes and not just individuals are involved in establishing legitimacy. In his consideration of power, control and leadership in organizations, Etzioni suggests another variety of legitimacy which should usefully extend Weber's typology and enhance its suitability in the study of socially-committed programmes. This relates to the normative base of a programme's valid exercise of personal formation towards change. Normative legitimacy derives from a shared set of broad cultural values encompassing both programme and participants. Obedience to the detail and specifics of a programme's procedures and ideals is forthcoming because they are perceived by the participants to be encompassed by, and in the final analysis consistent with, a set of beliefs to which they personally subscribe.

As well as different kinds of legitimacy there are also likely to be degrees to which a programme achieves legitimacy. Programmes differ in the ease with which they can establish legitimacy depending on the congruence between their world-views and educative processes and those of the society in which they operate, and on the epistemic status of the learning. In fact, it is useful to think of legitimation as a process that as well as strengthening in validity can also wane, and that this can occur selectively within a programme among its participants, providers, processes and content.

Charismatic legitimacy

Weber (1978, p.241) defined charisma as 'a certain quality of an individual personality by virtue of which he is considered extraordinary and treated as endowed with supernatural, superhuman or exceptional forces or qualities'. Because of the special demands in setting up new learning programmes it is expected that those who show initiative and leadership in this regard would require above average organizational and advocacy skills. But, when what is required is the legitimation of a particular world-view, which may well be deviant in terms of predominant definitions of reality, or the acceptance of the validity of a routine of learning experiences or the credibility of whoever is accorded responsibility for managing this learning, then it is easy to understand why charismatic legitimation, drawing on these 'supernatural', 'superhuman' qualities which Weber speaks of, should prove a particular if not a necessary asset. This is reflected in the profiles of the founders of some of the major adult learning initiatives, many of whom are described in religious terminology and are remembered as strong, larger-than-life personalities. Frequently, charisma is specifically mentioned.

A recent analysis of R.H. Tawney (Elsey, 1991) described him as the 'patron saint' of English adult education, and speaks of his contribution to its 'heroic age' and of his having been 'canonized in at least six biographies'. Tawney regarded systematic adult learning, particularly pertaining to political education, as the means by which workers would gain control and create a socialist order. He had strong religious convictions. For him, a fundamental tenet of christianity was a belief in a common humanity derived from a recognition of God as the Father of Man. In Tawney's legitimation, 'God represented a moral basis to the human condition which had to be achieved through personal awareness and collective action'.

The original idea for the Danish Folk High School movement came from a Lutheran bishop, N.F.S. Grundtvig. Alfred Fitzpatrick, a Presbyterian minister, was the founder of the Canadian Frontier

College. Moses Coady, a Roman Catholic priest and a central figure as guide, mentor and publicist for the Antigonish movement, has been described by one commentator as 'a saintly though forceful figure whose physical presence and searching intellect dominated most meetings he attended' (quoted in Crane, 1991). Laidlaw (1971, p.75), who worked with Coady at the extension department of St Francis Xavier University, concludes that 'under less spirited and courageous leadership than his, the Antigonish Movement could easily have been a milk and water affair with nothing to stir men's hearts and imaginations'. In fact, according to Crane (1991), a number of commentators have independently remarked on the charismatic nature of Coady's leadership. Myles Horton, the founder of Highlander, attended a theological seminary and had worked under the auspices of the Presbyterian Church. Many socially-committed programmes, in fact, have associations with religious bodies or quasi-religious movements, such as the temperance movement, or with organizations with a strong moral dimension such as the French Resistance. These religious convictions and associations contributed to their other-worldly and superhuman sense of mission and commitment.

The public speaking and lecturing styles of Tawney and Coady provide an insight into how disparate approaches, personalities and modes of self-presentation can succeed in establishing a similarly charismatic relationship with followers. Elsey (1991) quotes the following description of Tawney as a lecturer:

> He always had a script, done in his cramped handwriting, all loops and hooks, sometimes on the back of notepaper picked up in hotels, and he would declaim its rolling phrases with quiet intensity. He would steer gargantuan sentences to harbour because he had an unerring sense of the geography of a sentence, revealed in his meticulous punctuation. At the lectern, ash would drop onto his papers and sometimes he would, when transported, thrust his still burning pipe into a pocket of his tweed jacket.

Crane (1991) draws on a number of sources to give us an image of Coady's speaking style. He would begin haltingly, fumbling with a few notes and appearing unsure as to how he should develop his topic. Initially, his audience would wonder if he would talk at all. After a few minutes he would find his theme and words would come easily and effectively.

In the final analysis, as Nyomarkay (1967, p.11) remarks, 'no matter how extraordinary he may be, a person will not become a charismatic leader unless his extraordinariness is recognized by others. The transformation of extraordinariness into charisma depends on the political skills and magnetism of the potential charismatic leader and on his conviction of his historical role'. Charismatic legitimation doesn't follow from the attributes of individuals. It has to be accomplished in social interaction. It is a social product, a phenomenon created by actors in a social situation. Similarly, it has to be maintained and guarded against the threat of possible dilution. Willner (1984, p.4) stressed the accomplishment and maintenance of charismatic authority in observing that it is 'lodged neither in office not in status but derives from the capacity of a particular person to arouse and maintain belief in himself or herself as the source of legitimacy'.

Any attempt to understand charismatic legitimacy solely in terms of the attributes of an individual leader or authority figure is destined to being incomplete. A number of writers on authority have drawn attention to the intersubjective dimension of charisma, to the centrality of the relationship involved. Blondel (1987, p.54), in his study of political leadership, concludes that 'if there is one element of certainty about charismatic authority, it is that it is based on the direct relationship between followers and leaders'. Willner (1984) identifies three dimensions of this charismatic relationship—the leader-image dimension, the idea-acceptance dimension, and the compliance dimension. These dimensions emerge in Wallis' study of Dianetics and Scientology and, in particular, in the manner in which its founder, L. Ron Hubbard, generated and institutionalized charismatic authority. It is a case study of the accomplishment and maintenance of charismatic authority.

Acquaintances, Wallis (1976, p.248) tells us, remember Hubbard as a 'man of powerful personality', as someone who would 'make you feel things that you had never felt before'. He seemed to be always completely convinced of the validity of what he was doing, of the truth of what he said and of his own ability. Wallis says that he was unable to find an occasion when Hubbard admitted to making a mistake or apologizing: 'he seemed to lack the capacity to doubt, and in his personality and self-assurance others were able to see the strengths that they lacked, and thereby found it easier to believe'.

As the founder of Dianetics, Hubbard had a superior status in the movement. When others felt themselves to be equally competent

108

to develop and expand the movement, Hubbard's position became increasingly insecure. In response to this threat to his leadership, he developed Scientology which provided a transcendental basis for his leadership. He claimed to have 'penetrated the realm of the supernatural and there secured knowledge which would restore to men their long-lost spiritual abilities' (p.249). Hubbard was perceived to have privileged access to supernatural knowledge which overrode psychological and philosophical understanding. Wallis compares him to Buddha in that 'he had made available a route to Total Freedom' (p.250). As this knowledge was codified and a belief structure established the movement assumed a more self-consciously religious character.

While this analysis of Hubbard as a charismatic authority on Dianetics and Scientology is instructive, particularly in relation to the evolution of the legitimacy of his authority, his political and apparently manipulative strategy in maintaining himself in a position of authority may distract from its utility as a model of how charismatic authority can develop. He subordinated some potential leaders and expelled others. In the movement's publications he projected an image of himself as being superior in every way, someone to be sought after for advice and direction, and an authority figure with a capacity to arbitrate on members' knowledge and orthodoxy. If we distance ourselves from whatever strategic change was involved, and from whatever insincerity may be inferred, we are left with a case study of how feelings, ideas and behaviours are mobilized, and loyalty and attachment cultivated, in the changed circumstances of a movement's evolution.

In their early formulation Hubbard legitimated his programmes, and their underlying theories of human development and capacity, by means of his distinctive and striking personality and his ability to win attention and belief by virtue of his personal magnetism. But, these theories claimed to be scientific and therefore open to analysis, understanding and elaboration by whoever might develop a knowledge of them. Later, Hubbard became less the source and more the conduit through which transcendental knowledge, which is superior to mere mortal understanding, could be made public. This confirmed Hubbard's charisma, because of his supernatural relationship, but it also opened up the way for the systematization of a set of beliefs which were beyond scientific verification, but which invited assent in the context of a community of believers.

Texts have also generated their own charisma. This is achieved when texts act, not with a view to adding another perception or viewpoint to discourse, but to enhance emotional strength, give a depth of meaning, confirm within a particular tradition, confer or test loyalty or orthodoxy, rally support and focus cognitive and affective attention.

Texts that appear to have achieved a charismatic status would include *The Bible, The Prince, The Communist Manifesto, Small is Beautiful, The Second Sex,* and *Quotations from Chairman Mao,* to name but a few. These texts no longer rely on their authors for the strength of their attraction to successive generations. It is considered to be no adequate criticism that the writers who created these texts may have deviated from some of their precepts in their lifestyle, as might be argued in relation to Marx or Simone de Beauvoir, or that like Mao they have been politically discredited. Neither does it matter that the Bible may be dismissed as myth, or Schumacher as a primitivist romantic, or that Machiavelli may be elevated to the status of modern satirist. Charismatic texts take on a life of their own. Though the products of thinking, speculating, feeling or prescribing by flesh and blood individuals in real life situations they are nonetheless 'objects'. As such they are available to posterity in a static, unchanging, externalized format that makes no concessions to changing linguistic usage, social norms, cultural forms or definitions of the world. And while it is true that written language more than oral communication facilitates individual interpretation and varied personal meanings (Olson, 1977), texts do not always, as Smith (1985) argues, 'invite contention'. Those that have achieved a charismatic status invite reverence in the first instance and, later, assent. Within a community of believers they become sacred objects.

Charismatic texts are not cited to add to rational linear argument. For this reason they are used routinely by way of assertion rather that as a measured exposition of a particular thesis. Mary Daly, the American theologian and pioneer of radical feminist philosophy, recognized this use. Introducing her seminal study *Gyn/Ecology* (1979), she points to the problematic nature of the relationship between the intentions of the author and the uses to which a text can be put. While for her the writing of the book was part of the feminist project, she nontheless acknowledges that a book by its nature is 'an objectification of thinking/imagining/speaking', and that, while the dilemmas, contradictions and tensions 'of the living/verbing writer' are real, much of the problem relates to the manner in which books are perceived. 'If they are per-ceived/used/idolized as sacred texts (like the bible or the writings of chairman mao), then of course the idolators are caught on a wheel that turns but does not move. They "spin" like wheels on ice — a "spinning" that in no way resembles feminist process'.

The citation of key passages from charismatic texts and the introduction of characteristic phrases and words into discourse develop their own intersubjective realm of meaning. The following examples are illustrative.

Machiavelli's advice in *The Prince*:

> From this arises the question whether it is better to be loved more than feared, or feared more that loved. The reply is that one ought to be both feared and loved, but as it is difficult for the two to go together, it is much safer to be feared than loved, if one of the two has to be wanting. For it may be said of men in general that they are ungrateful, voluble, dissemblers, anxious to avoid danger, and covetous of gain; as long as you benefit them, they are entirely yours (reproduced in Jones, 1969, p.43).

Simone de Beauvoir's celebrated introduction to Book 2 of *The Second Sex* (1977, p.295):

> One is not born, but rather becomes, a woman. No biological, psychological, or economic fate determines the figure that the human female presents in society; it is civilization as a whole that produces this creature, intermediate between male and eunuch, which is described as feminine. Only the intervention of someone else can establish an individual as an Other.

Shaul, in his foreword to Freire's *Pedagogy of the Oppressed* (1972a, pp. 13–14):

> There is no such thing as a neutral educational process. Education either functions as an instrument which is used to facilitate the integration of the younger generation into the logic of the present system and bring about conformity to it *or* it becomes 'the practice of freedom', the means by which men and women deal critically and creatively with reality and discover how to participate in the transformation of their world.

In group sessions the declamation of key passages such as these induces a rhythmic effect. Their enactment generates a dramatic event. One's sense of membership derives from a recognition in the text of a meaningfulness in terms of one's biography and life situation. The chanting of slogans by the Maoist students is but a heightened and more stylized example of this phenomenon. Rational analysis and considered assent are not required, and where they are offered or suggested they may well be explicitly dismissed as a distraction under the guise of a spurious neutrality. They are equally likely to be disparaged as an amoral uncommitted orientation, as as technicist fetish or as a male way of interpreting the world and the significance of phenomena. Daly (1979) warns against this 'anti-cerebral' orientation: '"Feminist" anti-intellectualism is a mere reaction against moronizing masculinist education and scholarship, and it is a trap'.

If a trap, then also a very real dilemma that confronts strategy, method and ideological position, and not just in relation to feminist programmes. The more one intellectualizes the meaning to be extracted from a charismatic text the more its sacredness is dissipated. Once a text is found to yield multiple interpretations it becomes profane and no longer commands loyalty on the basis of its unique and reserved status. At this point a programme's legitimatory base may give way to a more traditional, normative or rational basis. Where this transition is successful, loyalty to the programme and the validity of its world-view may be put on a more secure basis since charisma is of its nature volatile. On the other hand, those who fail to make the transition may experience less commitment, a greater questioning or be lost to the programme.

There are few recorded analyses of how texts come to achieve a charismatic status for people, and fewer still where a more measured approach to the text subsequently evolved. For this reason, Okely's *Simone de Beauvoir. A Re-reading* (1986) is of particular significance to the understanding of the appeal and impact of charismatic texts. In her late teens Okely experienced Simone de Beauvoir as an intimate through contact with her writings, in particular *The Second Sex*. 'She was our mother, our sister and something of ourselves. Her name was a password and a slogan' (p.1). And also as a role model: 'Some of us modelled our lives on her pronouncements' (p.2). She quotes the writer Alice Schwarzer, '*The Second Sex* was like a secret code that we emerging women used to send messages to each other. And Simone de Beauvoir herself, her life and her work, was—and is—a symbol' (p.2). Some twenty years later Okely could write, 'today I can criticize de Beauvoir for her suspect generalization about "humanity's" spontaneous psychological reaction to the physicality of childbirth, but (then) I underlined it' (p.77). This is repeated in relation to de Beauvoir's Eurocentric, middle-class, urban, white bias, essentially that of mid-century French cafe society and the bourgeoisie, her partial success in challenging the mythologies about women which are to be found in the work of male authors, the tension between the biologically-determined and the socially-constructed interpretation of women, and her misreading of Freud, and Engels and Marx, in relation to the significance of the unconscious and macro-economic forms, respectively. In reflecting on a re-reading of *The Second Sex'*, Okely observed that while it 'now reads differently' the earlier reading cannot be easily set aside: 'I am astonished at how many phrases and ideas I consciously and unconsciously absorbed from *The Second Sex.*' Interestingly, these are illuminated by reference to marginal notes on the text made on an early reading. Okely concludes, 'some of these ideas are no longer appropriate but they are lying around somewhere in the back of my brain' (p.2).

Pure charismatic legitimacy relies totally on the magnetism of a person or text. As Berger and Berger (1976, p.289) point out, the instruction of Jesus 'you have heard it said—but I say unto you' epitomizes this appeal. In reality, charismatic legitimacy is usually supplemented by other bases for the legitimacy claims of agents and their message: the personal appeal of an individual or text remains but there isn't a total reliance on it.

Where this occurs the charismatic component attracts attention, commands engagement, mobilizes followers and provides a focus for the programme and the world-view involved.

Normative legitimacy

Normative legitimacy derives from a shared set of assumptions relating to bedrock issues fundamental to a programme's operation and objectives. To this extent, normative legitimacy is based on a consensus, and the greater the consensus and the more comprehensive its coverage the more established the legitimacy will be. Obedience to leaders within the programme is judged to be rightfully expected because they operate within this consensus. Where normative legitimacy operates, the validity of a world-view and the authority of individuals to transmit this world-view are dependent, not on rational analysis, not on appeals to history or tradition, not on the peculiar and unique personality of an individual, but on the fact that a particular group of people believes something to be true.

What this common belief might be can range from the transcendental, across cosmology, include theories of the origins of social problems, or be as basic as vocational reskilling. Such beliefs will be beyond the agenda of whatever analysis or speculation might operate within the programme since these are the core assumptions on which the programme is based. To allow that these assumptions might be open to question would be to undermine normative legitimacy, since to do so would be to dilute the normative character of the interaction. In such a case, where the 'certainties' lose their taken-for-granted status, their facticity, validity or correctness, and the normative base is eroded, another source of legitimacy has to be established if the programme is to continue to command allegiance.

Normative legitimacy incorporates what Newman (1973) referred to as the 'principle of dogma'. This use of the term dogma is not to be identified with closed-mindedness or autocracy or with any of the many negative associations which the term routinely evokes. Speaking of his own religious formation, Newman stressed that, while he had changed in many things, from the age of fifteen dogma had been the fundamental principle of his religion. Dogma relates to 'first principles of whatever kind' and for Newman the most momentous of these in the religious sphere would be the truths of divine revelation. These doctrines are, because of their origin, independent of human reason. He warned against 'the exercise of thought upon matters in which, from the constitution of the human mind, thought cannot be brought to any successful issue'. Accordingly, the 'anti-dogmatic' standpoint is mistaken because it involves 'subjecting to human judgement those doctrines which are in their nature beyond and independent of it' (p.193).

Dogma derived from divine revelation is a routine element of religious experience, and many great minds over the centuries have submitted to it, as Newman did, on the basis that it was a virtue of the intellect to know its limitations. As 'first principles of whatever kind', dogma, however, is not confined to programmes which aspire to change in relation to religious, transcendental or spiritual realms. Nor does it necessarily rely on some other-worldly authority to give it the status of dogma. It may be considered to be a bedrock assumption because of one's personal socialization to a value system, because of the dysfunctioning its questioning might occasion, or simply because first principles of some kind are necessary if social progress is to be made and nihilism avoided.

Hume's contention that values cannot be reduced to facts is relevant to the principle of dogma and normative legitimacy. It highlights a common misinterpretation and also provides a point of development. It is not uncommon for dogma to be identified exclusively with moral discourse, with prescriptions of how things ought to be, and set apart from scientific or factual enquiry. Similarly, Hume's distinction between fact and value is often expressed in 'naive empiricist terms which suggests that science is exclusively factual, while morals or politics are irremediably non-factual and evaluative' (Clarke, 1985, p.248). As Clarke goes on to rightly point out, even the most avowedly of factual analyses of the world are grounded on value judgements of various kinds—what is to be given priority as a research issue, the categories of knowledge according to which the world can be best interpreted, and what is to be preferred as a test of valid knowledge. Thus, Hume's distinction has a much broader application than is routinely understood. In all realms of enquiry there are values, and these cannot be justified except by reference to other value judgements. So also with assumptions. Schutz (in Wagner, 1966) points to a fundamental category of untestable assumptions—the lawfulness of the phenomena to be explained, the capacity of language to represent the world, the mutuality of mental engagement in a communicative encounter—when he argues that reciprocal awareness and communication presuppose a shared knowledge and a common world, including social relationships, and not the reverse. And this isn't even to touch on the distinguishing assumptions that give a programme its particular character. Similarly, all socially-committed programmes incorporate an element of dogma and it is from this, and its maximization, that normative legitimacy draws.

In their account of operating feminist group work Butler and Wintram (1991) describe how they sought to address the invisibility of women's experience and knowledge by reclaiming women's own history and language. For them a core assumption is that the personal is political. Since power disparity and exploitation are lived out in women's personal lives, they hope that a process of self-reflection and analysis will lead to an understanding of how social structures operate to confirm and perpetuate this exploitation. In this way women can come to understand, challenge and change patriarchy and the manner in which it systematically and in every domain of life oppresses women. For Butler and Wintram, the feminist beliefs on which their group work strategies are based are proclaimed 'with commitment rather than romanticism'. These 'core feminist beliefs ... are tried and tested, the corner stone of feminist thought and practice'. As they put it, 'our journey begins on the road of feminist philosophical principles' (p.6).

Other socially-committed programmes share this dogmatic element, in the sense that those involved in the interaction have already accepted certain validity or truth claims that are fundamental to it. For radicals, dogma takes the form of the class basis of society and the existence of alienation and exploitation. For democrats it is majoritarianism. Revolutionary movements accept the necessity of violence as a means of achieving their goals, be they emancipation, justice or liberation. For the peace movement, violence is anathema. Specifications on ecological balance and the relationship between people and nature are the first principles for environmental programmes.

Programmes vary in the challenges they face in establishing the dogmatic character of their fundamental tenets. McGuire (1982, p.251) points out that one of the hazards of being a cognitive minority is the tendency for the group's behaviour to be labelled as deviant. 'Strongly religious groups' such as the Jesus People, Moonists, Hare Krishnas and pentacostals are viewed as 'kooks', 'freaks', 'weirdos'. The application of these labels demonstrates the 'normative non-religiousness of the larger society'. In contrast, scrutiny of the assumptions on which literacy programmes are based is considered to be unnecessary. In modern society the inability to read and write strikes us as strangely pathological. Within a democratic system which places such emphasis on political participation it is an aberration. In an age of information and extended formal education it strains credulity that so many in western society reach adulthood without a mastery of such basic skills of communication. However, programmes committed to language change or revival throughout society are more likely to be normatively contentious.

Cultural responses of this nature change over time. In the case of peace, ecological and feminist movements we find evidence of a greater tolerance of their assumptions and first principles over recent decades. Their assessment of the world's problems and the priorities to be given to them are now less likely to be dismissed as extreme or as fringe concerns. To varying degrees the contentions of these movements have passed into the realm of the normative in society in general. When this stage has been reached, a programme's normative legitimacy faces a reduced threat from external definitions of reality. This isn't to imply that there would be widespread support for the principles involved but, rather, that they have come to be accepted as reasonable positions to take within the tolerated range of cognitive and moral positions within a society's culture.

Where the maintenance of normative legitimacy is problematic, a programme is likely to develop strategies to boost the most bedrock, at least, of its first principles. In her study of Pentecostal groups McGuire (1982, p.122) distinguishes between the factual nature of members' statements in giving testimony during group sessions and their meaningfulness. Some offered detailed mathematical calculations of the number to be saved on the last day, others spoke of the effects of the laying on of hands, all of which contradicted interpretations of official Catholic Pentecostal teaching. It may be, McGuire suggests, that the challenging of members' witnessing would strike at the heart of the group itself since a religious group bases its legitimacy on an understanding that what is being participated in is a shared religious experience. There is also evidence of this indulgent or lenient approach in the feminist group work experiences of Butler and Wintram (1991). There it can be explained in terms of its working-class context and the need to ease the working-class women, some of whom would have joined the groups against domestic and social resistance, into the mainstream of feminist principles.

Traditional legitimacy

Socially-committed programmes which aspire to significant social change are usually the work of minorities, particularly in their initiation and early formulation. In such cases, the critique of the existing social order and the vision of what should replace it are unrepresentative of the social thinking of their time. Such programmes are vulnerable to the accusation of being disruptive of society and of the personal lives of the people they influence. Those who initiate and enact them are frequently disparaged as 'disgruntled', 'political', or as *agents provocateur*. All of this is compounded by the fact that socially-committed programmes which have a strong social-reformist component usually proclaim, with varying degrees of emphasis, the virtues of democracy, popular participation, diffused power and egalitarianism. Yet, they can be readily accused of ignoring, in their strategies and educative processes, these same social and political virtues which their world-view proclaims. Where such tensions exist, a programme is presented with a particular challenge in establishing legitimacy since it must justify the socially-disruptive roles of its personnel as well as educative activities that are derived from an unrepresentative view of society. Advocates of radical change through education recognize this vulnerability. They are aware of the accusation that they are ' "politically-motivated activists", "committed to creating class conflict" where it does not exist and relentlessly ignoring "the freedom of individuals" to "live as they choose" ' (Thompson, 1980). Frequently, their response is to appeal to history. When Frank Milligan, a British innovator in adult education for the unemployed in the 1930s, was accused by a civil servant of being an agitator, he quoted John Stuart Mill's assertion, that 'nothing is more certain than that improvement of human affairs is wholly the work of uncontented characters' (Groombridge, 1976). Legitimation is established by placing the unrepresentative character of the programme in historical context. It is projected within a tradition of social activism and protest which over time has gained acceptability. Legitimation is by reference to precedent and antecedent. Persons, controversies, institutions and events are selected from the flux of historical space and brought into an evolving relationship with the programme being legitimated. The programme, in turn, is accorded a pedigree by being placed within a particular tradition, which allows it to be represented in terms of collective social change rather than as a manifestation of individual disenchantment, manipulation or agitation.

Maritain's (1963, pp. 139–146) concept of 'prophetic shock minorities' captures the imagery, sentiments and rationalizations of legitimatory discourse which appeals to traditions of dissent. The terminology of the concept is itself suggestive of this — prophecy as a vision of a better future, the shock of contestation, dissent and the disruption of established views, and the unrepresentative nature of minorities. Maritain is concerned with elements of a democracy which, though apart from its legal structures, are essential to its well-being, development and improvement. His premise is that the people need prophets, and democracy, he argues, cannot do without them. They provide 'the dynamic leaven', the energy that fosters political movements of a kind that cannot be legislated for or built into political structures since it is personal and experiential and based on individual initiative.

Maritain acknowledges that these prophets are usually self-appointed. Their mission originates 'in their own hearts and consciousness'. They lack the democratic mandate. In fact, as shock minorities their task is to operate as political and ideological shock troops. As pioneering minorities they seek to question, cultivate constructive dissent, and hold up the possibility of a better society. As such, they function not as representatives but rather as 'inspired servants' of the people.

> The people are to be awakened — that means that the people are asleep. People as a rule prefer to sleep. Awakenings are always bitter. Insofar as their daily interests are involved, what people would like is business as usual: everyday misery and humiliation as usual. People would like not to know that they are the people. It is a fact that, for good or evil, the great historical changes in political societies have been brought about by a few, who were convinced that they embodied the real will — to be awakened — of the people, as contrasting with the people's wish to sleep (p.142).

Maritain reaches back into history to find examples of this political and ideological awakening in the work of the pioneers of trade unionism and the labour movement, among anti-slavery campaigners and in national liberation, human rights and constitutional movements. He stresses their unrepresentative character: 'At the time of the Risorgimento, the great majority of Italians surely preferred not to be set free from the Austrian yoke. If a popular vote had been taken at the time of Samuel Adams, we may wonder whether the majority would have voted for the War of Independence. If a popular poll had been taken in France in 1940, it is highly probable that the majority would have voted for Marshal Pétain — they believed he hated collaboration with the Germans as they did' (p.142). In these and similar cases, he contends, the majority was wrong and the shock minorities were right.

In justifying social action on a post-factum basis, the legitimatory power of tradition is affirmed. We are invited to assess the rightness of a socially-committed programme, not in terms of the orthodoxy of its thinking or the standing of its key personnel, but in relation to similar initiatives, which in their time were equally unrepresentative and socially critical, and came to be recognized with the passing of history to have been in the best interests of humanity.

Where discourse seeks to legitimate a socially-committed programme by appeals to tradition there is an impulse to identify its antecedents, to create its own history. This may well involve revizionism, the rewriting of history in a manner that alters periodization, 'facts' and their significance, and, above all, their meaning. Discourse can, accordingly, be generative in a manner frequently identified by anthropologists in their studies of the functioning of myth as the rationale for a tribe's ideologies, political system and social structure. The manner in which a programme represents itself to itself and to others is rarely static. It will rework the past selecting, ignoring, adding and redefining. In this, the processes of demonizing, sanctifying, victimizing and martyrizing — the extracting of events, institutions and people from history and giving them a new meaning such that they can add to the potency of traditional legitimation — is central. Du Preez (1982, p.4) describes this process in relation to social movements, quoting Schlegel's assertion that 'historians are prophets in reverse':

> perfectly ordinary people, who were often involved in smuggling and thieving, became heroes. Insignificant events are often taken out of context to model relations between the collective and its opponents... A careful scrutiny of the history of any country will show many incidents... which have become symbols. These incidents confirm the existence of oppressors and can be used in calls on us to share the identity of the martyrs and to admit the implications of their identity.

Socially-committed programmes directed towards the interests of the working class have a long and geographically-dispersed tradition to draw on. It goes back in well-documented and widely-debated form to the beginning of the industrial revolution, and developments can be found in cultural settings as diverse as America, England, Scandinavia and Italy. Conveniently, since contemporary programmes which aspire to serving the interests of the 'workers' differ in terms of how this category within society is to be named and interpreted, this tradition varies widely in its strategies and understanding of the 'problem' which they seek to correct.

The Workers' Educational Association in Britain has been identified with the liberal approach, encouraging students to analyse the relative merits of competing ideologies, to adopt a questioning attitude, and to formulate their own evaluations and positions (Fieldhouse, 1989). In America, the Work People's College and the Labour College Movement, which were active from the beginning of the century, were based on an explicit class analysis of society. They sought to illuminate the excesses of capitalism for workers and to help them to develop skills which would allow them to further their immediate material interest in negotiating with employers, and ultimately to create a new social order. Danish Folk High Schools and the Antigonish movement in Nova Scotia cultivated the cooperative idea. O'Rahilly's workers' courses in Ireland were based on the contention that the workers' interests would be best served in a society organized according to Roman Catholic social principles. The Società Humanitaria de Milan was particularly innovative. Founded in 1893, in Lovett's (1989) description it 'convened the first European conference on unemployment; the first cooperative housing scheme; the first institution for the rehabilitation of the unemployed; trained cooperators; had a large "People's Theatre"; started the Italian People's Universities; started the first adult education unions; promoted People's Libraries — all before 1910'.

Accordingly, contemporary providers seeking to serve the needs of 'workers' have considerable choice if they wish to appeal to tradition to justify their programmes. An examination of how this tradition has been used to legitimatory effect in contemporary programmes provides considerable evidence of revizionism and, in particular, the practice of demonizing and sanctifying events and people where appropriate.

The Workers' Educational Association has been dismissed by the Labour College Movement as reformist, accused of teaching 'bourgeois social science' and 'of being incorporated into the status quo' (Brown, 1980). When in 1948, however, the Irish Trade Union Congress invited the General Secretary of the Workers' Educational Association to speak at a public meeting in Dublin, the occasion drew a strong protest from the Roman Catholic newspaper, *The Standard*. It warned workers that 'the activities of the adult education movement in Britain have been largely directed towards propagating Marxism' (quoted in Cathcart, 1989). *The Standard* commended the workers' courses offered at University College, Cork. The President of University College Cork, Alfred O'Rahilly, with whom these courses were identified, advocated their development and expansion by reference to insidious external threats: 'we are in a unique position in this country where the mass of the workers are faithful to their religion and have resisted subversive ideologies. Let us beware of complacency and apathy. Hostile forces are at work, all the more dangerous because they disguise themselves as neutral and liberal. Irish Catholic workers must bestir themselves lest leadership pass out of their control' (quoted in Cathcart, 1989). In an exchange with H.G. Wells, O'Rahilly situated his educational efforts in the context of anti-colonial and national independence struggles, referring to his 'Catholic forebears' who had suffered 'the persecution of Mr Wells' fellow-countrymen' (quoted in Gaughan, 1986, p. 245). In turn, O'Rahilly's diploma programmes have been dismissed as 'a series of courses for trade unionists on Catholic social teaching' (Whyte, 1984, p.160). Clearly, there is not just a history of workers' education but rather a series of programmes, personalities and events that can yield a variety of 'histories' with their characteristic symbols and their distinctive legitimatory potential. And this appears to be as true of academic accounts as it is of the competing narratives of the main protagonists. Brown (1980) contrasts Kelly's *The History of Adult Education in Great Britain*, a standard work on the topic, 'which contains a handful of insubstantial references to the Labour College movement, whereas it has a great deal of substance on the W.E.A.' with Simon's treatment which he describes as being 'hostile to the W.E.A., whilst containing much, often of an uncritical nature, on the Labour College movement'.

Some programmes build a retrospective component into their activities which establishes for the participants their location within a particular tradition. This has been greatly facilitated by the emergence of oral history as an acceptable method of inquiry. Yarnit (1980), the tutor organizer and co-ordinator of the Liverpool programme, Second Chance to Learn, records that the most frequent question from visitors to the programme was 'why so much History?'. Two-thirds of the timetable was given over to history, and history also formed a major topic for tutorial work and weekend seminars. Much of the written work had historical themes. He explains that history was the 'chosen vehicle' for exploring such key concepts as class, nation, race and sex within the context of a 'recognition that exploitation was the central feature of class society and that the purpose of education was to confront the student with his/her class position, helping them towards a critical understanding of their position'.

The rise and fall of Liverpool as a port and a city, the starting point of much of the programme's content, proved to be a fruitful avenue for exploring these concepts. This was because of Liverpool's link with Britain's imperialist era and third-world exploitation, with slavery, with racism and the Irish, and with industrial developments in the north of England. Contemporary autobiography, archives, newspaper and film, as well as interviews with people who had lived through these economic and social developments, were all used to construct accounts of the past.

The manifest function of this historical dimension was to help people to locate themselves in history with a view, not merely to understanding the social and economic forces that shaped their exploitation, but above all to position them intellectually and motivationally to act collectively to correct it. The legitimatory function of historicity, though less adverted to because of its latent nature, was equally important for the operation and success of the programme. By establishing that a history of dissent and protest exists, be it in relation to class, gender, nation or race, the discordant character of the programme was eased and its activities were made to seem more normal, proper and unremarkable than they otherwise might be. As the carrier of a tradition there was also a sense of a future which is essential for the creation of hope and the cultivation of motivation. Yarnit quotes Robert Owen's assertion with approval, that the working person has the right to 'learn what he is in relation to past ages, to the period in which he lives, to circumstances in which he is placed, to the individuals around him and to future events'.

Rational legitimacy

The most formal examples of rational legitimacy are to be found among legally-prescribed roles. While such roles are rare in adult learning relationships, the manner in which they become routinized and taken-for-granted is indicative of how more voluntary authority relationships can achieve acceptability.

In regimes with compulsory schooling pupils are obliged in law to submit themselves to formation, impinging on a wide spectrum of their behaviours, emotions, attitudes and beliefs, up to a specified age. Teachers are required to act as the agents of this formation. The obligations of both positions, and their complementary character, are asserted to be proper by reference to educational legislation. The teacher's role can be further extended by virtue of teachers being considered to be 'in loco parentis', a legal status that is also given to youth workers and scout leaders. Parents, themselves, despite a considerable dilution of their power since the time of the Roman *paterfamilias*, continue to be legally vested with substantial rights in relation of the formation of their children. This is recognized, sometimes adverted to as a matter for moral consideration, occasionally questioned, but it is only with regard to religious formation that it is contested with any regularity. Otherwise, the rights of parents in imposing their mark on the aesthetic, cultural, political and moral formation of their children is rarely a matter of debate. Even parents who are obsessive with regard to the cultivation of certain skills — sport and music are obvious examples — face little by way of a legitimatory crisis. This absence of questioning is even more paradoxical where offspring are perceived as the future hope of national, religious and communal movements, and to this end are placed in kibbutzim and the youth wings of paramilitary and fascist organizations (Bettelheim, 1969). However, a close reading of the changing emphasis in UNESCO declarations on children's rights since the 1950s (Oswanczyk, 1985) suggests that, at that level of discourse at least, parental authority is less robust than it used to be.

Legally-prescribed authority relationships rarely find it necessary to appeal to the justification of law to achieve and maintain legitimacy. Only in times of crisis, disputation or disagreement do parents, teachers, youth workers and scout leaders refer to the legal basis of their duties, obligations and power. The routinization of these formal roles over time helps to explain this. They are enacted widely throughout society and in a semi-public arena. In some cases, they represent transitional events in the lifecycle — starting and finishing school, moving from one level to the next. Their legal standing exists as a component of the stock of cultural knowledge, known in such a public and taken-for-granted sense that its proclamation is rarely necessary.

Legal status can be signified by means of ritual and symbol as a feature of this routinization process. Titles, modes of dress and insignia set teachers and scout leaders apart from those over whom they legally exercize their authority. But, as well as differentiating between participants in the encounter, ritual and symbol 'construct a framework of meaning over and beyond the specific situational meanings' (Bernstein, 1975). Thus, award ceremonies, uniforms, saluting the flag, morning prayer and induction procedures function to relate the individual 'to a social order, to heighten respect for that order, to revivify that order within the individual and, in particular, to deepen acceptance of the procedures which were used to maintain continuity, order and boundary and which control ambivalence towards the social order' (Bernstein, 1975). And this is only to draw on the 'flat view' of ritual in the tradition of Durkheim and the functional anthropologists who interpret ritual as 'reflections' of key features of the social structure. A more fluid generative view of ritual, ascribing to it the capacity to shape, structure, create meaning and redefine relationships between groups (McLaren, 1986), will be introduced in Chapter 6 where we explore the associative character of socially-committed programmes.

A more general source of rational legitimacy, widespread where adults are involved, is the involvement of 'experts' in a programme. Those who are recognized as having expertise have usually achieved this status by virtue of formal training and the possession of established credentials. The degree of professionalization of a role is also important. The longer the training, the greater the degree of induction into a moral code relating to client service, and the more there is self-government, the more likely the role will be vested with rational legitimacy. For Weber rational legitimacy was bound up with bureaucratization with its focus on the 'office'. This involves clearly specified obligations and areas of competence, and predictable and non-emotive functioning.

In socially-committed programmes the identification and specification of needs by 'experts', be their authority identified with professionalism or bureaucracy, is the prime example of a practice that routinely attracts rational legitimacy. When this occurs the formative intentions of the programme and its wider social aspirations are perceived to be acceptable because they have been prescribed in the service of participants' needs by those who, because of their knowledge, training and judgement, are deemed to be competent authorities. As Lawson (1979, pp. 36–37) points out, the concept of need gives the impression of providing the organizer of a learning programme with an objective basis on which to make judgements. To say that one is meeting a need is deemed to be a fitting justification for a programme's immediate objectives. 'The logic of "need" statements', he argues, are 'similar to that of some statements involving the word of "God" or its analogues. To say of a situation that "it represents the will of God" or "it is the will of Allah" is to cut short all further comment'. There is nothing else to be said because concepts like God represent 'logical stopping points' in that 'they are at the very edge of what can be said'.

Leagans' (1964) suggestions on how needs in relation to rural and agricultural change might be determined is an example of this appeal to rational procedures. For Leagans, needs represent 'an imbalance, lack of adjustment, or gap between the present situation or status quo and a new or changed set of conditions assumed to be more desirable'. Needs are the difference between what is and what ought to be. The determination of both of these statuses is treated by Leagans as an empirical exercize. 'What is' can be determined by a study of the situation, involving a careful selection, analysis and interpretation of facts. 'What ought to be' can be determined by research findings and the value judgements of those knowledgeable in relation to agricultural and rural change. According to Leagans, the central task facing leaders of agricultural extension programmes 'is that of helping people recognize what their behaviour is like, what their farm and home practices and conditions are like, and what their communities are like (each in relation to what they could and ought to be) — and seeing all of this in relation to the knowledge, skill and effort necessary to help people make changes that are possible and desirable'. The entire process is presented as following logical, considered and non-contestable procedures. It is assumed that the practice of need-identification is in the interest of the potential participants, who are being put in touch with the reality of their situation and with the steps they must take if they are to improve themselves and their communities. This assumption that there is no intrusion from the values of those who conduct the analysis of need is essential to the establishment of rational legitimacy.

Viewed in this manner as a technical exercize, the specification of need is deceptively simple and unproblematic. Most commentators, however, acknowledge that, as a concept, need is extremely complex. There are methodological problems of isolating, identifying and labelling needs, but most of all there is the 'value' problem, since the concept of need is ultimately a normative issue. Examples of the advocacy of two disparate forms of social change — modernization and liberation — illustrate how embed-

126

ded in value judgements the specification of need can be. These are derived from the recommendations of the Murphy Reports on the kinds of need which required a response in the interest of the modernization of Irish society, and from the writings of Paulo Freire based on his conscientization work in Brazil and Chile.

The final report of the Murphy committee, *Adult Education in Ireland* (1973), identified needs in relation to agricultural, industrial, commercial, social and religious roles. These included the 'topping up' of basic education, day-release courses, vocational training, courses in trade union organization and industrial relations, political education, education for leisure, and education for christian values. The most static version is to be found in the interim report, *National Adult Education Survey* (1970): education should initially aim at enabling the poor 'to live better in their domestic economy, even within their low income situation' (p.20), and later to provide a means of improvement for individual poor people. For housewives, educational activity was seen as a means to ameliorating their 'unnecessarily hard' routine characterized by budgetary problems and confinement to the home (p.21). A more dynamic view of the needs of poverty groups is to be found in the final report where the emphasis is on the exploration of the conditions which facilitate and sustain poverty and related social problems, though it does appear to confine its explanatory perspective primarily to the growth of bureaucracy. In both reports, however, a consensus view of role prevails in which what is expected of individuals and social positions is considered to be settled and beyond dispute, and therefore not demanding critical reflection. For instance, Irish values, beliefs and culture are assumed to be homogeneous and are presented throughout both reports as the 'given' established yardstick for evaluating innovation and change, rather than being acknowledged as suitable objects for analysis, justification and possible modification.

What remains unexplicated in the specification of role needs is the fact that they reflect a particular model — that of social change through personal improvement — of the function of adult learning programmes in society. This model assumes that, in providing for personal improvement, individuals become more knowledgeable, happier and fulfilled, and in turn contribute to a better society by their greater efficiency, consideration and sensitivity in the acting out of their social roles. There is a broad satisfaction with the structure of society. According of this view, the necessary improvements are capable of being effected by better role performances by individuals rather than by changes in role definitions or relationships between roles. Above all, the individual's self-fulfillment and society's needs are seen to be complementary.

Adaptation needs are outlined throughout the final Murphy report in the context of a rapidly changing Irish society. The following is a typical example of a sentiment that is repeated throughout the report: 'the adaptability needed to develop one's true potential, especially in a rapidly changing society, must be nurtured throughout one's lifetime by systematic adult education' (p.4). Where the need for preparing individuals to interpret, evaluate and actively determine their response to change is recognized, a distinct selectivity appears to operate. New ideas, particularly those emanating from the mass media and from a 'Europe committed to economic and merely human objectives' (final report, 1973, p.20), are considered to demand a critical orientation. Yet, adults 'should be able to see and grasp' the opportunities produced by technological advances (interim report, 1970, p.13), and provided with 'programmes of a liberal education which may help to avoid the dehumanising effects of repetitive manipulation of products and machines' (final report, 1973, p.73).

Selectivity in directing the critical reflection of others, by means of the designation of aspects of social change as either dangers or challenges, must always raise questions as to whose interests are being served. In fact, the specification of adaptation needs reflects another hidden value system, that of adult education as social adjustment. This involves fostering individual adjustment to social and technological change, helping individuals to cope with the phenomenon of change and with temporary phases of unemployment, and forming adjustable, mobile and trainable persons. Change is seen as inevitable and benign once the necessary adjustments are made. Individuals are perceived as passive unreflecting objects adjusting to rather than influencing the direction of change. A person's main task is to respond to the challenge of change and to modify and adjust to reap the potential benefits.

Liberating needs have been identified by Paulo Freire (1972, 1972a) in the context of his conscientization programmes in Brazil and Chile. He perceives it to be the function of adult education to respond to the need of those attending these programmes to be freed from their unequal position in society. For this to be successful the individuals involved must alter their view of soci-

128

ety, of themselves and of the type of person (based on material possessions, colour, area of residence, educational level, etc.) they perceive themselves to be, to develop self-confidence and to organize themselves to change their relationships with other sectors of society. This involves facilitating the analysis of one's social location, and in particular the ideologies which support it, fostering group awareness and solidarity, and motivating political action in association with others similarly located for the purpose of changing fundamentals of one's social, economic and political situation.

According to this model of the function of adult education — consciousness-raising — society is perceived in terms of exploitation and domination. In this view the function of adult education is to help the oppressed to recognize their exploited condition, to identify their oppressor and to cultivate personal confidence to engage in collective action with a view to achieving their liberation.

As a concept, need directs attention to the clients of a programme and appears to allocate a central position to their requirements in course planning. Discourse in official reports and prospectuses can appear as client-centered with minimal reference to the models of adult learning and social change which inform the specification of participants' needs. The value judgements and the social interpretations involved thus remain unexplicated and concealed. In this manner, the value positions relating to personal formation and social change acquire the robustness of taken-for-granted constructs, and the associated individual needs assume an existence and a plausibility of their own. At the legitimatory level, need provides a construct by which power, knowledge, and its distribution are justified. The issues of who is to be given access to what forms of educational experience, and whose views are to prevail in this regard, become technical problems of assessment while the ideological aspects go unrecognized.

Conclusion

The four varieties of legitimation — charismatic, normative, traditional and rational — considered in this chapter are ideal types. Programmes will rarely confine themselves to any one of these appeals. The extent to which they are drawn on, and in what combination, will vary with what a programme accepts as truth criteria, how pervasive are its designs on the person of its participants, the allocation of power among its agents, its relationship to institutionalized reality, and its stage of development.

At the early stages of a programme's operation charisma is a distinct asset. Establishing legitimacy can be particularly challenging at the point of first declaring the existence and intention of a programme and inviting participation. At the initial stage of its existence its world-view and strategies are most likely to be competing with those of more established programmes and institutionalized realities. If a programme is to impress people as being more meaningful than existing demands on their minds and emotions it helps if its appeal has a distinctive character about it and, particularly, if this appeal is focused on a personality or a text.

Charisma, however, will rarely sustain legitimacy as a programme evolves and systematizes. Operationally, established programmes will supplement charisma, where it exists, with other bases for the legitimatory claims of their message. The point can be arrived at when a charismatic initiator dies or is discredited, or where a text is demystified to the status of being no more than another account or interpretation. A programme may cope with this threat to its legitimacy by proclaiming that it is 'larger than individuals' or that it is not ideologically static or fundamentalist in its attachment to a particular text. Where charismatic legitimacy expands it usually takes the form of charismatic normative legitimacy in the first instance. This usually results from the systematization of its world-view to the point where a common membership of an intersubjective community, rather than a dynamic personality or sacred text, is the referent in legitimation. Dogma then becomes the prime basis for justifying the expectations of allegiance to the programme's message and personnel.

Charismatic traditional legitimacy is also a common transitional stage where the appeal to a person or text is supplemented by appeals to history. This has the effect of expanding the legitimation retrospectively, rather than laterally as with the dogma of a community of believers. And it achieves this in a manner that often retains the appeal of strong personalities, but ones drawn selectively from the course of history.

Like charisma, tradition merges with other bases of legitimacy particularly where the programme involves dissent and can appear vulnerable to the accusation of being the work of disgruntled unrepresentative characters.

Rational legitimacy is most likely to operate independently and, while it can be found to coexist with other appeals, there are particular impediments to the operation of charismatic rational legitimacy. This is because rational legitimacy is derived from legal and expert prescriptions and embodies a strong bureaucratic ethos which is anathema to the personalism, affectivity and un-predictability of charisma.

Overall, a programme's legitimatory discourse is never static. It is like a web that reforms and reconstitutes itself, influenced by a programme's epistemic intent and psychological designs on participants, and, when successful, stabilizing the objectivity of its vision and the authority of its agents where its relationship with the wider society generates doubt or dissent.

6 The learning encounter: associative forms

Introduction

The significance of the associative character of socially-committed programmes has arisen at a number of points in previous chapters. This has been most notable in relation to the conditions necessary for the efficient transmission of a more epistemically-complex substance and for the concomitant success of role/identity and interpretive change among programme participants. The nature of the interpersonal relationships within programmes has also arisen in delineating their legitimatory strategies. The associative quality of an encounter refers to the character of the relationships between the actors involved. Thus, induction, ritual, intersubjectivity, language, solidarity, historicity, role-modelling and dependency, all of which recur in our analysis of representation and recruitment, personal change and legitimation in socially-committed programmes, are relevant.

The force and direction of the analysis so far is that if socially-committed programmes are to increase their efficiency and to maximize the likelihood of their achieving their personal and social objectives, certain associative qualities are necessary.

Studies of learning programmes involving adults tend to neglect their associative qualities. In the case of more formal adult learning settings, a number of studies of classroom atmosphere, ethos and environmental press are available. Power relations between participants are often used to describe and characterize the broadly-based learning environments involved in the socially-committed programmes under consideration here. The exercize of authority might be described as authoritarian, democratic or egalitarian, the learning style as collaborative or didactic, and the education as that of equals or unequals. The associative quality that recurs as a contested characteristic of socially-committed programmes with any regularity is their individual/collective emphasis.

This emphasis refers to both the processes and the outcomes of a programme, though this distinction is rarely adverted to. Learning programmes can address the needs of individual learners and assist them, for instance, in gaining literacy skills or educational qual-ifications, in developing themselves personally or in facilitating occupational mobility or social improvement. Alternatively, the collective rationale takes as its unit of intervention a particular social class, race or sex rather than individual members of these groupings. It determines needs in the light of group requirements for collective awareness, self-confidence, mobilization and social action. The Council of Europe (1974) evaluation of pilot projects on permanent education in Europe draws on this distinction. It links education for individual development with the liberal tradi-tion of adult education, in which social and economic inequalities were perceived to be remediable by means of better educational opportunities for 'disadvantaged' individuals. Collective change, as an objective in adult learning programmes, seeks to change society through its social, political and economic structures, and as such has a more radical pedigree.

Mezirow (1989), in responding to criticism about the radical status of his theory of transformative learning, has forcefully argued that the concept of collective action is inadequate in analysing the varieties of social change that are possible in the wake of emancipatory meaning perspectives. Relatedly, he contends that the personal distortions which emancipatory learning needs to confront can be psychic and epistemic as well as socio-cultural, and that 'each of these three dimensions involves different and variable modes of interaction and action'. Thus, 'transformative learning is profoundly intersubjective but it is not exclusively group mediated. In therapeutic learning, which involves psychic distortions, the relationship is often one-to-one. Epistemic learning may be either group or mentor mediated. Socio-cultural learning may involve either group or collective learning experiences'. In highlighting the different modes of interaction through which personal transformation is facilitated, Mezirow is drawing attention to the associative character of socially-committed programmes.

Associative forms

Some conceptual refinement is required if the particular forms that association between participants can take are to be adequately delineated and named. Sources for this conceptualization are to be found in writings on the individual and society, solidarity, social integration and collective action that reach back to the beginnings of sociology. The conceptualization that follows draws explicitly on a tradition that spans more than a century and includes Tonnies, Weber, Cooley, Davis and Giddens. This scheme distinguishes between seven varieties of association — categorical, atomistic, collective, primary, dualist, exclusionary and activist.

Categorical association

Social categories are no more than statistical groupings. They involve the linking of people through an act of classification and delineation. They exist conceptually rather than experientially. Characteristics such as income level, age, height and shoe size provide a basis for categorical association. Typically, the characteristic shared is not perceived by those represented to have any significance for how they might relate to one another. Accordingly, they see no necessity to meet, interact or pursue goal-directed behaviour. There is no sense of mutual interest, common values or a shared life-situation. All that can be said of categorical association, that has a significance for the analysis of socially-committed programmes, is that it has potential for mobilization and transformation to higher forms of association which are likely to have an impact on personal formation.

Atomistic association

Social aggregates share a common focus that may involve no more than the coming together of people. There is no necessary sense of sharing. The relationship between the participants is atomistic. Those watching a television programme at any one time, a queue waiting for a bus, a cinema audience, those being transported in a lift, or motorists in a traffic jam are examples. While there is likely to be an awareness of the existence of others, the goal of the moment doesn't require that any cognizance be taken of one another apart from whatever is demanded by the rules that apply to such encounters — waiting one's turn, not jumping the queue or quietness in the cinema. Though atomistic, if the people involved share a common focus and physical space, transformation to more socially-significant associative forms is a possibility. A large student group in a lecture theatre exemplifies this. From the students' point of view the focus is on the lecture. The encounter doesn't require communication, empathy, or solidarity between students. The goals of the learning programme can be effectively achieved by maintaining an atomistic stance. Yet, if the encounter persists over time it is likely that, through attraction and repulsion, a sense of common interest, and social contact outside of lectures, a higher-order associative form will develop.

In educational contexts atomistic association is most clearly found among students of distance learning programmes. Relationships with staff, as well as with other students, are significantly more restricted than in conventional educational programmes. It also gives the student more control over the learning experience. As social atoms they have no ties of obligation, friendship or common interest which might constrain their behaviour. Their invisibility reduces the possibility of surveillance. Taking the programme on their own terms, and integrating the learning into their own interpretive schemes, is more an option than in educational programmes incorporating more direct and interactive forms of association. As Harrison puts it in relation to the Open University in Britain, 'if our own students tend to be isolated from their teachers, at least they are not distanced from their own local and personal life patterns: they remain sturdily themselves, which may not be so easy for the bright working-class lad from Rochdale who "gets through" to Cambridge' (quoted in Rogers, 1977, p.173).

For this very reason, because atomistic association allows participants to 'remain sturdily themselves' it is inappropriate, even to the point of being dysfunctional, in socially-committed programmes where the requirement is that fundamental change occurs in a predictable direction.

Collective association

Collectivities, on the other hand, experience the existence of a bond — a common grievance, allegiance, set of values or heritage. There is an awareness of a common membership, though those who share this collective identity do not require physical contact. In the case of such collectivities as nationalities or religions, frequency of interaction involving the total collectivity would be impracticable. Collective association can make inroads on the private and personal. One may be required, or indeed feel obliged, to submerge personal interest or inclination in favour of the goals of the collectivity. Equally, the identities highlighted and made salient and socially relevant through collective association may well conflict with established allegiances, values and inclinations. Collective association is a basic requirement in a socially-committed programme if it is to have a realistic hope of achieving its objectives.

The pivotal associative transition in consciousness-raising type programmes is the cultivation of a sense of collectivity where a lower-order associative form previously existed. Freire's programmes sought to awaken a realization among poor peasants in Latin America that they shared a common exploited condition within the socio-economic and cultural system. This required a fundamental redefinition whereby participants in a social aggregate or those who occupied a similar social category came to perceive themselves in other than atomistic or statistical terms. In consequence, the poor peasants would see themselves as members of a particular class, sharing a characteristic set of interests. Identities that had been submerged through repression or a lack of cultural awareness should then emerge as cultural and political forces. The collectivization of aggregates and social categories provides the associative basis for mobilization and social action.

A similar process is to be found in the women's movement and the American civil rights movement, both of which also use the terminology of consciousness-raising. But the associative transition involved in collectivization is equally to be found among the physically and mentally impaired, homosexuals, nomads, council tenants and students, as they strive to kindle the communality of their social situation and erode whatever sense of individual inadequacy, limitation or marginalization they may be experiencing. This is an essential first step in making the personal political.

Peace building programmes which seek to reduce conflict and

tension between groups or nations provide a heightened example of attempts to bring about social change through collective association. In Ireland, the success of cross-community (Protestant, Loyalist/Catholic, Republican) and cross-border (Northern Ireland/Irish Republic) linkages is dependant on established identities being eroded, or at least being perceived as less significant in influencing inter-group relationships than the common interests and concerns which these linkages build on and seek to make manifest in the forging of collective association.

A recent study of peace-building programmes has referred to economic, social and sporting links between Northern Ireland and the Irish Republic, which create formal and informal relationships but which are to a large extent independent of political tensions, as Track Three Diplomacy (Murray and O'Neill, 1991). This follows Montville (1987) who coined the term Track Two diplomacy to describe 'unofficial, informal interaction between representatives of adversary groups or nations which aims to develop strategies and create an environment which could contribute to the resolution of their conflict'. With Track Three Diplomacy it was felt that the very lack of political intent might well prove to be the programmes' greatest strength since contact would occur in a non-threatening milieu. The experiences of those involved in these linkages reveal something of how collectivist association develops as well as some of the supportive and restraining factors involved.

The authors recognized that in talking about cross-border contact there was a danger of reifying the border and thus failing to see it as a political creation, as a negotiated product of historical factors. At an obvious level, they point out, 'nationalists perceive the border as a frustration of their aspirations while unionists see it as a safeguard of theirs' (p.30). They give the example of the Gaelic Athletic Association's response to their questionnaire to the effect that they didn't recognize the border and therefore didn't engage the cross-border activities! Members of this association, committed to the promotion of gaelic games and cultural pursuits, because of their all-Ireland activities would share a common sense of heritage, values and objectives. For them, the political existence of the border represented no impediment to their collective identity as Irish men and women.

For many, however, forging a collective sense of association between individuals in Northern Ireland and the Irish Republic and between Protestant/Loyalist and Catholic/Republican communities would face a range of impediments typical in inter-group conflict. These include mutual ignorance, stereotype and suspicion. But, most of all, it involves a set of existing collectivist associative forms based on religion, cultural identity and political traditions which would appear to be diametrically opposed to and threatened by the formation of an identity that transcended religion, culture or politics, and had the potential to relegate them to a lower status in social mobilization and action. The success of cross-community and cross-border mobilization of individuals and groups was found to be more likely where the mutual benefits outweighed any anxieties about the potential erosion of existing identities. This was reflected in the ease with which campaign-based groups established contact, developed working relationships and recognized mutual interests: their campaign issue was their mission and the cross-border dimension was an opportunity to advance the achievement of their goals.

> Personnel in the Women's Centre, for example, claimed that the common concerns of women transcended political difference and division. They did see contact lessening isolation and frustration but, of more importance, was the fact that it provided a combined (and therefore a stronger) lobby. In this same vein, the Trade Unions of Ireland stated that within a common concern for the unemployed, 'we have more problems that unite us than those which divide us'. And again, the National Gay Federation claimed that the many areas of concern shared by gay communities all over the world, make political and cultural differences seem trivial (p.14).

Identities formed through collective association support one another, compete or become more or less salient depending on the social context.

Primary association

Groups, like collectivities, have a sense of membership, an obligation to fellow members and collective loyalties, and a common sense of values. But they exhibit the additional characteristic of frequency of interaction. The most heightened manifestation of these characteristics is to be found in what have been called primary groups. Cooley's classic definition is as follows:

> By primary groups I mean those characterized by intimate face-to-face association and cooperation. They are primary in several senses, but

138

chiefly in that they are fundamental in forming the social nature and ideals of the individual. The result of intimate association...is a certain fusion of individualities in a common whole, so that one's very self, for many purposes at least, is the common life and purpose of the group. Perhaps the simplest way of describing this wholeness is by saying that it is a 'we'; it involves the sort of sympathy and mutual identification for which 'we' is the natural expression (quoted in Davis, 1969).

Rather than talk in terms of primary groups as opposed to secondary groups, Davis is of the view that it is more appropriate to refer to the primary character of association defined by closeness, smallness, durability, intimacy, intensity and solidarity.

A predominant tendency among socially-committed program-mes which incorporate group work in some form is to strive towards the cultivation of a high degree of primary association in their social encounters. This is reflected in a range of related aspirations and values which is common in such situations. Group encounters of this nature physically structure themselves so as to be small, frequent and face-to-face. They seek an atmosphere that is warm, non-threatening, supportive and affirming. They value power structures that are democratic, non-hierarchical and egalitarian, and social interaction that results in bonding, solidarity and communality. These are reflected in Wagner's proposals for good group-work practice in women's discussion circles as applied by German women's groups in Frankfurt and Freiburg (cited in Gieseke, 1992).

- The group is composed of women only.
- The best size is five to seven women.
- The group must not be open to any newcomer at random.
- The group should meet at home, in turns, once a week for some two or three hours.
- All group members should always participate in discussions.
- There is no group leader.
- The group agrees on a subject before each session, and then each women in turn tells of her experiences.
- Each woman is free to decide what to tell and what not to tell.
- She must not be interrupted during her narrative.
- Her narrative is then referred to by the other members who try to understand better, share and give feedback.

139

- Narratives must not be criticized unless the narrator expressly asks for critical comments.
- No advice should be given.
- 'I' and not 'one' should be used.
- Once all the woman have told their tale, everybody listening attentively, the group should take half-an-hour for joint discussion.

Primary association achieved by means of practices such as these, and the principles and values which they embody, have a dominant sense of humanity, personal integrity, non-intrusiveness and individual fulfillment. But, if criticisms of the best-known primary group in society, the family, are to be heeded, other examples of primary association need to be similarly explored for dysfunctional features. Cooper (1976, pp. 24–29) claims to have isolated some of the factors that operate within the family 'often with lethal but always with humanly stultifying consequences'. These factors include the 'glueing together of people based on the sense of one's own incompleteness', allowing freedom that is 'totally enjoined' and 'minutely prescribed' within set relationships, unnecessary social control and a series of rituals and taboos. And all of this occurs despite the fact that those involved are 'the kindest, closest, best-intentioned people in the world' (p.63).

Nor is it entirely fanciful to point to the similarity between the physical organization of participants in the archetypal group discussion and the panopticon, Bentham's design for the ideal prison in the mid-nineteenth century. Circular in shape, its main feature was the location of individual cells around its perimeter. A central observation tower allowed for the observation of prisoners at all times, though the guards, through the use of blinds, could make themselves invisible to the prisoners. Rogers (1977), in a standard text on adult learning strategies, emphasizes the significance of seating arrangements for communication within a group. She points out that the physical distance and lack of eye contact associated with the serried rows of the traditional classroom retard whatever inclination students may have to talk to one another. On the other hand, in 'the opposite type of group, by sitting close to people and facing them, it is extremely hard *not* to talk to them'. Apart from encouraging communication by seating participants in a circle, a statement is also being made about authority and power within the group: 'equality of participation can be encouraged through recognition of direct and symbolic forms of structuring group processes' (Butler and Wintram, 1991, p.78). Being more visible, participants are under constant surveillance and the creation of a private sphere in the physical sense is impossible, except by making a symbolic public statement by physically withdrawing. Rogers (1977, p.105) quotes the following description of a 'professional moaner' in such a group: 'if things do not go his way he starts getting impatient and saying in effect that he can't stand our company any longer. As the evening goes on he pushes his chair farther and farther out of the circle. If he's really feeling irritable he ends up yards away!'

In Goffman's (1969) terminology, there is no 'back region' in the circle of participants where one can switch off, relax, withdraw, act out of role or generally show any kind of covert reaction that one would not wish to defend.

More significant than the fact of surveillance facilitated by the physical organization of the group is the range of personal exposure that is considered to be appropriate where primary association prevails. The more primary the association the more limited will be the aspects of one's personality and social situation that are considered to be inappropriate to raise in group sessions. Thus, paralleling the physical visibility, participants also find themselves in an associative form which deems personal visibility to be proper and normal. In fact, nondisclosure, reticence and nonparticipation will be regarded as deviant behaviours in such settings and explained as a lack of personal readiness to be receptive to the group's mission.

Garfinkel (1967) describes an experiment in which he asked students to spend from fifteen minutes to an hour in their homes acting out the assumption that they were boarders. They were to behave in a circumspect but polite manner, avoid getting personal, use formal modes of address and speak only when spoken to. In other words, they were being asked to behave in a manner that would be considered inappropriate within primary association. The following confrontation, typical of what ensued, represents the kind of group rules, expectations, reprimands and penalties through which control operates within encounters defined by primary association.

A father followed his son into the bedroom. 'Your mother is right. You don't look well and you're not talking sense. You had better get another job that doesn't require such late hours'. To this the student replied that he appreciated the consideration, that he felt fine and that he wanted a little privacy. The father responded in a high rage, 'I don't want any more of that from you and if you can't treat your mother decently you'd better move out!'

The possibility that egalitarian and client-centred learning strategies might well incorporate control dimensions that remain opaque, even beyond the first flush of innovative enthusiasm and missionary zeal, has been demonstrated in relation to progressive pedagogies in the primary school (Sharp and Green, 1975). It is, of course, the central theme of Foucault's (1977) *Discipline and Punish* that structures of control, through surveillance, internalization and definitions of normality, persist in organizations and professions that would regard themselves as human, caring and emancipatory.

Dualist association

Dualist association is characterized by dyads, or social pairings, of emotional intensity and psychological significance. Psychological exchange, the mutual fulfillment of needs, is involved. The need to dominate, direct or lead complements the need to be sheltered, shepherded, a follower. There is a submersion of ego. One hands over an element of oneself, though the 'receiving' partner in the dualism may be unaware of this. The conception of power to be found in critical social science is pertinent: 'power is dyadic in the sense that all of its many forms invoke the self-understandings of the powerless as well as the powerful ... Power, like all social interactions of active beings, is rooted in part in the reflections and will of those interacting, both the powerless as well as the powerful' (Fay, 1987, p.130).

Examples of dualist association are likely to be found wherever primary association is a feature of socially-committed programmes. This is a hidden feature of many socially-committed programmes which many providers and leaders would deny, appealing to their egalitarian, open and non-hierarchical principles and values. An analysis of the formation and operation of women's groups in Milan, which followed the principle of leaderless group work, acknowledged that the groups were nearly always formed because one or two women took the initiative. These 'were acknowledged by others just because of their activity and gained special status in the group'; these leaders, nonetheless, 'claimed to be equals among equals for the sake of harmony and avoidance of conflict' (Gieseke, 1992). This example is no more than a mere intimation of what providers of socially-committed programmes would have difficulty in recognizing. Dualisms can equally be based on intimacy, emotional attachment, charisma, knowledge or achievement.

A distinctive function of dualist association within socially-committed programmes is indicated by Berger and Luckmann (1973, p.174) in relation to strategies for maintaining an individual's sense of subjective reality.

> On the whole, frequency of conversation enhances its reality generating potency, but lack of frequency can sometimes be compensated for by the intensity of the conversation when it does take place. One may see one's lover only once a month, but the conversation then engaged in is of sufficient intensity to make up for its relative infrequency. Certain conversations may also be explicitly defined and legitimated as having a privileged status — such as conversations with one's confessor, one's psycho-analyst, or a similar 'authority' figure. The 'authority' here lies in the cognitively and normatively superior status that is assigned to these conversations.

Psychologically, dualist association may well be essential in socially-committed programmes, as a replacement for relationships with significant others from previous social formations which are necessarily severed as a consequence of participation in the programme. A key question is the extent to which the more dependent partner ever moves on to form an independent identity, and the degree of facilitation and encouragement in this regard provided by the more dominant partner in the dualism.

Exclusionary association

Goffman (1968) described the phenomenon of the 'total institution' as an organizational form in which the fulfillment of the members' full range of needs and the enactment of their daily routine are confined to its social parameters and purview. As he puts it, 'every institution captures something of the time and interest of its members and provides something of a world for them; in brief, every institution has encompassing tendencies' (p.15). An associative version of the 'total institution' is to be found where the relationship is structured so as to exclude a specific or comprehensive set of external experiences. Exclusionary association is identifiable not merely by solidarity among members but, characteristically, by a sense of distancing, and even segregation, from adversarial, dysfunctional or potentially contaminating forces. In socially-committed programmes it can be employed to fulfil a variety of programme needs and functions.

Exclusionary association may be considered a necessary prerequisite for the operation of a programme and the means towards the achievement of its objectives. Describing the beginnings of the women's education programme in Southampton in the mid 1970s, Thompson traces some of its inadequacies — a restrictive view of women and a concern with their therapeutic control rather than the cultivation of critical awareness — to the presence of men 'who, if they had understood anything about "consciousness raising" among women, would have appreciated the unhelpful and inappropriate imposition of their presence' (Thompson, 1983, p.150). The logic of exclusionary association, implied in some feminist programmes, is to be found in the philosophy of the Women's Education Centre in Southampton as proclaimed by Thompson: 'we have the opportunity to provide not only a programme of women's education which is a reflection of women's experience and knowledge, culture and political concerns, but also to create a social and emotional environment which can celebrate and confirm collective and feminist principles as a real alternative to hierarchical and patriarchal relationships' (p.188).

Whether or not women need this sheltered atmosphere, and the extent to which its practice serves to reify and confirm the very social and personal conditions — lack of self-esteem, denial of confidence and expertise, emotional/cognitive attributions and marginalization — which feminists seek to challenge, is being currently debated in a most uncompromizing manner in the light of action research on women's groups in Germany and Italy (Gieseke, 1992).

By cultivating an ingroup/outgroup distinction exclusionary association enhances solidarity among members. Threats to a programme's operation from outside forces heighten the need for mutual support, the recognition of common interests and the transcending of differences. Such threats may be real, imagined or contrived. Erikson's (1966) study, *Wayward Puritans*, describes how in a New England puritan community phases of witch hunting and public fear of attack from forces hostile to the community coincided with the dissolution of religious orthodoxy, loyalty and the internalization of the community's beliefs among its members. The sense of siege, apparently contrived, had an integrating effect in making salient and affirming the social, moral and religious rationale for the community's existence. Within socially-committed programmes exclusionary association often establishes its rationale by adversarial means — their social goals become the removal or erosion of a targeted social fact. For O'Rahilly, the threat of totalitarianism in the late 1940s and 1950s seemed very real, particularly in its communistic form. So also did the 'false' ideologies of secularism and liberalism. In arguing for the application of Roman Catholic social principles — subsidiarity, familism, the diffusion of property — to social and political organization, and their dissemination by means of adult learning programmes, O'Rahilly railed against these alien forces which he projected as having designs on the minds of the Irish people. The stridency to be found in O'Rahilly's writings in this regard is typical of the discourse of exclusionary association.

> 'Once more men are facing the great decision: Christ or Cæsar';
> 'More fortunate in this country, we must yet beware lest this secularist naturalist view creep into our education';
> 'It is time for humanity to assert itself against this agnostic dogmatism masquerading as science';
> 'The alternative to Rome is Moscow' (all quoted in O'Sullivan, 1989a, pp. 166–167).

A similar stridency, sometimes supported by moral panics and a demonizing of adversary forces, can be found in programmes as varied as those which set themselves against pollution, patriarchy, secularism and physical violence. Heretics, doomsday scenarios and moral outrage are particularly functional in social movements with a widely-dispersed membership. Heightening the emotional and cultivating a sense of urgency serve to compensate for the absence of primary/dualist association, with its intense, regular face-to-face contact and mutual support, and help to sustain identification with the movement and loyalty to its objectives. Exclusionary association through ingroup/outgroup delineation also sharpens a movement's profile when, in its early stage, it seeks to publicly establish its identity and mission and appeal to potential members. What Donoghue (1992, p.157) said of the practice of cultural nationalism in his Irish schooling — 'we defined ourselves by not doing certain things' (English games, music, religion) — is equally recognizable in the mobilizing strategies of religious believers in a secular world, pacifists in a violent society and 'greens' in relation to the environmentally-unenlightened.

Where interpretive change is involved, exclusionary association is often used to assist in the establishment of what is 'real and proper'. Ryan (1970, p.221) points out that people are more likely to consider that their own beliefs are shared by everyone else, that there is a cognitive and moral consensus, if they have 'only evidence of agreement, and no evidence of disagreement'. He illuminates this by reference to the Greek historian Herodotus who recorded that when those who ate their dead ancestors were introduced to those who cremated theirs there was a good deal of mutual surprise and confusion! Exclusionary association can function to reduce the shock and confusion that is caused by the abrasion of interpretive sub-worlds. In modern culturally-diverse and mobile society, with its sophisticated communication media, this represents a challenge of a kind that wouldn't have existed in a more homogeneous, static and isolated world. In some instances, exclusionary association may take the form of physical segregation or avoidance. Contact with carriers of competing world-views, be they family members, friends or business acquaintances, is discouraged and the participant in the programme is drawn into a new social network that embodies or supports the programme's interpretive world. If physical segregation is not possible, Berger and Luckmann (1973, p.178) suggest that the segregation can be achieved by definition, that is 'by a definition of those others that nihilates them.'

> The alternating individual disaffiliates himself from his previous world and the plausibility structure that sustained it, bodily if possible, mentally if not. In either case he is no longer 'yoked together with unbelievers', and thus is protected from their potential reality-disrupting influence. Such segregation is particularly important in the early stages of alternation (the 'novitiate' phase).

Where physical contact is unavoidable, and the nihilation of competing definitions of reality difficult to achieve, exclusionary association may be established through what Guskin and Guskin (1970, p.56) referred to as 'immunization'. If given 'a mild dose of opposing arguments ... to ward off strong opposing arguments', participants can be protected against contamination from physical and psychological contact with 'unbelievers'. In this manner exclusion operates through a gradual strengthening and broadening of the legitimatory capacity of participants with regard to the rationale of the programme. The doubt and self-questioning that can arise through contact with representatives of other realities, and the openness to a belief that there might be a basis for dialogue with them, is progressively eroded.

Activist association

Activist association involves goal-directed behaviour on the part of the participants. It requires a reaching out beyond the confines of their own inter-relationships with a view to altering some aspect of society beyond themselves and their personal world. In this sense it differs from relationships directed towards mutual support, self-help or personal development. Also, unlike the goals of such relationships which are process-based, the goals of activist association are product-based, in that the social action of the individuals involved is directed towards a specific concrete change in society. One's personal world is unlikely to remain unaffected, however, by collaborative social action. In that sense, to invert the well-known consciousness-raising slogan, it is difficult to avoid the political impinging on the personal. To enter into an activist association is to make a statement about one's aspirations for social change that is more public than any of the processes of learning, analysis or reflection engaged in through participation in socially-committed programmes. Through involvement in deputations, lobbying, marching, demonstrating, sit-ins, civil disobedience or violence, one is publicly proclaiming one's disposition towards social institutions and authority figures. There is a signalling of political intent and an identification with particular ideologies. Potentially, the implications for the individual's personal trajectory are far-reaching in that the manifestations of activist association represent a 'coming out'. As bridge-burning events they can precipitate a reworking of one's relationships with family, friends and work associates, together with the assumption of a new public identity. Andrews (1991, p.164) echoes many of these consequences of activism in her analysis of lifelong radicals:

Activism is not merely something which the respondents do, nor even just a part of them. It is them. During their long accumulated years of engagement, they have come to define themselves through their activism... just as respondents' beliefs are expressed through their actions, so do their actions reaffirm their beliefs. A corollary of this is that the very doing of the political action enables respondents to perceive of themselves as politically engaged.

Despite these implications for the self, one's public identity and social relationships, most advocates of socially-committed learning see nothing problematic about social action following in the light of reflection and critique. On the contrary, the failure to act where there has been a learned awareness of unsatisfactory social arrangements is frequently disparaged as truncated intervention — knowing, but not doing.

Giroux (1979), in his criticism of 'one-sided and ideologically frozen' versions of so-called radical educational experiences, spares neither process-based nor content-based pedagogies. The former, he contends, do no more than 'enrich our existential selves with moments of collective warmth and cheery solidarity'. This he dismisses as 'a form of depthless psychology rather than a form of radical praxis'. The latter takes the form of 'information, issues, and alternative world views designed to break through the ideological encrustations that hold the "oppressed" in a helpless state of political ignorance'. By failing to develop a theory of liberation, that incorporates a critical understanding of the interplay of pedagogy, ideology and social change, Giroux concludes that they both end up depoliticizing the very people they intend to liberate.

Similarly, sociologists committed to radical change through education criticize the potency of 'social awareness' or 'social criticism' as suggested by some exponents of the 'new' sociology of education associated with Young (1971). Whitty (1977) cautions that they tend to exaggerate the power of 'multiple accounts of the world to subvert ... conventional notions of reality.' Within such claims, he suggests, 'there seem to lie shades of the young Hegel's remark that "once the kingdom of ideas is revolutionized, reality cannot hold out"'. He points out that 'the over-emphasis on the notion that reality is socially constructed seems to have led to a neglect of the consideration of how and why reality comes to be constructed in particular ways, and how and why particular constructions of reality seem to have the power to resist subversion'. This is the basis of Freire's (1972a) warning that awareness does not create reality and that political action must remain a central element in conscientization. And Harris (1979, p.173), who recognizes the importance of what we have described as interpretive change in socially-committed learning, acknowledges it only as a first step: 'there would be little point in getting people to see how their consciousness is formed, and if necessary making them aware that their consciousness was false and distorted, unless the intention was to do something about it'. Mezirow (1989), who himself has been criticized because his conceptualization of adult learning as perspective transformation is said to lack a theory of social action (Collard and Law, 1989), responds:

> The educator may encourage the learner to critically reflect on specific taken-for-granted relationships which appear dependency-producing or oppressive, but the learner makes his or her own decisions about specific actions to be taken, if any. The educator can be a partisan, but a partisan only in a commitment to fostering critical reflection and action; the what, when and how of the action is a decision for the learner.

In making this distinction between facilitating reflection and encouraging social action, Mezirow is typical of those advocates of socially-committed programmes who feel that, in such programmes, participants retain a personal autonomy when it comes to determining what the implications for social action of their newly-constructed meaning systems, critical awareness or restructured realities might be. Few seem to recognize that the more successful they are in bringing participants to a particular view of the world, the less autonomous is the personal action that is likely to follow. Brookfield (1987, p.65) rightly contends that there seems to be little awareness that those who 'seek to encourage critical thinking have an ethical duty to point out to those involved the risks accompanying actions springing from this new state of awareness'. In his view, 'helping people explore the often contradictory and ambiguous nexus where private troubles and public issues meet often entails making clear the connection to social action' (p.62). He raises some of the 'crucial ethical issues' (p.65) involved in changing another person's world-view with reference to a community development project in Africa. Having established the link between their oppressive social and political structures and the local economic conditions, the participants decided on a programme of resistance only to have almost the entire village murdered in a machine-gun attack. Rarely are the consequences of programme-led social action so dramatic or tragic. Nonetheless, Brookfield acknowledges that cultivating a view that one is marginal or oppressed can be a 'profoundly destabilizing act' carrying the 'risk of harsh consequences as well as of life-changing victories' (p.63).

Thus far, we have considered a programme's associative forms in terms of its evolution, requirements for goal attainment and demands on participants once accepted as members. It is now necessary to explore more fully what is involved for the individual in entering into these associative forms, that is to analyse the experience of membershipping.

Membershipping

The membershipping of participants into the various associative forms is an essential and recurring task for socially-committed programmes. This involves integration into the character of the new relationship, ensuring the participants see themselves as part of it, and making the required adjustments in terms of behaviour, identity, values, perceptions and social action. Seen in terms of personal biography, membershipping requires a status change for the individual involved.

Altering one's associative relationship with others is an important experience in social transition. For the person involved it can provoke tension, doubt and anxiety. For the socially-committed programme, the ease with which the transition is managed will influence the stability of the programme and the smooth operation of its processes of recruitment, engagement and influence. Turner refers to the point of mid-transition in status change as its liminal state, derived from the latin *limen* meaning a threshold. He stresses its sense of associative anomie that is a distinguishing characteristic of it.

> During the liminal period, the characteristics of the *liminars* (the ritual subjects in this phase) are ambiguous, for they pass through a cultural realm that has few or none of the attributes of the past or coming stage. Liminars are betwixt and between... Liminars are stripped of status and authority, removed from a social structure... Much of what has been bound by social structure is liberated, notably the sense of comradeship and communion, or communitas (quoted in McLaren, 1986, pp. 258–259).

But this unloosening of bonds, this decoupling from the past, though an essential prerequisite for the formation of new associations, can nonetheless create the conditions for a sense of displacement, isolation and marginalization. Viewed in a developmental light, liminality can be seen as an opportunity for personal stocktaking, biographical reflection or relatively uncluttered cultural analysis; negatively, it can precipitate uprooting and normlessness.

Some of the possibilities that exist for associative change once the liminal stage has been reached are discussed by Negt (in Holzapfel's summary translation, 1992) in the light of his research on workers' education in Germany. Negt traces the problem of workers' mobilization and consciousness-raising back to their unstructured situation and the absence of guiding patterns for the interpretation of their social and economic existence. For this reason Negt considers it essential that the 'worker-existence as social aggregate phenomenon' becomes a point of intervention for educative efforts. By this he means that the subject of workers' education must not be confined to the wage issue; it is the psychic phenomenon, which arises from the lived condition with all its tensions and contradictions, that produces the possibility of consciousness-raising through education. For Negt, education must begin with workers' consciousness of conflict but it must also strive to take into account the origins of alienated consciousness. Its goal is to translate atomistic association into collective association by cultivating and maintaining a common consciousness derived from the examined condition of being a worker. Negt, however, was conscious of the fact that other possibilities were available to workers. They could strive for greater wage increases or better working conditions. This Negt interprets as a form of social and economic levelling that would ultimately dissipate the category of worker as a meaningful construct for collective mobilization. Feelings of collective association could be cultivated in relation to others involved in one's place of production — directors, managers, supervisors — based on the common bond of social interest or national objectives. These are dismissed by Negt as vicarious compensations, but they nonetheless represent other possibilities for association once workers have been brought to the point where associative change is possible.

Accounts of women's groups point out that women often attend in the face of opposition from family members, frequently spouses or partners. In many of these instances, the women involved can be said to be in a dualistic association, with considerable disparities of power and associated problems of dependency. In these circumstances, liminality is likely to be particularly traumatic, representing a transitional crisis that may be resolved by entering into a dualistic association within the programme, in effect transferring one's dependency to a leader or another participant (Breakwell, 1986). For others, the experience of reflection and personal stocktaking may provoke a personal crisis with the questioning of taking-for-granted principles and practices from long-established relationships. Gieseke (1992) quotes an Italian woman on a second-chance learning programme who responded to a feminist interpretation of the world in the following terms:

> My first reaction to this text is rejection: I reject the theory that we women have always been instrumentalized and administered by the male and his history. I am aware that my protest serves to protect myself, but for a women who is past the mid-point of her life and who has always believed that she has done her best, it is tragic if she is told (I use my own words): 'Everything you have done in your life was wrong; the values you believed in, like the family, children, conjugal fidelity, purity, even your household chores — everything wrong, the outcome of a subtle strategy brought forward from one generation to the next for the eternal exploitation of women'. I repeat: I can only be dismayed.

Gieseke poses the question as to how much pain one is allowed to cause in a learning process that isn't therapeutic, and how a previous lifecourse can be corrected without calling into question a person's life as a whole, thereby endangering the 'self'. As she puts it, 'if all past life must be called into question and, at the same time the bounds imposed by society prevent a fresh beginning, the road to a new identity is bumpy'.

In ecological programmes, similarly, participants are being invited to display, at the very least, collective association based on a common habitation of a fragile and finely-balanced ecosystem, and to identify with future generations in terms of the environmental legacy to be bequeathed. This may require disengagement from less universal collectivities such as trade union membership, local workers or the unemployed whose interests, in particular the placing of a greater emphasis on the creation of employment, may be in conflict with those of environmentalists.

Where definition and redefinition of the world is involved, as is frequently the case with higher-order associative change, Schutz (in Wagner, 1973, pp. 252–262) has pointed to the possibility of transition shock. According to Schutz, people are vulnerable to such a shock as they move between 'provinces of meaning' upon which they 'bestow the accent of reality'. In fact, for Schutz people are not ready to abandon a particular interpretation of the world without having experienced a specific *shock* which impels them to break through the limits of a particular province of meaning, and 'to shift the accent of reality to another one'. The more insulated a person's experience and the more unreflective their formation, the more acute will be the sense of transition shock. To live in a socially-limited world that is epistemically sealed is to have a restricted awareness of the range of possible realities. And, for those for whom there has been only one reality, even the possibility that there might be others must itself be fundamentally unsettling.

The higher-order the associative change required in a socially-committed programme and the more this transition produces tension-provoking liminality, the more a programme must incorporate within its strategies and processes a means of smoothing the induction of new participants and of easing the crisis. By taking Garfinkel's (1956) 'degradation ceremonies' and inverting them and the conditions that make them successful, it is possible to conceptualize the practices which many programmes use to manage the integration of new participants. Garfinkel described 'any communication work between persons, whereby the public identity of an actor is transformed into something looked on as lower in the local scheme of social types' as a 'status degradation ceremony'. Here we are concerned with status change — in the sense of an altered mode of association between actors — and the ceremonies by which it is made real to the participants.

- The subject of the status change must be 'removed from the realm of their everyday character and be made to stand as out of the ordinary'.
- Those managing the transition (it can equally be singular) must so identify themselves and establish that they are acting, not on their own behalf, but rather as representatives of the programme 'drawing on communally entertained and verified experience'.
- The 'supra-personal values of the tribe' must be made 'salient and accessible to view'.

- Those managing the status change must succeed in establishing their right to represent the values and rationale of the programme.
- The subject experiencing the status change must be ritually integrated and made to feel a member.
- There must be evidence of a 'fixing' of the status change in the behaviour of the representatives of the programme.

Socially-committed programmes enact these ceremonies often in an unobtrusive fashion, but with nonetheless telling effect. They meet requirements for successful status change in disparate ways. Unsolicited and unpersonalized circulars, personalized documentation, modes of address, invitations, agreements on meeting arrangements, sharing confidences, public declarations, demonstrations, styles of dress and physical contact set people apart and make salient new associative possibilities. By these means, subjects can be made to experience differentiation from the great mass of humanity as they are brought into a new association with others. Roles, titles, use of 'we' and 'us', slogans and banners serve to identify the bearers of new associative principles and values. Mission statements take the form of manifestos, rules, constitutions, lore and histories. Positions, titles, life situation, and biographical accounts establish the authority of whoever among the programme's providers, leaders and facilitators represents it to the new member. Through inclusion on mailing lists, membership cards, letters, telephone calls and proclamations, the change of status is publicly declared. The programme mirrors this status change to the new member through giving attention, asking for advice, holding expectations for behaviour, delegating responsibilities and nomination as representative/spokesperson.

A number of features of socially-committed programmes appear to be relevant to the successful management of status change, in this instance the effective integration of individuals into a particular associative form. Four features of membershipping ceremonies — organization, ritual, language and holism — merit consideration.

154

Organization

Wheeler (1966) has constructed a typology of interpersonal settings which can be usefully drawn on to describe how socially-committed programmes vary in the manner in which they organize the induction of new members. This typology is based on whether the recruit is facing a new setting alone or in the company of others (their individual/collective status), and whether or not the recruit has access to others who have been through the same process (disjunctive/serial processing). Applied to socially-committed programmes the typology would distinguish between the following:

	Individual	Collective
Disjunctive	A widely-dispersed, once-off, rare or emerging social movement, recent recruits being unkown or inaccessible.	Summer school/study week of a distance-learning programme; inaugural group-based programmes; once-off demonstrations, deputations; conferences.
Serial	New recruit to an established social movement, politicial party, religious or other ongoing grouping.	Recurring housed programmes; typical mainstream educational institutions.

With disjunctive/individual induction there is the minimum of interpersonal support in that there are neither fellow recruits to share with nor role models to give advice or be emulated. Individuals are obliged to rely more on their own resources and are sustained in their membershipping because of strength of personality, conviction or life situation.

Since there is peer support available with disjunctive/collective induction, but not the advice and support of established and experienced participants, the character of the programme is less stable and the recruits more likely to impress their own collective influence on it.

Serial/individual induction is more conducive to the smooth integration of the recruit into the programme. Its resources can be targeted on the single recruit who is more amenable to influence because of his or her isolation. In fact, studies of social pressure suggest that the presence of just one other like-minded person can significantly strengthen one's resistance to conformity (Asch, 1952).

Potentially, serial/collective induction provides for the possibility of two independent socializing forces, one internal to the incoming group, the other operating from the established members. The degree to which these act in tandem, opposition or independently will depend, among other factors, on the commitment and openness to the programme's influence among the incoming group and on the degree of solidarity and diversity among existing members.

Ritual

Ritual, in its many interpretations, can be identified in socially-committed programmes. The 'flat view' of ritual was introduced in relation to the achievement of rational legitimacy in Chapter 5. This understanding of ritual sees it as a reflection of deeper meanings and social structures. The more fluid, generative view of ritual is necessary if the part it plays in realizing status change in socially-committed programmes is to be recognized and attributed. According to McLaren, (1986, p.48) rituals 'must not be seen as transparent vehicles that house pre-packaged signifieds'. Power, interest, interaction and ideology are involved in the interdependence of symbols (signifiers) and signified. Ritual practices can stabilize or change in meaning: 'as forms of enacted meaning, rituals enable social actors to frame, negotiate, and articulate their phenomenological existence as social, cultural and moral beings'.

Rituals exhibit such qualities as repetition, stylization and evocation which involve the incarnation of symbols, metaphors and cultural models for behaviour.

The ceremonies by which status change is managed in socially-committed programmes embody ritual practices. The making salient of the liminal status of the presenting member, the self-presentation of the programme, the public representation of its beliefs, proclaiming the acceptance of existing members, and the ultimate loss of liminal status all operate to structure experience in a way that shapes consciousness. But, if these processes are to be mutually supportive and operate in a manner that is functional to the operation of the programme, it is essential that the actor's understanding of 'what is happening' as these practices are being enacted is sympathetic to the intended status change. There is always the possibility that the meaning or import of the practice will be redefined by the presenting members. This can occur as a collective response or through negotiation in interaction with existing members. A requirement for the successful operation of ritual, from the programme's point of view, is that the 'official' structuring of consciousness is the one that is experienced by the incoming member.

Students on a return to study programme recalled the experience in the following humorous fashion, apparently inverting ritualizing meaning in a way that restrains associative change and subverts the personal learning that one assumes to have been the object of the programme.

> When I started at the Poly I did suffer from culture shock and panic attacks at first, not forgetting eyestrain and writer's cramp. 'Rationalism' meant nothing to me and Weber was a neighbour I used to know. The language used by lecturers is still rather strange and a scrambler is a definite advantage, but once you realise that intellectualism is just an excuse for an ego trip you're alright. At present my grant is £2,700 a year plus £370 travelling expenses and is definitely better than work/social security. Now I'm only answerable to myself for what I spend the money on — no social security snoopers, no loss of pay through illness — just extra hard work to catch up from someone else's notes.
>
> However, we are beginning to wonder if all the important stuff is done in secret at lunchtime when all the working-class students are up the refectory eating their peas off their knives (quoted in Thompson, 1983, p.192).

To be successfully introduced to higher education is to be socialized into a general academic community. Associative forms include a collective sense of student identity, the atomistic character of large lecture settings, and the primary nature of tutorial and informal friendship groups. For students coming from backgrounds under-represented at advanced levels of education, there is likely to be an exclusionary dimension as boundaries, and later barriers, are established between themselves, friends and even family members. Substantively, there is the induction into the academic world-view of a general as well as a subject-specific kind. These transitions are ritualized by means of a number of practices: through the privileged

access to knowledge represented by the common use of specialized terminology and a familiarity with established authorities;
participation in set encounters and experiences such as tutorials,
production of essays and term papers, and student activities; and
official recognition through grant awards with their requirements
and obligations.

The students on the return to study programme quoted above
appear to have failed to take the official meaning from such rituals, or to submit to them in the anticipated sanctioned manner
by which a working-class adult publicly becomes a fulltime student. If this reinterpretation of institutional rituals is firmly based
and capable of attracting support from like-minded peers or even
staff, the consequences could range over withdrawal, token and
instrumental participation or, depending on institutional stability,
fundamental adaptation of the programme itself. An alternative
interpretation of these students' accounts of being introduced to
the ritual practices of induction into student life is that the tongue-
in-cheek self-disparagement is a coping disposition by which the
anxiety, doubt and uprooting which characterizes the liminal state
is managed. In fact, it is possible for programmes to harness stylized subversion to the point at which it operates as a ritual release
of tension for new members. Where this occurs, what appears as
overtly dysfunctional to a programme is more likely to be deeply
integrative.

Language

The significance of language in the process of status change is to
be found in the initial reaction of a working-class woman from the
East End of London on meeting radical feminists for the first time:
'*I* was who they were talking about, but I didn't understand a word
they said' (quoted in Thompson, 1983, p.139). In this woman's
experience, the language of feminism represented an impediment
to induction into a collective association with other women. Yet,
where a specialized terminology and distinctive way of speaking
exists, as often is the case where the associative transition embodies
higher-order epistemic substance, it produces a means by which the
status change can be facilitated and confirmed. Language is very
prominent in the enactment of the ceremonies by which status
change is effected. The more it appears special and unique to the
status to be adopted the clearer will be whatever accession is pub-

licly proclaimed. For this to occur, however, it is necessary that the distinctive language of the programme becomes the language of the presenting member. In fact, such a change of language can be interpreted as ritual submission, a symbol of 'yielding' to the influence of the programme and its membershipping ceremonies (Samarin, 1972). An extreme manifestation of an identifying language is the 'speaking in tongues' to be found among some religious groups (McGuire, 1982) but the phenomenon is sufficiently widespread in secularized belief-systems and encounters to be vulnerable to the following caricature by Axmacher (quoted in Alheit, 1992):

> Authentic, encouraging, charismatic, dynamic, emphatic, feminine, holistic, hedonistic, interactive, creative, pleasure-seeking, communicative, normative, optimistic, participative, rhetorical, spiritual, team-orientated, visionary, truthful, forward-looking: feeling good, working better (afterwards), having understood nothing at all.

And this is to target the 'private languages' of only a number of perspectives. Their private nature is due not so much to linguistic inaccessibility. It has more to do with the manner in which their use, and the representation and communication which they embody, are bound up with an intersubjective view of reality. To participate with conviction requires interpretive change as well as linguistic competence. But definitions of the world depend on language to categorize, delineate and name the distinguishing features of their accounts of reality. Language and what is 'real' are inseparable.

To be without a distinctive language impedes the representation of one's perceptions. Collectively, it limits the formation of intersubjectivity. The centrality of 'naming' has been repeatedly identified by individual women as an element in the emergence of their collective sense of womanhood, as well as in the mobilization of women to higher associative forms within the women's movement. Cullen (1987) recalls how, in the absence of a terminology by which to identify and confront patriarchy and stereotype, she experienced 'anxiety and insecurity' about her identity: 'there has been no accepted vocabulary available to girls and woman who become uneasily aware of their status as outsider in the perspective of the 'I' of western culture ... I had never heard of patriarchy or stereotypes. I literally had no words with which to define or think through the trauma'. This, of course, is a personal manifestation of what Friedan (1983) in *The Feminine Mystique* referred to as the problem without a name.

As an impediment to a programme's capacity to attract and integrate new members, the absence of a distinctive language has been recently noted in relation to programmes of political change in central and eastern Europe. Speculating on the possibility of basing social policy on a collective sense of common citizenship, de Deken (1992) cautions: 'forty years of Marxism Leninism has discredited the conceptual tools of the advocates of the "social citizenship" model. It has left Social Democracy without a vocabulary for mobilizing its fragmented electorate'.

Holism

Membershipping ceremonies that are holistic engage the total person. Not confining themselves to exercizing the mind, they excite the feelings and emotions, invite movement and expression, and provoke zeal, vision and faith.

A number of analyses of socially-committed programmes have explicitly pointed to the limitations of the unidimensional integration of members. In his commentary on programmes of political education and paid educational leave in Germany, Holzapfel (1992) has warned against the danger of being 'too cognitivist', and advocates the use of art, drama and video production. Shor (1986) has identified creative and imaginative activities as valued features of Freire's approach to bringing students into a solidary and codetermining relationship with their teachers.

Pointing to the limits of rational change, Fay (1987) claims that even where the cognitivist approach works best, where behavioural dispositions are formed as a result of learning cultural ideas, it is still inadequate. This is because it fails to take account of the impact on social relations of what he refers to as somatic learning, the education of bodies. He sees the significance of somatic learning as being particularly evident in the formation of a soldier where physical drills and routines are used to cultivate the proper bearing, head alignment and movement of the feet. He contends that this is not peripheral to the process of socialization to a new identity:

> This bearing is important not simply to fit some aesthetic ideal extraneous to the task of being a good solider; learning to have the proper bearing is in part to acquire the dispositions and attitudes, essential to carrying out the duties of a solider.

Equally, according to Fay, what is true in armies also applies to the training of monks and street gang members, to draw on disparate examples. And while this process of bodily training is less conscious and organized in the education of priests, prisoners and doctors, the process is essentially the same since 'to become a person of a certain sort is to acquire a body and a set of bodily dispositions appropriate to this sort'.

In fact, many programmes recognize the benefits of holistic membershipping in their practices. Literacy programmes in Latin America, the Caribbean and Africa have often been organized as 'mass' events, using song, dance, mime and folk practices, frequently in a carnival atmosphere. Evans (1980), writing on the growth of writers' workshops in working-class communities, believes that for many of those involved they are 'as much an expression of working-class consciousness as an educational experience'. This is clear from the following piece by Mary Casey, one of the writers quoted by Evans.

> Why do you care what class I'm from?
> Does it stick in your gullet like a sour plum?
> Well, mate! A cleaner is me mother
> A docker is me brother
> Bread pudding is wet nelly
> And me stomach is me belly
> And I'm proud of the class that I come from.

Not alone does creative writing such as this celebrate a working-class identity but it does so with exclusionary intent. There is a confirmation of boundaries and a disdainful resistance to assimilation.

Also operating with holistic effect during the membershipping process are a number of 'confessional' practices. Described as sharing, situating, bonding or affirming exercises these involve considerable self-exposure. They include the giving of accounts of the development of one's religious, cultural, political, feminist, ethnic or cultural awareness and 'conversion'. A comprehensive range of the self is revealed in these accounts as the new members admit to doubts and anxieties, reveal conflicts and tensions, and celebrate personal awakenings in their biographical path to the membershipping stage. What appears as spontaneous and untutored in these members' accounts, however, may well be the product of a retrospective reconstruction of events in the light of the programme's ideology (Beckford, 1978).

Conclusion

All of the associative forms described in this chapter can be found in learning relationships: the atomistic character of distance learning, the dualism that can develop between tutor and student, and the activism of experiential and action-based learning are but examples. Within socially-committed programmes the imperatives of personal change and legitimation are such that the higher-order associative forms are likely to prevail. These associative forms are analytical categories and the act of considering them individually and in isolation from one another may obscure the real life flux of relationships to be experienced in the career of a socially-committed programme. In fact, different associative forms will co-exist, compete, merge or fade in different combinations and sequences. In consciousness-raising an essential task is the transformation of categorical association into, at least, collectivist association. And the process rarely stops there. Intentionally, groups characterized by strong primary association are formed, dualisms may develop and a programme of social action often follows. Exclusionary association has been noted as a characteristic feature of socially-committed programmes which represent minority or threatened world-views, or whose providers feel that their task of bringing about social change is a particularly daunting one. Successful identity and interpretive change may demand dualist association reminiscent of the dependency and emotional intensity of the parent-child relationship. For providers of socially-committed programmes the activist dimension is indispensible, be it as a feature of the programme or as a consequence of it. Advocates of activist association would argue that there is no point in changing people's perception of reality and role capacities if they are not to act in the light of these personal changes and bring about the requisite adjustments to society.

Because of their significance for the success of socially-committed programmes, considerable energy will be invested in establishing and maintaining appropriate associative forms and in achieving the smooth induction of new members.

Two qualifications are appropriate. Associative forms do not exist without a content. People do not interact in an epistemic vacuum. As well as variation in the character of the relationship between participants in socially-committed programmes they also vary in the substance of the personal and social change which is the purpose of their existence. Equally, it needs to be stressed that individual socially-committed programmes, like other forms of collective activity, can take on a life of their own and for any number of reasons operate dysfunctionally in relation to the achievement of their stated objectives. How a programme copes with a specific variety of dysfunction — the doubts, disbelief, dissent or incapacity of participants — is considered in the next chapter.

7 Coping with dysfunctional response

Introduction

Many providers of socially-committed programmes declare themselves to be conscious of the dangers of dogmatism in their view of the world. They claim to recognize the potential to impose on participants, in a manner that does violence to the interpretations and understandings they bring to the programme, a perception of reality that treats them as passive objects in the learning process. This is particularly true of programmes which see their mission as liberationist and emancipatory. Fay (1987, p.105), in advocating educative action as a means of facilitating self-understanding and enlightenment, recognizes that 'a major danger for anyone who aspires to alter the way people think, feel, and act is dogmatism degenerating into tyranny'. Freire (1972a, pp. 66–67) warns that

> in their desire to obtain the support of the people for revolutionary action, revolutionary leaders often fall for the banking line of planning a programme content from the top down. They approach the peasant or urban masses with projects which may correspond to their own view of the world but not to that of the people. They forget that their fundamental object is to fight alongside the people for the recovery of the people's stolen humanity, not to 'win the people over' to their side.

Freire goes on to argue that the notion of winning the people over should not be part of the vocabulary of revolutionary leaders. Throughout their account of operating women's groups according to feminist principles Butler and Wintram (1991) acknowledge that, as paid workers occupying white middle-class status positions in society, there are impediments to be recognized in their efforts to demonstrate the applicability of their principles to the life situations of women who differ from them on such grounds as financial security, social status and racial identity. As they put it, 'we should never lose sight of the argument ... that theoretical intricacies can only ever be an approximation to reality' (p.6). And even those programmes which legitimate their actions by reference to truths outside their rational choice — religious dogma, received tenets, 'scientific' political principles — would reject the charge that they were seeking to impose their own world-view on passive unthinking participants.

The extent to which these aspirations of non-imposition and anti-dogmation pervade the practice of socially-committed programmes can be explored by considering how a programme treats participant response which is perceived to be dysfunctional to its mechanisms and aspirations. Being able and willing to distinguish between legitimate and illegitimate rejection of one's theory of society is, according to Fay (1987), essential if a programme's transformative mechanisms are not to become manipulative. If this distinction isn't a feature of the thinking of a programme any rejection of its world-view, he argues, 'can then be interpreted as indicating that its rejecters must continue to be manipulated in an instrumentalist manner ... until they are supposedly "rational enough" to respond to the theory in a reflective and coherent way, for which read: until they accept the critical theorist's analysis of their situation' (p.105). But to allow that participant rejection of one's world-view might be genuine and tenable is to accept the possibility that the vision on which the programme is based is invalid, worthless or false. Since the providers of socially-committed programmes are predisposed to reject both the charges of manipulation and error, a theoretical paradox arises that demands explication. So also does it experiential manifestation: we are required to explain how providers of socially-committed programmes, which distance themselves from imposition and dogmatism, fail to produce instances where they have experienced significant transformation in the light of contact with the lived experience of participants.

In examining how a programme responds to expressions of disbelief, rejection, doubt, role distance or incapacity and, in particular, how it interprets and labels dysfunctional response, how it reacts to it and how it contains it, we can begin to unravel these theoretical and experiential paradoxes.

Interpreting dysfunctional response

Quarrelsome dissent

To interpret dysfunctional response as quarrelsome dissent is to individualize it. Any suggestion that it might have significance beyond the behaviour of the participant is dismissed. No underlying structural forces are considered to be at work. The explanation, such that it is, is to be sought in the personality of the individual or in the interpersonal dynamics of the programme.

Where a programme successfully labels dysfunctional response as quarrelsome dissent it effectively neutralizes and depoliticizes whatever doubt or criticisms relating to the programme are being proclaimed. Since the explanation is seen to reside in individuals, whatever constitutes dysfunctional response is considered to be without implications for the programme, be it in relation to the validity of its objectives or the character of its formative strategies. Moreover, since there is a suggestion of irrationality and contrariness on the part of the individual, this deflection of attention and analysis from the programme is confirmed. In such circumstances, a programme cannot be expected to be unduly concerned about dysfunctional response or to entertain the possibility that it might have contributed to it in some, however unthinking, manner. The culpability of the individual rather than some putative inadequacy of the programme is what is highlighted.

Any programme that finds itself repeatedly attributing dissent to the quarrelsome nature of the perpetrators needs to examine the possibility that it is indulging in diversionary tactics.

Tranformative resistance

There is an extensive body of analysis which interprets dysfunctional behaviour in educational settings as resistance to domination and manipulation. According to this interpretation, the

educational system in capitalist societies is entrusted with the responsibility of reproducing an unequal social and economic order.
In Althusser's (1971) view, the school's task is to reproduce both
the forces of production and the existing relations of production:

> It (the school) takes children from every class at infant school age,
> and then for years, the years in which the child is most 'vulnerable',
> ... it drums into them, whether it uses new or old methods, a certain
> amount of 'know how' wrapped in the ruling ideology.... Each mass
> ejected *en route* is practically provided with the ideology which suits
> the role it has to fulfil in class society: the role of the exploited... the
> role of the agent of exploitation ... of the agent of repression... or of
> the professional ideologist.

To perform these tasks effectively any suggestion of exploitation
must be disguised. Those who are being treated unequally must
believe that the educational system is acting fairly, and that any
limited access to resources or life chances they might experience
has been determined by an open meritocratic process. Bourdieu
(1973) has argued that of all the mechanisms that have been
used throughout history to transmit power and privilege 'there
surely does not exist one that is better concealed ... than that
solution which the educational system provides by contributing
to the reproduction of the structure of class relations and by
concealing, by an apparently neutral attitude, the fact that it
fills this function'. In particular, Bourdieu contends that this
concealment is a requirement of societies 'which tend to refuse
the most patent forms of hereditary transmission of power and
privilege'.

Occasionally, the students see through this ideology and recognize the process for what it is, a mechanism of ideological imposition, economic exploitation and curtailed opportunity. But,
lacking a language of critique or a familiarity with the discourse
of radical political theory, their experiential recognition of this exploitation is communicated by means of truancy, class avoidance,
disruptive behaviour and anti-school responses. Corrigan's (1979)
ethnographic account of the school experience of working-class
youth in Sunderland, *Schooling the Smash Street Kids*, offers such
an interpretation of dysfunctional response. There is said to be
much evidence in the words and actions of the Smash Street Kids in
relation to schooling that points to 'a resurgence of revolutionary
feeling about education among youth itself' such that one might

'see the working-class youth as capable of questioning, and maybe overthrowing, the conception of education inherent within capitalism, and replacing it with one that is much more capable of meeting the needs of working people'.

The interpretation of dysfunctional response as transformative resistance has been theoretically expanded in the work of radical theorists such as Apple (1979) and Giroux (1983). They stress the need to acknowledge the capacity of individuals to resist oppression and chart the different forms which such resistance can take.

But those who interpret dysfunctional response as transformative resistance do so in relation to programmes which they oppose and of which they are critical. For providers of socially-committed programmes to even entertain the possibility that what they are doing is exploitative, and that dysfunctional response might represent an unmasking of the reality of the programme, would be self-discrediting. And, yet, it might well be that dysfunctional response could be the mechanism for uncovering and illuminating anti-human aspects of a programme which otherwise remain hidden to the providers.

Reactionary resistance

Where dysfunctional response is interpreted as resistance, it is more likely to be viewed as reactionary rather than transformative. According to this interpretation, participants resist the formative efforts of the programme due to some characteristic in their make-up which they bring with them from previous experience.

This finds its most pronounced form in programmes which seek to eliminate false consciousness, ignorance or distorted realities. In such cases reactionary resistance is to be expected since the characteristics which give rise to it are themselves a feature of the participants' psychology and social situation which the programme has set out to correct. In fact, for many such programmes the dislodgement of what motivates reactionary resistance is at the very heart of the programme's activities. As well as providing the most heightened examples of reactionary resistance, programmes which assume false consciousness on the part of participants also advance an explanation as to why the resistance can be so deep-rooted. Fay (1987, p.98) contends that those who attempt the critical transformation of people 'must expect resistance from their audience because of the kind of ignorance they are trying to eliminate'. But since these misunderstandings about themselves and the society in which they live are usually shared by others who occupy the same social position, 'they constitute an important element of the conceptual scheme in terms of which these people talk about themselves and their social world. Furthermore, they are illusions and not merely false ideas … In other words, these self-misunderstandings are attempts to satisfy certain important needs and desires of the people who hold them, and this means they have a great power in their psychological economy'. Since dislodging these illusions requires the transformation of self-concepts and practices which give direction and meaning to people's lives, 'it involves acquiring a new identity'.

But, reactionary resistance can equally be imputed in programmes with less dismissive attitudes to the world-view of participants where it can be attributed to dependency, attachment, loyalties, a lack of faith or political naivety.

Reacting to dsyfunctional response

Cognitive respect or psychological strategy?

Berger (1976) argues that conflicting definitions of reality and their representatives should be approached with an attitude of cognitive respect. There are impediments to treating dysfunctional response in this way since, in the final analysis, the intention of socially-committed programmes is to change people and society in a particular direction.

Berger criticizes consciousness-raising type programmes for their failure to adopt such an attitude of cognitive respect towards those whose consciousness is to be raised. Consciousness-raising, he argues, is a project of higher-class individuals directed at lower-class people, and the consciousness that is targeted is the consciousness which the latter has of its own situation: 'thus a crucial assumption is that lower-class people do not understand their own situation, that they are in need of enlightenment on the matter, and that this service can be provided by selected higher-class individuals.' This lack of cognitive respect is not confined to left-wing activists, according to Berger. It can equally be found among those who are right-wing or middle-of-the-road in their perceptions of an ideal society: ' "They don't understand what is good for them" is the clue formula for all "consciousness raising", of whatever ideological or political coloration …put differently, the concept allocates different cognitive levels to "them" and to "us" — and it assigns to "us" the task of raising "them" to the higher level'.

Harris (1979, pp. 170–171) concedes that an incomplete understanding of their situation and true needs 'is the clue formula for consciousness raising', since 'in certain political situations, ideology, and education, bring about the conditions whereby people do not understand the situation in which they live, nor do they understand what is in their best interests'. Harris is interpreting consciousness-raising in the Marxist sense of false consciousness and contends that 'there are good grounds whereby one ideology or set of beliefs can be judged as being a better or worse representation of the world than other ideologies or sets of beliefs', and that such judgements can be made on the basis of acceptable and valid criteria. Relatedly, Harris contends that 'it is quite possible to have a vanguard whose consciousness is developed to the extent that it can make such judgements of critical preference'. Jarvis (1991a), however, argues that while the Marxist concept of false consciousness implies a 'cognitive hierarchy', the idea of conscientization does not. Equally, Fay (1987) argues that Freire's programmes incorporate significant protection against elitism. According to Jarvis, Berger fails to understand that Freire's method is about 'problematising reality rather then imposing another "superior" reality upon that already held by the learners'. Where strict cognitive respect operates, however, it would be considered invalid to select one view of reality over another as being in need of problematizing, or to assume that any particular individual or group possessed such a vantage point on reality as to make unproblematic their specification and targeting of who could benefit from consciousness-raising.

An attitude of cognitive respect to those who respond in a dysfunctional way to socially-committed programmes can easily be confused with a strategic approach. In the strategic approach, dissent, a lack of cooperation or doubt are treated in a lenient, tolerant and considered manner with a view to bringing the perpetrators around to the desired point of view.

The following quotation from the *Selected Works of Mao Tse-tung* spells out clearly the strategic approach to dysfunctional response:

All work done for the masses must start from their needs and not from the desire of any individual, however well-intentioned. It often happens that objectively the masses need a certain change, but subjectively they are not yet conscious of the need, not yet willing or determined to make the change. In such cases, we should wait patiently. We should not make the change until, through our work, most of the masses have become conscious of the need and are willing and determined to carry it out (quoted in Freire, 1972a, p.67).

Fay (1987, pp. 98–108) identifies four strategies which can help to break down resistance to educational transformation. Firstly, the message or world-view must 'speak to the felt needs' of participants, 'with the result that it must be grounded in their self-understandings even as it seeks to get them to conceive of themselves and their situations differently'. Secondly, there must be an attempt to show how participants' ideas are operating against their own best interests. Thirdly, participants' understandings can be related to the social conditions which created them. Fourthly, a programme can provide the necessary pedagogical conditions for reflective self-enlightenment. Fay commends the women's movement for the manner in which it has utilized all of these mechanisms in dealing with the problem of resistance.

In the strategic approach the error of the participant is never in doubt. But, since in any learning situation it makes good sense to start where people are, dissent, doubt etc. must be given sufficient credibility to allow them to become the object of analysis, as a stage in a process that is ultimately directed towards their dissipation or refutation.

Containing dysfunctional response

How do providers and participants sustain the feeling that the experience of a programme is not manipulative or constraining in the context of programmes which, if they are to survive, must nonetheless ensure that dysfunctional responses don't threaten the stability of the programme? A programme's legitimacy, depending on the form it takes, requires a foreclosing of debate on certain ideas, an acceptance that selected principles are beyond question, or a receptivity to the pronouncements of key individuals. The epistemic nature of the substantive change to which a programme directs its energies can incorporate assumptions regarding the function of knowledge and the basis on which truth can be tested and validated. The necessary psychological change can be such that an affective nonrational disposition is required. The associative requirements may involve holistic immersion in the programme. And, yet, adults need to feel that, as adults and as voluntary participants, everything is up for debate and they are not the object of manipulation and predetermined agendas for change.

This is a particular case of the universal problem of the tension between agency and culture in human behaviour. Archer (1989, p.xi) points to the 'tension to be resolved ... between the fund of ideas which in a real sense we will feel free to accept or reject, and the fact (sometimes known, but sometimes happening behind our backs) that the pool itself has been restricted or contaminated and that our sensed freedoms can be more a matter of manipulated feelings than of genuine liberty'.

How do socially-committed programmes sustain this necessary sense of freedom among participants while at the same time fulfilling the requirements of containment, management, foreclosure and holistic immersion that follow from, in particular, the legitimatory, epistemic, formative and associative imperatives of a programme?

Paradigms: concepts, terminology, themes

A discreet ongoing mechanism for the management of dysfunctional response, and all the more effective because of its discretion, utilizes the controlling power of a programme's paradigm. Paradigmatic control takes the form of regulating the parameters of the thought processes of participants. In particular, it serves to contain dysfunctional response within acceptable cognitive limits, while giving participants the feeling of a sensed freedom to draw on an infinitive pool of ideas that Archer speaks of. An understanding of how this control operates can be gained by considering the manner in which some key components of a paradigm — concepts, terminology and themes — structure an individual's thought processes.

Concepts are boundaried categories of thought. They represent filters through which the world is known and internalized. They differentiate and integrate what would otherwise be experienced as a buzzing mass of stimuli. Concepts are cultural and historical phenomena and can be seen to vary between cultures and over time. It follows, in theory at least, that it should be possible to interpret experience in the light of the totally novel set of concepts. In fact, culturally-prescribed concepts are invested with considerable power: they define boundaries of normality and demand allegiance for the purpose of meaningful social contact. To deviate conceptually may well result in a disruption of social life, a lack of comprehension and perhaps even attract the label of genius or schizophrenic. To analyse why certain concepts dominate at any one time and the processes by which they change requires a consideration of the belief systems involved and the social interests represented. At its most fundamental there is an ontology implicit in a repertoire of concepts in that 'concepts reflect and embody in their meaning beliefs about how the world operates' (Fay, 1987, p.44).

It follows, therefore, that for a programme to regulate the conceptual framework through which reality is known and interpreted is to exercize control at a deep and hidden level of structure. This derives from a conceptualization's normative power, cultural embeddedness, connotations of reality, and the social interests involved. Where the conceptual apparatus sanctioned by a programme's paradigm is internalized, any subsequent dissent or contestation is restrained by the fact that even the very act of formulating such an assault has to make use of the conceptual framework of one's adversary.

Concepts, however, are abstractions and maintain a very precarious claim on reality in the absence of being labelled. The relationship between language, concepts and reality is much disputed. Positivism, structural linguistics, semiology and linguistic analysis all suggest their own interpretation and differ in the location of their emphasis. To what extent is the world available to be known as something 'out there' independently of the modes of knowing (e.g., concepts, language) of the knower? Is the understanding of what is true, valid or real a function of the structure of the language we use to describe the world? Can we really justify the depsychologizing of the sending and receiving of signs — is the system of social signification all that really matters in determining meaning? Or is the issue really a conceptual one that can be settled by the analysis of the concepts used by people in living life and making sense of the world (Winch, 1958; Kearney, 1986; Fay, 1987)?

In sanctioning a particular terminology to label and transmit its conceptual organization of the world, a programme's paradigm operates to effectively bracket these questions. The complex contestation they embody is excluded. Not alone, therefore, does the terminology of a programme's paradigm give a reality and sense of permanence to its conceptual repertoire, it also confers on it a taken-for-granted sense of ordinariness and normality.

Themes are topics that, when spoken of, can be reasonably expected to make sense to the participants in the communicative encounter. They are observational sentences or utterances that are recognized and understood. They constitute valid elements of discourse. Themes are what can be spoken of in a specific inter-subjective community. Themes may at times appear as elements of 'idle talk' — snap judgements, careless evaluation, ill-considered opinion — that functions to fill aural space and ease social interaction rather than to advance authentic communication (Heidegger, 1962). Yet, even in idle talk there is a testing of the cognitive and communicative tolerance of a theme. And it constitutes a testing ground that involves no statement of intent or commitment. As such, idle talk allows for themes to be filtered into a programme's discourse without suggesting doubts about a participant's orthodoxy or threatening the programme's direction.

In the operation of paradigmatic control within socially-committed programmes, these components of concept, terminology and theme are difficult to disentangle. They come together in discourse where their controlling power is more likely to be recognized by theorists or dissident former participants, rather than by current participants and providers who remain culturally immersed in the programme.

The existence of conceptual dissonance between providers and participants can render the conceptualization of a paradigm more visible and available for analysis. An example of how participants might fail to conceptualize a programme in the manner envisaged by the providers is described by Rockhill (1987). Drawing on life history interviews with working-class hispanic women in Los Angeles as part of a project on literacy, she contrasts the radical interpretation of literacy as power, which she sees as dominating most discourse on literacy, and the lived experience of women as it relates to being literate. While the women yearned to learn English and felt it was necessary for getting ahead, they believed they could get by without it and were unlikely to learn enough of it to make any difference to their lives. According to Rockhill, 'conceptions of empowerment, resistance and rights do not capture the way the women we interviewed talk about their longing for literacy;

174

how they think about their lives, what is meaningful to them, or the conflicts they live'. These conceptions, she found, did not make contact with the material conditions, the relationships or the dreams of the women; they addressed public spheres, such as politics and the economy, rather than the private one of the home, including religious, family and gender relations. As she put it, 'to frame literacy in terms of equality of opportunity, rights or empowerment is absurd in the face of a fist — or, less dramatically, in a gendered society where the conception of rights is alien to women who have been told all their lives that they must obey and care for others'. Since conceptual control can be so pervasive where it operates successfully in a programme, we are forced to rely on examples of conceptual dissonance to highlight its existence and effectiveness.

A crucial mechanism in the structuring of a person's conceptual organization of the world is linguistic usage. Where a reconceptualization of reality is necessary if a socially-committed programme is to be successful, and this is true to some degree of most socially-committed programmes, induction into a new representation of experience is required. The imaging of reality through language, and the curtailment exercized by this process of imaging through the selective use of language, advances the participant's reconceptualization (and deconceptualization) of the world. In this way, according to Ball (1990, p.25), who draws on Baudrillard's process of 'imposition of the real', 'discourse is self-generating, self-reinforcing ... where the opposition between things as presented and what's really going on begins to dissolve. Signs take on a life of their own, their own circulation.'

To control language, if we follow Wittgenstein, is to control the boundaries of what is thinkable and unthinkable. It is to determine what is said and what is left unsaid. In the preface to the *Tractatus*, Wittgenstein (1961) contends:

What can be said at all can be said clearly: and whereof one cannot speak, thereof one must be silent. Thus the aim of the book is to draw a boundary of thinking, or rather — not of thinking, but of the expression of thoughts: for in order to draw a boundary of thinking, we should have to be able to think both sides of the boundary (we should have to be able to think what cannot be thought). It will therefore only be in language that the boundary can be drawn, and what lies on the other side of the boundary will be plain nonsense.

At various points in previous chapters the significance of having a method of naming experience, and thus delineating and drawing boundaries around components of reality in such a way as to objectify and confirm them, has been mentioned. Language thus opens up possibilities of regulating participants' organization of the world and their experience of it. In so doing, there is the less public experience of unnamed realities being regulated to a limbo world of intuitions, feelings and hunches which, lacking a means of representation and communication, maintain a tenuous hold on reality as it is understood within a particular group. The controlling function of language is recognized by Sartre, as is its capacity for social disruption and change: 'Words wreck havoc when they find a name for what had up to then been lived namelessly' (quoted in Bourdieu, 1977).

In advancing the course of their projects, a number of writers have recognized the role that language can play in assisting or retarding their efforts. In his critique of the family as a conditioning device, Cooper (1976, p.29) laments: 'I have perforce used a language that I find archaic, essentially reactionary and certainly discrepant with my thinking. "Family words" like mother, father, child … The connotation of "mother" takes in a number of biological functions, primary protector functions, a socially over-defined role, and a certain legal "reality" '. Because of this, Cooper feels constrained in his efforts to question 'the fatuity and danger of the fetish of consanguinity' while confined to a language that underlines roles defined by a blood relationship. But he does not suggest a new language. Somewhat like Derrida (1978), he is using 'discourse which borrows from a heritage the resources necessary for the deconstruction of that heritage itself'. Derrida's practice of *sous rature*, usually translated as 'under erasure', is designed to advance this deconstruction from within a tradition. The idea is that since the word is inadequate it is crossed out, but since it is necessary for communication it remains legible.

Daly (1979), on the other hand, feels that the distorting capacity of male language is so great that a new terminology has to be constructed, what she refers to as a gynomorphic vocabulary.

The controlling arena of concepts is that of the idealist realm. Terminology influences through the structuring capacity of language. Thematic control incorporates more material regulation. Roles, interpersonal relationships, ethos and context are all involved in determining what themes will be introduced to discourse and what will remain unsaid. As Foucault (1981, p.62) puts it, 'we know very well that we are not free to say anything, that we cannot speak of anything when and where we like, and that just anyone, in short, cannot speak of just anything'.

To speak of prohibition and exclusion in relation to what topics are discussed, and what lines of speculation, inquiry, explanation and action are considered useful to pursue, may give the impression of conscious action and conspiratorial intent on the part of programme leaders. On the contrary, thematic control is a manifestation of how illusory communicative symmetry can be, and an indication of the many sources other than disparities of behavioural power that can shape what is uttered in a communicative encounter. In a programme with transcendental or spiritual objectives, secularism will be dismissed as delusion. In a poverty action programme, to blame the poor for their poverty would be to attract disbelief and wonderment at the presence of the speaker in the programme. Exaggerated, heightened or stylized versions of reality may pass unquestioned if they advance a movement's political aims. New members and those experiencing doubts or anxieties may occasionally introduce themes, normally disallowed, but which are strategically tolerated. McIlroy (1990) identifies some to these features of control in the operation of trade union educational programmes in Britain. He argues that the tendency has been for trade union education to become 'less democratic, for education to become increasingly *delivered* as a *service* by a specialized bureaucracy, *provided* for rather than created and developed by students' self-organization'. And while the use of participatory pedagogy in the classroom is seen as a vital means of skill development and the cultivation of confidence for wider union involvement, 'rigorous, critical scrutiny of union democracy itself, bureaucratism, rank and fileism, as distinct from "this is the union structure", approach has found little place in trade union education'.

Concepts, terminology and themes operate at the pre-discursive level of a programme's activities. As such, they are not routinely the subject of discussion but they shape what is. Their control over the discourse of a programme will be influenced by the degree to which the paradigm they represent tightly frames the consciousness of the participants.

Paradigms: framing

The framing of a paradigm refers to its boundaries and how weak or strong are their definition. Framing relates to the degree to which the components of a paradigm are set apart from whatever concepts, terms, and themes are considered to be external to it. This is most obviously a matter of consciousness, of how reality is conceptualized and understood. But, it isn't a 'free-floating' or 'bodyless' consciousness: it is socially grounded, embedded in biographies and social space and manifesting symbolic and material power.

Framing is at its strongest when a paradigm attains a hegemonic status. This is the ultimate in framing in that there is no awareness of another reality outside of the paradigm. The conceptualization and explanation of the world represent the boundaries of common sense and normality. It experiences no challenge because there is no world-view, interpretation or vision to be set against it. In fact, so deeply structured is a hegemonic paradigm that its existence as a paradigm is unknown to those whose consciousness it regulates.

Bourdieu's (1977) distinction between doxa and orthodoxy expands on the tightness of the definitional capacity of a paradigm's boundaries. And it achieves this in a manner that qualitatively distinguishes between different kinds of framing and the tensions involved in maintaining them, and the distinctions between them, in existence. Doxa refers to the universe of what is undiscussed and, therefore, undisputed, 'the sum total of theses tacitly posited on the hither side of all inquiry, which appear as such only retrospectively when they come to be suspended practically' (p.168). It incorporates the absolute form of legitimacy 'since it is unaware of the very question of legitimacy, which arises from competition for legitimacy, and hence from conflict between groups claiming to possess it'.

Orthodoxy, on the other hand, refers to the universe of discourse, the realm of available opinions and arguments, but in a manner that explicitly defines some ways of thinking as erroneous or untrue. When the limits of doxa are pushed back, and its arbitrary character revealed, it becomes necessary for those who subscribe to the established view to systematize and rationalize it. Orthodoxy involves the answering of questions which under doxa remain unposed. Orthodoxy requires legitimation of positions in a way that doxa does not.

178

As Bourdieu points out, the control exercized by orthodox positions, in sanctioning some world-views and opposing others, conceals a more fundamental censorship that operates through maintaining a distinction 'between the universe of things that can be stated, and hence thought, and the universe of that which is taken for granted' (pp. 169–170).

Where a programme succeeds in being silent about its characteristic paradigm as a paradigm, what constitutes contestation will operate within functional limits. Whatever questions, doubts or disputes arise will not be subversive of the programme. Rather, the appearance of open discourse allows participants to feel that they are drawing on an uncontaminated corpus of ideas. They experience themselves as agents: willing, influencing, determining. The more tightly framed a programmes's paradigm the more its contestability is obscured, while what contestation occurs operates within unsensed constraints.

Conclusion

All programmes of educative action experience, in some degree and kind, participant response that impedes the attainment of their objectives. This can take many forms and include incapacity, unresponsiveness, doubt, dissent or resistance. Dysfunctional response of this nature has the potential to destabilize a programme by dissipating consensus regarding its intentions, proclaiming counter definitions of reality, threatening legitimacy, and disengaging from forms of association which are necessary for the personal change required by the programme.

Because of this, socially-committed programmes must find ways of coping with dysfunctional response before it disseminates and takes effect. Yet, few providers of socially-committed programmes will wish to be regarded as dogmatic in their world-view and dismissive of criticism and alternative realities. Programmes that claim to be emancipatory, progressive or modernist will know that even a hint of elitism or dogmatism will render them vulnerable to the accusation of hypocrisy. For their part, participants must not experience the programme's coping mechanisms as oppressive or manipulative, or in any sense threatening their status as free and wilful adults.

How a programme explains dysfunctional response, and how

it reacts to it is a more accurate indicator of how anti-elitist and anti-dogmatic it really is than its protestations in this regard. To interpret the dysfunctional response of participants as quarrelsome dissent or reactionary resistance on their part is to individualize the attribution of motive in the form of a personal psychology or incapacity. It is to proclaim that the programme itself, its message, processes and agents are beyond interrogation. The doubts, dissent or unresponsiveness of participants are defined as having no validity as counter realities. Their status does not require the programme to question itself in the light of their emergence and manifestation. Dysfunctional response is traced to forces external to the programme which itself remains unproblematic to its providers; it is regarded as a form of consciousness to be explained rather than entertained.

The fact that this is to treat participant consciousness about the programme with little cognitive respect can often be disguised where programmes adopt a strategic approach to deviation from their world-view and formative strategies. This involves a toleration of a degree of deviation on the basis that one should start with the felt needs and self-understandings of participants, whatever they might be, if their consciousness is to be engaged and ultimately opened to the formative mechanisms of the programme. In the strategic approach the error of the participant is never in doubt to the provider. It is based on the view that it makes for effective learning to start when people are, though the only kind of credibility their dysfunctional response is given is as a temporary stage of consciousness, as a means towards its own dissipation and refutation. For providers who come to their commitment in a manner that allows them to acknowledge or be aware of only their own reality, the dismissal of deviance is likely to be regarded as an obligation, at worst infused with a disposition of paternalism towards the participants.

The strategic approach to dysfunctional response allows participants to feel that they are, if not quite equal partners in a dialogue, at least accorded some degree of authenticity and credibility in interpreting the content and processes of the programme. Paradigmatic control performs a similar task even more discreetly. By controlling the thought processes of participants through the designation of sanctioned concepts, terminology and themes it allows for a kind of flexibility, deviation and choice which poses a minimal threat to the programme. In the participant's experience there is a sense of freedom. For the programme, the paradigmatic insulation contains deviance within functional limits.

8   Conclusion

Introduction

This has been an analysis of socially-committed programmes defined as systematic efforts to bring about social change through educative action. The focus is the subjectivity of the participants which it seeks to establish as an object of moral concern in its own right rather than as a medium, to be acted on and through, in the interests of social change. Throughout the analysis particular examples of socially-committed programmes have been selected for consideration in the light of the six questions posed at the outset.

- How do people come to be committed to the active pursuit of a particular kind of change?
- How visible is the underpinning logic of the motivation to bring about change?
- What is the epistemic status of the desired change?
- How is the legitimacy of the programme established?
- What is the associative character of the interaction?
- How is dysfunctional response on the part of participants coped with?

The specific programmes drawn on could in many instances have been augmented with examples from socially-committed programmes of a different kind. Those selected serve to illuminate a particular point; personnel in other programmes are invited to interrogate themselves and their programmes in a similar manner. Some types of socially-committed programmes figure more than others. Consciousness-raising type programmes involving women, the disadvantaged and community action are examples of efforts to bring about social change through educative action that recur throughout the book. This is because such efforts have been documented in ways that provide responses to the six questions forming the conceptual framework of the analysis. Many other kinds of socially-committed programmes lack such analysis. Methodologically, what this points to is the need to generate an ethnography of socially-committed programmes that would make visible the kinds of features identified by this conceptual framework. Summative evaluation, adopting the black box approach to the dynamics of the programme, is inadequate for this purpose. What is required is a focusing on the microworld of programmes in operation with a view to providing conceptually elaborated accounts rather than untheorized narratives.

We now return to the three sets of issues raised towards the end of Chapter 1: human agency, structural forces and ideology. Not alone are these major themes of debate within social analysis, they also provide the broad parameters to the conceptual framework we have used to interrogate socially-committed programmes.

Human agency

Human agency refers to the individual person's involvement in the direction of social affairs. To stress the role of agency in social change is to locate the motor of change within the individual. It regards the course of human events as a product of wilful, meaningful and purposeful social action.

It would be easy to interpret socially-committed programmes as manifestations of agency in operation. They involve a distinct emphasis on the individual. They proclaim themselves to be people-driven and people-centred. They are instigated by individuals, they address the subjectivity of participants and they declare themselves to be in the interests of people. Yet, as our analysis of socially-committed programmes progressed from the motivating forces of their initiators through their representation, epistemic status, legitimation and forms of association, and concluding with how they coped with dysfunctional response, we encountered many examples of impaired or submerged agency.

We adopted a biographical approach to the origins of personal conviction and the forces that translate it into an activist commitment to engage in educative action for the purpose of changing society. This followed a consideration of political socialization, particularly in its broader interpretation which encompassed formal and informal learning, politically-relevant learning in non-political settings, and spanned the lifecycle. Even with this loose interpretation of political socialization, there is an inbuilt disguising of human agency derived from a traditional perspective on socialization which sees it as something that is acted upon individuals. The merit of this perspective, however, is that it recognizes the power of early formation. In particular, it highlights the capacity of the family, through its own agency and the experiences outside of the family which it can regulate, to exert a lasting influence on the individual. For this reason, where commitment can be traced to family experience, the strength of agency in the direction and enactment of the commitment can be justifiably questioned. In such a case, socialization, conceived as a series of external forces forming the individual, is an appropriate construct.

Of the four models of commitment extracted from the biographies of social activists and campaigners, linear commitment draws most heavily on early socialization. Linear commitment derives from family formation, its regulation of non-family influences during early life, and subsequent self-selection of influences in the light of dispositions and world-views carried forward from childhood and adolescence. Linear commitment involves an attachment to causes that is maintained throughout the lifecycle, and invokes a sense of integrity and consistency which makes assumptions about the agency of the actors involved. The actors are believed to be constantly reassessing and affirming the direction of their commitment. An alternative interpretation, that their early socialization has been propulsive or that it has integrated with other forces of formation in the maintenance of psychological and social congruence, might be equally valid. Such an alternative interpretation would signal entrapment rather than agency.

Sectoral commitment, derived from dispositions or needs originating in the family, can be submitted to a similar interrogation though it is likely that, in this case, the agency of individuals would be submerged only where the psychological orientations are particularly strong. Equally, where commitment is derived from later influences such as school, peer group or voluntary associations, the power of external forces on the individual is likely to be greatest where the contribution of the particular sector satisfies the needs of the person at the point at which their trajectories meet.

Flashpoint commitment, the sudden reorientation of one's life in the light of a dramatic event, appears to have very little of the wilful self involved, but it remains the least understood of ways of coming to commitment. At present, one cannot say how the susceptibility to flashpoint events might be the product of earlier experiences and influences.

Reactive commitment has the greatest claim to human agency since of its nature it involves taking stock of events, reflection, due consideration and action.

When participants submit themselves to the influence of a socially-committed programme as adults, too many assumptions relating to full knowledge, voluntarism, rationality and power are made such that there is an inflated sense of their taking control of their lives. Participants are often motivated by a range of affective and relational needs, which may well be satisfied by the programme, but which have little to do with its formal intentions, and may be recognized and understood only in an intuitive or haphazard manner, if at all. Relatedly, people do not select from an infinite range of programmes. Social, economic and personal circumstances influence participation. The assumption that participation in socially-committed programmes involves the grasping of opportunities to move one's life forward according to a distinct plan of personal development or social reform is not consistent with the research on adult participation in learning opportunities.

When it is differentiated in terms of purpose, cosmic function, truth criteria and forms of meaning, the substance of personal change aspired to in socially-committed programmes emerges as an epistemically diverse experience that has implications for the restraining of individual action. There is a distinct difference between 'knowledge how', procedural knowledge, and 'knowledge that', propositional knowledge, that parallels the distinction between instruction and education. The emancipatory function demands personal change that affects the individual in a deep, experiential and comprehensive manner. In contrast with the technical function of knowledge, which is directed to the domestication of the natural environment, it embodies a persuasive imperative for action in one's personal life and social relationships. The transmission of religious truths requires a suspension of the truth criteria of the physical sciences. In common with aesthetic experience, and to a lesser extent moral judgement, it involves immersion in an intersubjective community where characteristic verities are imbued with the status of first principles because of revelation, inherited tradition or trust. To seek symbolic or synoptic change is to desire to alter the manner in which an individual understands, names, orders and interprets reality across all its physical, social and transcendental dimensions. This is because symbolics are the necessary means of representing reality while synoptics 'gather up' and integrate all the other forms of meaning.

Segmental change, which involves the alteration of no more than a particular facet of a person's make-up, is unlikely to be adequate to effect the level of epistemic change required in socially-committed programmes. The conditions for successful role/identity change can be quite invasive for the individual. Interpretive change will be required, in some form, in successful socially-committed programmes. The more pervasive the interpretive change, the more the transformation assumes some of the characteristics of the parent/child relationship, such as those of affectivity and power disparity, which diminish the adult status of the individual.

In establishing the credibility of its agents and world-view a programme can appeal to a number of bases for its legitimacy. We identified four generic types: charismatic legitimacy, normative legitimacy, traditional legitimacy and rational legitimacy. Where they each diminish agency they do so in distinctive ways.

Pure charismatic legitimacy relies totally on the unique magnetism of a person or text. Assent is given in the sense that one is caught up in the distinctive appeal of the relationship. The compelling nature of the appeal may be inexplicable. With normative legitimacy, agency is affected by the range of the dogma, the first principles constituting the bedrock assumptions of the programme's operation, which is considered to be beyond the agenda of the reflection. To allow that these assumptions might be open to question would be to dilute the normative character of the interaction. The wider the range of these certainties the less there is available for personal scrutiny. Traditional legitimacy locates the participant in history. An awareness of being located within a particular tradition of social analysis and action situates the consciousness of the participants in a flow of forces, events and ideas that immediately impresses as being larger than individual action and will. With rational legitimacy one is handing over a layer of one's self-determination to those who are legally given authority or who are designated as experts.

In collective association inroads can be made on the private and personal. There may be a requirement, or a sense of obligation, to submerge one's personal inclinations in favour of the goals of the collectivity. Where the encounter embodies primary relationships there are the added components of closeness, smallness, intimacy and durability. There is a strong sense of communality and solidarity. Within primary relationships dualisms frequently emerge in which there is a submersion of ego, a ceding of an element of oneself to the dominant partner. Activist association appears to have all the hallmarks of agency. It can be readily interpreted as action following in the light of reflection. What is difficult to disentangle from the apparent individuality of social action is the propelling force of a programme's world-view, once it has been successfully inculcated. In managing status change from one form of association to another, holistic strategies engage the total person and deprecate undue reliance on the cognitive.

No socially-committed programme will be without a degree of doubt, dissent or resistance among its participants. A programme needs to find ways of containing dysfunctional response, if it is to maintain loyalty and avoid its disruptive potential being realized more widely throughout the programme. Socially-committed programmes routinely interpret dysfunctional response as quarrelsome dissent or reactionary resistance in a manner that devalues the individuality of the participant. The action of the *I*, in Mead's conceptualization, is designated in pathological terms rather than being credited with any integrity or insight that might have implications for the operation of the programme. At its most accepting, the reaction of a programme to dysfunctional response would be strategic, according it a temporary credibility as the programme works towards its refutation and dislodgement. A particularly effective mechanism by which dysfunctional response is contained deploys the controlling power of a programme's paradigm. The concepts, terminology and themes sanctioned by a paradigm operate at a pre-discursive level to shape the character of discourse. And when a paradigm is tightly framed, its conceptualization, naming and thematizing of reality represents the boundaries of common-sense and normality. Where this occurs, whatever questions, doubts or disputes might emerge from the individual response of participants will operate within unsensed constraints. Participants will continue to experience themselves as agents, wilfully drawing on an apparently uncontaminated corpus of ideas, but failing to recognize the containment of the programme's paradigm.

Agency refers to the making of society through individual action. To vary the emphasis, and theorize on the person in relation to society, is to raise the question of personal autonomy. Autonomy is associated with being self-directive. It assumes that values and priorities are subjected to critical scrutiny and that one is not the unthinking agent of another's designs. It equally requires the release from 'self-incurred tutelage', the habit of passivity, acqui-escence and uncritical thinking, mentioned in Kant's essay 'What is Enlightenment' (in Kant, 1959). The demands and components of autonomy are eloquently outlined by Berlin:

> I wish my life and decisions to depend on myself, not on external forces of whatever kind. I wish to be the instrument of my own, not other men's, acts of will. I wish to be a subject, not an object; to be moved by reasons, by conscious purposes, which are my own, not by causes which affect me, as it were, from outside. I wish to be somebody, not nobody; a doer — deciding, not being decided for, self-directed and not acted upon by external nature or by other men as if I were a thing, or an animal, or a slave incapable of playing a human role, that is, of conceiving goals and policies of my own and realising them (quoted in Lukes, 1973, p.55).

Drawing on our consideration of the subjectivity of the partici-pant in socially-committed programmes, and their features which appear to impair human agency, it is possible to identify the fol-lowing potential threats to the realization of these conditions for autonomous involvement:

- those who initiate socially-committed programmes may themselves be entrapped through socialization, and from the need to maintain psychological and social consistency in their personal lives;
- the failure of programmes to fully declare their objectives and intentions in a manner that establishes effective and symmetrical communication;
- the submersion of rationality required by some forms of

epistemic change, the pervasiveness of psychological formation through role/identity and interpretive change, and the invasiveness of the conditions necessary for their success;

- the requirement in charismatic legitimacy that one submits to the indefinable dynamic of the relationship, the granting of special status to first principles as being beyond scrutiny in normative legitimacy, one's submersion in history through traditional legitimacy and, in rational legitimacy, designation of others, as experts, as having a privileged capacity to specify one's true needs;
- the enveloping communalist orientation of a programme as it progresses towards the higher order associative forms — collective, primary, dualist, exclusionary, activist — and the hidden persistence of surveillance and internalization in apparently humane and people-centred encounters and membershipping strategies;
- the dismissal of participants' doubts, anxieties and questionings as quarrelsome dissent or reactionary resistance, and giving them a hearing, not because of their credibility, but only as a means to their refutation, together with the unsensed constraints operating through the sanctioned concepts, language and themes of a programme's paradigm.

Structure

As Giddens (1990) has acknowledged, the tension between agency (or to use his term, human action) and social structure is a basic theoretical dilemma in sociology that has existed since modern social thinkers first attempted to systematically explain human behaviour. To adopt the structural approach is to explain behaviour in terms of social forces external to individual actors. It sees people as constrained in what they can do, and assumes that regularities in human behaviour can be anticipated and explained in the light of a knowledge of the social forces operating on individuals as they seek to meaningfully give direction to their lives. The structural approach emphasizes recurring patterns of action, interaction and collective configurations, as well as the different forms of institutional life and symbolic activity, and the role they play as 'social facts' that operate independently of the individual. While they may not actually determine behaviour, it is believed that they certainly compromize the choices which people realistically have available to them when they seek to act in an intentional, individualized and authentic manner. And what makes this dilemma between agency and structure all the more difficult to analyse experientially is that structural forces operate most effectively when we are unaware of their constraining or foreclosing impact on our social action.

As our interrogation of examples of socially-committed programmes proceeded it became clear that many of the features of the programmes identified in the process were imperatives: they were structural requirements necessary if the conditions for the achievement of the objectives of the programme were to be realized. As such, they owed less to the choice or viewpoint of individuals directing a programme and emerged as built-in essentials derived from the nature of the programme's objectives. One of the implications of interpreting the activities of socially-committed programmes as a series of interrelated structural imperatives is to dismiss, as simplistic and individualistic, the manipulative or conspiratorial interpretation of the many examples of submerged human agency and threatened autonomy outlined in the previous section.

The initiation and provision of socially-committed programmes could benefit from being treated as a social process that cannot be reduced to wilful human action. The strong personalities who initiate and lead such programmes may not be conduits through which structural forces realize themselves, or epiphenomena of underlying forces shaping their actions, but neither are they aloof from these influences. Biographical analysis allows for a situating of these influences over the full span of one's development and provides a spectrum and vantage point on the translation of one's personal conviction into a commitment to change others and, through them, society.

In turning to the participants, their first point of contact with a socially-committed programme is likely to be the proclamation of its intentions. From our analysis of the representational discourse of socially-committed programmes we found it to be general, non-specific and vague, to be inspirational rather than communicative. We identified many threats to the self-declaration of the courtship analogy, to the meeting of minds required in communicative consensus, and to the symmetry in dialogue, disputation and power of the 'ideal speech situation'. But there is little to be added to our understanding by attributing these threats to the evasiveness or deceit of the providers. These impediments to communication derive largely from the character and function of the representational discourse of socially-committed programmes. They have to do with the need to recruit participants, generate allegiance and cohesiveness among those involved and cope with goal-conflict and tension. Their source is likely to be the symbolic integration demanded in loosely-coupled systems and the stirring of the imagination to which utopian ideologies aspire.

The epistemic status of the substance of change aspired to is pivotal to the strategies adopted in socially-committed programmes. In differentiating between the substance of change in terms of its immediate purpose, cosmic function, truth criteria and forms of meaning, the substantive change which socially-committed programmes seek to effect was revealed as an epistemically diverse experience. To maximize the specific epistemic change required, a programme needs to ensure that psychologically appropriate personal change occurs. A few examples should serve to identify the nature of the structural link between epistemic content and psychological process in socially-committed programmes. Propositional knowledge, scientific or axiomatic knowledge, and empirics can require induction into distinctive roles and interpretations of reality, though they superficially appear to require no more than an addition to one's stock of knowledge. Interpretive change is essential if the transmission of emancipatory-motivated knowledge, religious knowledge and synoptics are to be successful. Role/identity change is versatile in the epistemic change that it can instigate, but segmental change has a low epistemic capacity. For this reason, any socially-committed programme, with even the most modest of designs on society, will need to achieve substantial psychological change among its participants, at least involving an alteration of their role capacity and identification, and most likely a change in their interpretation of reality, if it is to be successful. To set a socially-committed programme in motion, therefore, is to aspire to changing people in a psychologically significant fashion. How fundamental that psychological change will need to be depends on the epistemic substance of the programme, in particular its cosmic function, truth criteria and forms of meaning.

Successful role/identity change will, in turn, make demands on a programme's strategies of formation with implications for the supportive nature of its atmosphere, the availability of suitable

191

role models, together with the disengagement from competing models, and the provision of inducements. Since interpretive change during the adult years is most likely to involve induction into sub-worlds of reality, their plausibility must be established and maintained and, through restricted contact, nihilation, disparagement or immunization, threats from competing definitions of reality must be reduced.

Where these conditions are put in place they will, of course, have been the creation of human actions. The leaders, facilitators and organizers of the socially-committed programme will have directed and determined the arrangements. But in doing so, their real options will have been greatly circumscribed by the structural imperatives that link epistemic substance, psychological change and formative strategies. These imperatives are not determined by the people who put in place the requirements they signal.

This set of structural imperatives is but a miniature template of the complex of relationships, interdependencies, prerequisites and conditions linking all the aspects of socially-committed programmes considered in this book which structure a more wideranging and interrelated set of imperatives.

In establishing its legitimacy a programme is declaring the basis on which it assumes the entitlement to influence people and society. Without a satisfactory legitimatory base a programme would fail to recruit new members, lose the allegiance of existing participants, and subsequently wither away. Each of the four bases of legitimation considered — charismatic, normative, traditional and rational — has its own strengths and appropriateness in serving a programme's goals of survival and expansion. It is unlikely that a programme can achieve the initial dynamism to get it successfully launched without some element of charisma. Normative legitimacy, the acceptance of dogma, first principles of whatever kind, within a community of believers, is required where the epistemic demands of the programme do not allow for validation by means of the truth criteria of the physical sciences. Traditional legitimation is particularly functional where a programme needs to establish a pedigree for its activities and world-view, reach back into history to broaden its constituency of support, and dissipate any suspicion or accusation of unrepresentativeness or disruptiveness. Where a programme has a formal or legal basis for its activities, rational legitimacy will be a constituent feature of the organization of the programme. Role relationships between provider and participant that are legally constituted, or that are specified within statutory organizations, may supplement their legitimation in other ways, but in the final analysis they have to appear justifiable in terms of their rationality.

Demands are also made on the associative character of a socially-committed programme in maximizing its efficiency. The associative quality of an encounter refers to the character of the relationships between the actors involved, and emerged as a significant feature of socially-committed programmes throughout the analysis. Participants cannot be allowed to 'remain sturdily themselves' in programmes that seek to change people in predictable directions, and for this reason atomistic association is inappropriate. The achievement of collectivist association through the bonding of heritage, or a common set of values or grievances, is a basic requirement in socially-committed programmes. It is pivotal at the point of transition from lower-order associative forms in consciousness-raising type programmes, where the cultivation of a common identity is a prerequisite for the dissipation of false consciousness and the mobilization of cultural and political action. Such dissipation and mobilization will demand the primary association of the small intimate group. The intensity of dualist association may be necessary to compensate for infrequency of contact or, psychologically, to replace relationships with significant others from previous social formations which are severed as a result of participation in the programme. Exclusionary association provides conditions necessary for the dilution of the impact of competing world-views, and is particularly important at the 'novitiate' phase of membershipping. Advocates of activist association would argue that there is no point in changing people's perceptions of reality and role capacities if they are not to act in the light of these personal changes, and make the requisite adjustments to society.

The higher order the associative change demanded in a socially-committed programme, and the more these transitions provoke tension and anomie, the more the membershipping process has to incorporate strategies, usually drawing on the power of group influence, ritual, language and holistic engagement, to smooth the induction of new participants and to ease the sense of crisis.

Providers and participants of socially-committed programmes must sustain the feeling that the programme is not manipulative or constraining. Yet, programmes must ensure that whatever constitutes dysfunctional response, be it doubt, resistance, or incapacity, must not be allowed to threaten the stability of the programme. Paradigmatic control of ideas, the means by which a programme regulates the thought processes of its participants, is ideally suited for this purpose since it provides for the experience of having options but conceals their foreclosing in a manner that is functional to the objectives of the programme.

Ideology

Even if we go back no further than the ideologues of the French Revolution, to whom the contemporary usage of the concept is conventionally traced (Hall, 1978), ideology has generated a litany of meanings and associated controversies. The following meanings are pertinent to our present discussion:

- Ideology as prescription: proposals pertaining to political options relating to systems of government or to major societal institutions such as the economy, religion, education or the family;
- Ideology as socially-constructed knowledge: the attribution of meanings to phenomena in a manner that is shaped by the material and social forces impacting on a culture;
- Ideology as deception: a consciousness that operates against one's objective interests.

Ideology, in its prescriptive meaning, is a central feature of socially-committed programmes. This follows from our working definition which stressed the manner in which socially-committed programmes are premised on the desire to contribute to the stability, modification or fundamental alteration of the existing social order. The educative action involved is not an end in itself but is rather subordinated to the social vision which predates the existence of the programme. This social vision is intended to be relentlessly pursued in that its consideration, analysis or critique isn't meant to form a meaningful feature of the programme. In this sense, socially-committed programmes can be said to be ideological, which is no more than to acknowledge their normative character.

Ideology, considered as socially constructed ideas, moves beyond description and incorporates the position that knowledge is a reflection of forces external to the individual. To suggest that a socially-committed programme is ideological in this sense is to utter a truism, since one's awareness and interpretations of the world cannot remain aloof from one's material and social position in it. This returns the analysis to the influences of political socialization on the consciousness and social action of the providers and initiators of socially-committed programmes.

To interpret ideology as deception, however, is to assume that objective interests can be determined. If this is to have any real application, it requires that some understandings of the world and of personal needs must, at least, be less ideological than others, i.e. that some forms of consciousness must not suffer from deception and be privy to as true and as real an understanding of events as the human mind can achieve.

Socially-committed programmes vary in their prescriptions for the good life and for a better society. Yet, they are equally confident about their special vantage point on society, about not being deceived themselves, and, indeed, about the morality of their intentions to free others from self-deception. Accordingly, the same set of learning experiences may be regarded as exploitation by some and emancipation by others. As I indicated at the end of Chapter 1, it isn't within the disciplinary perspective of this book to sit in judgement on questions relating to the validity of knowledge, on what constitutes true and valid understandings of the world and on what is to be regarded as deception. The sociological exploration of the ideological character (considered as deception) of socially-committed programmes seeks to identify the aspects of a programme which impede the access of participants to that vantage point of objective awareness of the programme's processes, objectives and effects which this interpretation of ideology assumes to be possible.

This is to consider the extent to which participants are ideologically empowered in relation to their engagement by the programme, the degree to which they are positioned, as effectively as anyone can be, to distinguish between real and spurious needs, between valid and incomplete knowledge, between true and false consciousness, and between liberating and exploitative influences. Empowerment of this nature requires the possession of the following varieties of attributes and capacities:

■ Instrumental: literacy, communication skills, knowledge;

- Expressive: confidence, assertiveness, free from dependency;
- Critique: the capacity to pursue and question dispositions beyond the prescribed horizons of one's society or group;
- Activist: the motivation to take action in the light of critical awareness.

In considering the ideological empowerment of a programme's participants in relation to its impact on their subjectivity, the issues of human agency, structure and ideology are brought together. It would appear, from the listing of the diverse ways in which socially-committed programmes function to impair human agency and threaten personal autonomy, that they do not operate in ways that are conducive to the ideological empowerment of participants. The communication of programme intent was found to be typically inadequate. The more fundamental the psychological change involved, the more the adult status of the participants in terms of power and affectivity was diminished. Legitimation involved the handing over of an element of one's self-determination to others on the basis of personal dynamism, dogma, tradition or expertise. The membershipping of participants to the higher-order forms of association in socially-committed programmes demanded a submission to collective interests, a submersion of ego and a holistic immersion of a kind that deprecates undue reliance on the cognitive. Through the ideological control of a programme's paradigm what constitutes criticism is contained within unsensed limits.

But since these impediments to the ideological empowerment of participants are features that follow in the light of the structural imperatives of socially-committed programmes, providers and leaders are confronted with a dilemma.

Efficient socially-committed programmes cannot afford to incorporate the conditions that are necessary for the ideological empowerment of participants. To do so would be to endanger the programme by diluting the features — recruitment, psychological impact, legitimacy, association, paradigmatic control — that are necessary for its existence. The more a socially-committed programme builds into its operations safeguards against the kinds of threats to personal autonomy outlined earlier, the more its effectiveness will be eroded. The price of efficiency in advancing one's social cause is the invasion of the personal autonomy of

196

participants; the consequence of ideologically empowering participants is to inadequately satisfy the structural imperatives of socially-committed programmes.

My emphasis in suggesting a resolution of this dilemma is grounded in a model of social critique that has much in common with that of Eder (1990):

> Social theory... is only one possible way of interpreting the social world. It is only one attempt to decipher the objective meaning of a historic situation. But as such it is part of the collective learning processes it reconstructs historically. Social theory as critical theory is an intervention into the interpretations of those trying to shape the course and direction of collective learning processes. Such a conception of critique is of a 'therapeutic' nature. And this means that professional socio-scientific analysis has the task of dissolving all rationalizations that pervade social action.

Eder describes sociologists as 'specialists in interpretations'. Their task is 'to push new interpretations beyond those to which we have become accustomed... by deconstructing the illusions of the rationality, or its substitutes, ascribed to a society or to a social class or to a social group'.

It is suggested that the providers and initiators of socially-committed programmes put their trust more in the ideological empowerment of people than in the efficiency of their programmes. If their programmes have the validity they claim for them, whatever they might lose in the short-term modification of people's consciousness and actions, they are set to gain in the long-term from the attachment and enhanced commitment to their cause of those who are ideologically liberated. Furthermore, the endorsement of their social objectives by those whose autonomy hasn't been compromised should affirm the validity claims of their world-view.

These interpretations of socially-committed programmes are offered to those who are committed to social change through educative action. Overall, it is concluded that providers will need to become a good deal more self-interrogatory about the programmes they initiate and lead, and that this disposition and habit of reflexivity should necessarily encompass their own biography of commitment to social change through educative action. It is hoped that the conceptual framework of this book, and the manner in which it has been differentiated and expanded in terms of categories, schemas and questions, will contribute to this spirit and practice of reflexivity.

Bibliography

Abbott, W.M. (ed.) (1966), *The Documents of Vatican II*, Guild Press, New York.

Adult Education in Ireland (1973), Final Report of the Murphy Committee, The Stationery Office, Dublin.

Alcock, P. (1987), *Poverty and State Support*, Longman, London.

Alemayehu, R. (1988), 'Adult Education and the Third World: An African Perspective', in Lovett, T. (ed.), *Radical Approaches to Adult Education: A Reader*, Routledge, London.

Alheit, P. (1992), 'The Biographical Approach to Adult Education', in Mader, W. (ed.), *Adult Education in the Federal Republic of Germany: Scholarly Approaches and Professional Practice*, Centre for Continuing Education, University of British Columbia.

Almond, G.A. and Verba, S. (1963), *The Civic Culture*, Little, Brown and Co., Boston.

Althusser, L. (1971), 'Ideology and Ideological State Apparatuses', in Althusser, L. *Lenin and Philosophy and Other Essays*, New Left Books, London.

Andrews, M. (1991), *Lifetimes of Commitment*, Cambridge University Press, Cambridge.

Apple, M. (1979), *Ideology and Curriculum*, Routledge and Kegan Paul, London.

Archer, M. (1989), *Culture and Agency*, Cambridge University Press, Cambridge.

Asch, S.E. (1952), *Social Psychology*, Prentice-Hall, New Jersey.

Bair, D. (1991), *Simone de Beauvoir. A Biography*, Vintage, London.

Ball, S. (1990), *Politics and Policy Making in Education*, Routledge, London.

Barker-Lunn, J.C. (1970), *Streaming in the Primary School*, NFER, Slough.

Beauvoir, S. de (1977), *The Second Sex*, Penguin, Harmondsworth.

Beckford, J.A. (1978), 'Accounting for Conversion', *British Journal of Sociology*, vol. 29, pp. 249–262.

Berger, P. (1976), *Pyramids of Sacrifice*, Doubleday, New York.

Berger, P.L. and Berger, B. (1976), *Sociology: A Biographical Approach*, Penguin, Harmondsworth.

Berger, P.L. and Luckmann, T. (1973), *The Social Construction of Reality*, Penguin, Harmondsworth.

Bernstein, B. (1975), 'Ritual in Education', in Bernstein, B., *Class, Codes and Control, Volume 3*, Routledge and Kegan Paul, London.

Bettelheim, B. (1969), *The Children of the Dream*, Thames and Hudson, London.

Bettelheim, B. (1986), *The Informed Heart*, Penguin, Harmondsworth.

Blondel, J. (1987), *Political Leadership*, Sage, London.

Blum, A. (1971), 'Methods of Recognising, Describing and Formulating Social Problems', in Smigel, O. (ed.), *Handbook on the Study of Social Problems*, Rand McNally, Chicago.

Bourdieu, P. (1973), 'Cultural Reproduction and Social Reproduction', in Brown, R. (ed.), *Knowledge, Education and Cultural Change*, Tavistock, London.

Bourdieu, P. (1977), *Outline of a Theory of Practice*, Cambridge University Press, Cambridge.

Bourdieu, P. and Passeron, J.C. (1977), *Reproduction. In Education, Culture and Society*, Sage, London.

Breakwell, G. (1986), *Coping with Threatened Identities*, Methuen, London.

Brim, O. (1966), 'Socialization through the Life Cycle', in Brim, O. and Wheeler, S. (eds.), *Socialization after Childhood*, Wiley, New York.

Brim, O. (1968), 'Adult Socialization', in Clausen, J.A. (ed.), *Socialization and Society*, Little, Brown and Co., Boston.

Bromley, D.B. (1977), *The Psychology of Human Ageing*, Penguin, Harmondsworth.

Bron-Wojciechowska, A. and Bron, M. (1990), 'Adult Education for Democracy in Europe', *International Journal of University Adult Education*, vol. 29, pp. 66–83.

Brookfield, S. (1983), *Adult Learners, Adult Education and the Community*, Open University Press, Milton Keynes.

Brookfield, S. (1987), *Developing Critical Thinkers*, Open University Press, Milton Keynes.

Brown, G. (1980), 'Independence and Incorporation: The Labour College Movement and the Workers' Educational Association before the Second World War', in Thompson, J. (ed.), *Adult Education for a Change*, Hutchinson, London.

Browne, N. (1986), *Against the Tide*, Gill and Macmillan, Dublin.

Burgess, P. (1971), 'Reasons for Adult Participation in Group Educational Activities', *Adult Education*, vol. 22, pp. 3–29.

Butler, S. and Wintram, C. (1991), *Feminist Groupwork*, Sage, London.

Cathcart, H.R. (1989), 'Adult Education, Values and Irish Society', in O'Sullivan, D.(ed.), *Social Commitment and Adult Education*, Cork University Press, Cork.

Centre for Contemporary Cultural Studies (1981), *Unpopular Education*, Hutchinson, London.

Charters, A.N. and Hilton, R.J. (eds.) (1989), *Landmarks in International Adult Education. A Comparative Analysis*, Routledge, London.

Clarke, D. (1985), *Church and State*, Cork University Press, Cork.

Clausen, J.A. (ed.) (1968), *Socialization and Society*, Little, Brown and Co. Boston.

Collard, S. and Law, S. (1989), 'The Limits of Perspective Transformation. A Critique of Mezirow's Theory', *Adult Education Quarterly*, vol. 39, pp. 99–107.

Cooper, D. (1976), *The Death of the Family*, Pelican, Harmondsworth.

Corrigan, P. (1979), *Schooling the Smash Street Kids*, Macmillan, London.

Corson, D. (1986), 'Policy in Social Context: Collapse of Holistic Planning in Education', *Journal of Education Policy*, vol. 1, pp. 5–22.

Corwin, R.G. (1967), 'Education and the Study of Complex Organizations', in Hansen, D.A. and Gertsl, J.E. (eds.), *On Education, Sociological Perspectives*, Wiley, New York.

Council of Europe (1974), *Permanent Education: Evaluating Pilot Experiments. Interim Report*, Strasbourg.

Courtney, S. (1992), *Why Adults Learn*, Routledge, London.

Crane, J.M. (1991), 'Moses Coady and Antigonish', in Jarvis, P. (ed.), *Twentieth-Century Thinkers in Adult Education*, Routledge, London.

Cullen, M. (1987), 'Knowledge and Power: Patriarchal Knowledge and the Feminist Curriculum', in Cullen, M. (ed.), *Girls Don't Do Honours*, Women's Education Bureau, Dublin.

Daly, M, (1979), *Gyn/Ecology*, The Women's Press, London.

Danziger, K. (1971), *Socialization*, Penguin, Harmondsworth.

Davis, K. (1969), *Human Society*, Collier-Macmillan, New York.

Deem, R. (1978), *Women and Schooling*, Routledge and Kegan Paul, London.

Deken, J.J. de (1992), 'Social Policy and the Politics of Solidarity', *Sociological Review* (Prague), vol. 28, pp. 351–368.

Denzin, N.K. (1971), 'Symbolic Interactionism and Ethnomethodology', in Douglas, J.D. (ed.), *Understanding Everyday Life*, Routledge and Kegan Paul, London.

Derrida, J. (1978), *Writing and Difference*, Routledge and Kegan Paul, London.

Donoghue, D. (1992), *Warrenpoint*, Jonathan Cape, London.

Dreitzel, H.P. (ed.) (1973), *Childhood and Socialization*, Macmillan, New York.

Durkheim, E. (1956), *Education and Sociology*, Free Press, New York.

Durkheim, E. (1982), *The Rules of Sociological Method*, Macmillan, London.

Dworkin, A. (1992), *Mercy*, Arrow, London.

Eco, U. (1980), *The Name of the Rose*, Secker and Warburg, London.

Eder, K. (1990), 'The Rise of Counter-Culture Movements against Modernity', *Theory, Culture and Society*, vol. 7, pp. 21–47.

Elsey, B. (1991), 'R.H. Tawney—" Patron Saint of Adult Education"', in Jarvis, P. (ed.), *Twentieth-Century Thinkers in Adult Education*, Routledge, London.

Erikson, K. (1966), *Wayward Puritans*, Wiley, New York.

Etzioni, A. (1964), *Modern Organizations*, Prentice-Hall, New Jersey.

European Centre for Human Rights Education (1992), *General Information*, Prague.

Evans, D. (1980), 'Writers' Workshops and Working-Class Culture', in Thompson, J. (ed.), *Adult Education for a Change*, Hutchinson, London.

Fay, B. (1987), *Critical Social Science*, Polity Press, Oxford.

Fieldhouse, R. (1989), 'Great Britain: Workers' Education Association', in Charters, A.N. and Hilton, R.J. (eds.), *Landmarks in*

International Adult Education: A Comparative Analysis, Routledge, London.

Foucault, M. (1973), *The Order of Things*, Vintage Books, New York.

Foucault, M. (1977), *Discipline and Punish*, Penguin, Harmondsworth.

Foucault, M. (1981), 'The Order of Discourse', in Young, R. (ed.), *Untying the Text*, Routledge and Kegan Paul, London.

Freire, P. (1972), *Cultural Action for Freedom*, Penguin, Harmondsworth.

Freire, P. (1972a), *Pedagogy of the Oppressed*, Penguin, Harmondsworth.

Freire, P. (1978), *Pedagogy in Process: The Letters to Guinea-Bissau*, Seabury Press, New York.

Friedan, B. (1983), *The Feminine Mystique*, Penguin, Harmondsworth.

Garfinkel, H. (1956), 'Conditions of Successful Degradation Ceremonies', *American Journal of Sociology*, vol. 61, pp. 420–424.

Garfinkel, H. (1967), *Studies in Ethnomethodology*, Prentice-Hall, New Jersey.

Gaughan, J.A. (1986), *Alfred O'Rahilly 1: Academic*, Kingdom Books, Dublin.

Giddens, A. (1990), *Sociology*, Polity Press, Oxford.

Gieseke, W. (1992), 'Feminist Target Groups as a Form of Work', in Mader, W. (ed.), *Adult Education in the Federal Republic of Germany: Scholarly Approaches and Professional Practice*, Centre for Continuing Education, University of British Columbia.

Giroux, H. (1979), 'Paulo Freire's Approach to Radical Educational Reform', *Curriculum Inquiry*, vol. 9, pp. 257–272.

Giroux, H. (1983), *Theory and Resistance in Education*, Heinemann, London.

Goffman, E. (1968), *Asylums*, Pelican, Harmondsworth.

Goffman, E. (1969), *The Presentation of Self in Everyday Life*, Penguin, Harmondsworth.

Grace, G. (1978), *Teachers, Ideology and Control*, Routledge and Kegan Paul, London.

Greenfield, T.B. (1978), 'Organization Theory as Ideology', *Curriculum Inquiry*, vol. 9, pp. 97–112.

Groombridge, B. (1976), 'The Wincham Experiment', *Studies in Adult Education*, vol. 8, pp. 113–133.

Gurvitch, G. (1971), *The Social Frameworks of Knowledge*, Blackwell, Oxford.

Guskin, A.E. and Guskin, S.L. (1970), *A Social Psychology of Education*, Addison-Wesley, Massachusetts.

Hall, B.L. (1988), 'Adult Education and the Peace Movement', in Lovett, T. (ed.), *Radical Approaches to Adult Education: A Reader*, Routledge, London.

Hall, S. (1978), 'The Hinterland of Science: Ideology and the "Sociology of Knowledge"', in Centre for Contemporary Cultural Studies, *On Ideology*, Hutchinson, London.

Harris, K. (1979), *Education and Knowledge*, Routledge and Kegan Paul, London.

Havighurst, R.J. (1953), *Human Development and Education*, Longmans, Green, New York.

Heidegger, M. (1962), *Being and Time*, Blackwell, Oxford.

Heyman, R.D. (1974), 'A Theoretical Look at Knowledge, Schools and Social Change', *Comparative Education Review*, vol. 18, pp. 411–418.

Hirst, P. (1974), *Knowledge and the Curriculum*, Routledge and Kegan Paul, London.

Hogan, P. (1990), 'The Academy, the Market and the Courtship of Youthful Sensibility', in Mullins, T. (ed.), *Proceedings of the John Henry Newman Centenary Symposium*, Department of Education, University College, Cork.

Holroyd, M. (1988), *Bernard Shaw 1. The Search for Love*, Chatto and Windus, London.

Holzapfel, G. (1992), 'Experiential Approaches in Adult Education', in Mader, W. (ed.), *Adult Education in the Federal Republic of Germany: Scholarly Approaches and Professional Practice*, Centre for Continuing Education, University of British Columbia.

Hull, J.M. (1992), 'Religion and Education in a Pluralist Society', in Lane, D.A. (ed.), *Religion, Education and the Constitution*, The Columba Press, Dublin.

Inglis, T. (1990), 'Could We All Come Down Out of the Clouds Again?: Frank C. Laubach and World Literacy', *International Journal of University Adult Education*, vol. 29, pp. 1–21.

Inkeles, A. (1969), 'Social Structure and Socialization', in Goslin, D.A. (ed.), *Handbook of Socialization Theory and Research*, Rand McNally, Chicago.

Ireland. National Adult Education Survey (1970), *Interim Report*, (Murphy Committee), The Stationery Office, Dublin.

Jackson, B. and Marsden, D. (1966), *Education and the Working Class*, Penguin, Harmondsworth.

204

Jarvis, P. (ed.) (1991), *Twentieth-Century Thinkers in Adult Education*, Routledge, London.

Jarvis, P. (1991), 'Paulo Freire', in Jarvis, P. (ed.), *Twentieth-Century Thinkers in Adult Education*, Routledge, London.

Jones, W.T. (1969), *Masters of Political Thought, Volume 2*, Harrap, London.

Kagan, J. (1969), 'The Three Faces of Continuity in Human Development', in Goslin, D.A. (ed.), *Handbook of Socialization Theory and Research*, Rand McNally, Chicago.

Kant, I. (1959), *The Foundations of the Metaphysics of Morals*, Bobbs-Merrill, Indianapolis.

Kardiner, A. (1945), *The Psychological Frontiers of Society*, Columbia University Press, New York.

Kearney, R. (1986), *Modern Movements in European Philosophy*, Manchester University Press, Manchester.

Kempe, R.S. and Kempe, C.H. (1978), *Child Abuse*, Fontana/Open Books, London.

Kerouac, J. (1967), *Satori in Paris*, Andre Deutsch, London.

Kimmel, D.G. (1974), *Adulthood and Aging*, Wiley, New York.

Komisar, B.P. and McClellan, J.E. (1961), 'The Logic of Slogans', in Smith, B.O. and Ennis, R.H. (eds.), *Language and Concepts in Education*, Rand McNally, Chicago.

Kuhn, T. (1962), *The Structure of Scientific Revolutions*, University of Chicago Press, Chicago.

Kumar, K. (1991), *Utopianism*, Open University Press, Milton Keynes.

Laidlaw, A.F. (1971), *The Man from Margaree. Writings and Speeches of M.M. Coady*, McClelland and Stewart, Toronto.

Langton, K. (1969), *Political Socialization*, Oxford University Press, New York.

Lawson, K.H. (1979), *Philosophical Concepts and Values in Adult Education*, Open University Press, Milton Keynes.

Leagans, J.P. (1964), 'A Concept of Needs', *Journal of Cooperative Extension*, vol. 2, pp. 89–96.

Lee, J. (1973), *The Modernization of Irish Society*, Gill and Macmillan, Dublin.

Long, H.B. (1991), *Early Innovators in Adult Education*, Routledge, London.

Lovett, T. (1975), *Adult Education, Community Development and the Working Class*, Ward Lock, London.

Lovett, T. (1980), 'Adult Education and Community Action', in Thompson, J. (ed.), *Adult Education for a Change*, Hutchinson, London.

Lovett, T. (1989), 'Adult Education and the Working Class', in O'Sullivan, D. (ed.), *Social Commitment and Adult Education*, Cork University Press, Cork.

Lukes, S. (1973), *Individualism*, Blackwell, Oxford.

Lukes, S. (1974), *Power. A Radical View*, Macmillan, London.

McCarthy, T. (1988), *The Critical Theory of Jurgen Habermas*, MIT Press, Cambridge, Massachusetts.

McGuire, M.B. (1982), *Pentecostal Catholics*, Temple University Press, Philadelphia.

McIlroy, J. (1990),'"If Rightly Understood ..." Trade Union Education and Democracy', *International Journal of University Adult Education*, vol. 29, pp. 85–101.

McLaren, P. (1986), *Schooling as Ritual Performance*, Routledge and Kegan Paul, London.

McLellan, D. (1977), *The Thought of Karl Marx*, Macmillan, London.

McPherson, A. and Raab, C.D. (1988), *Governing Education. A Sociology of Policy since 1945*, Edinburgh University Press, Edinburgh.

Maritain, J. (1963), *Man and the State*, University of Chicago Press, Chicago.

Martin, B. (1988), 'Education and the Environmental Movement', in Lovett, T. (ed.), *Radical Approaches to Adult Education: A Reader*, Routledge, London.

Mateju, P. and Rehakova, B. (1992), 'From Unjust Equality to Just Inequality?', *Sociological Review* (Prague), vol. 28, pp. 293–318.

Mead, G.H. (1934), *Mind, Self and Society*, University of Chicago Press, Chicago.

Merelman, R.M. (1972), 'The Adolescence of Political Socialization', *Sociology of Education*, vol. 45, pp. 134–166.

Merleau-Ponty, M. (1969), *Humanism and Terror*, Beacon Books, New York.

Merton, R. (1968), *Social Theory and Social Structure*, Free Press, New York.

Mezirow, J. (1978), 'Perspective Transformation', *Adult Education*, vol. 28, pp. 100–110.

Mezirow, J. (1989), 'Transformation Theory and Social Action. A Response to Collard and Law', *Adult Education Quarterly*, vol. 39, pp. 169–175.

Mills, C.W. (1970), *The Sociological Imagination*, Pelican, Harmondsworth.

Mohr, L.B. (1973), 'The Concept of Organizational Goal', *American Political Science Review*, vol. 67, pp. 470–481.

Montville, J. (1987), 'The Arrow and the Olive Branch: A Case for Track Two Diplomacy', in McDonald, J.W. and Bendahamana, D. (eds.), *Conflict Resolution: Track Two Diplomacy*, Foreign Service Institute, Washington, D.C.

Moore, W.E. (1969), 'Occupational Socialization', in Goslin, D.A. (ed.), *Handbook of Socialization Theory and Research*, Rand McNally, Chicago.

Morrison, J. (1989), 'Canada: Frontier College', in Charters, A.N. and Hilton, R.J. (eds.), *Landmarks in International Adult Education. A Comparative Analysis*, Routledge, London.

Morrison, A. and McIntyre, D. (1971), *Schools and Socialization*, Penguin, Harmondsworth.

Muller, V. (1991), 'Legitimation: A Key Term in Sociological Theory or "Argomento Rituale"?', *Sociological Review* (Prague), vol. 27, pp. 742–750.

Murphy, J. (1993), *Rio De La Plata and all that ...*, Dedalus, Dublin.

Murray, D. and O'Neill, J. (1991), *Peace Building in a Political Impasse: Cross Border Links in Ireland*, Centre for the Study of Conflict, University of Ulster at Coleraine.

Natriello, G., McDill, E.L. and Pallas, A.M. (1990), *Schooling Disadvantaged Children*, Teachers College Press, New York.

Neugarten, B. (1963), 'Personality Changes during the Adult Years', in Kuhlen, R.G. (ed.), *Psychological Background of Adult Education*, Centre for the Study of Liberal Education for Adults, Chicago.

Newman, J.H. (1973), *Apologia Pro Vita Sua*, Sheed and Ward, London.

Nyerere, J.K. (1968), *Freedom and Socialism: A Selection of Writings and Speeches, 1965–1967*, Oxford University Press, Dar es Salaam.

Nyomarkay, J. (1967), *Charisma and Factionalism in the Nazi Party*, University of Minnesota Press, Minneapolis.

O'Connor, F. (1963), *The Lonely Voice*, Macmillan, London.

Okely, J. (1986), *Simone de Beauvoir. A Re-Reading*, Virago, London.

Olson, D. (1977), 'From Utterance to Text. The Bias of Language in Speech and Writing', *Harvard Educational Review*, vol. 47, pp. 257–281.

Ó Murchú, M. (1989), 'Alfred O'Rahilly and the Provision of Adult Education at University College, Cork', in O'Sullivan, D. (ed.),

Social Commitment and Adult Education, Cork University Press, Cork.

O'Sullivan, D. (1973), 'Schools and Political Socialization', *Administration*, vol. 21, pp. 105–116.

O'Sullivan, D. (1989), 'Adult and Continuing Education in the Irish Republic: A Research Synthesis', *International Journal of Lifelong Education*, vol. 8, pp. 211–234.

O'Sullivan, D. (ed.) (1989a), *Social Commitment and Adult Education*, Cork University Press, Cork.

Oswanczyk, E.J. (ed.) (1985), *Encyclopedia of the United Nations and International Agreements*, Taylor and Francis, London.

Parsons, T. (1961), 'The School Class as a Social System', in Halsey, A.H., Floud, J. and Anderson, C.A. (eds.), *Education, Economy and Society*, Collier-Macmillan, London.

Paulston, R.G. (1972), 'Cultural Revitalization and Educational Change in Cuba', *Comparative Education Review*, vol. 16, pp. 474–485.

Perrow, C. (1979), *Complex Organizations*, Scott-Foresman, Oakland, N.J.

Phenix, P.H. (1964), *Realms of Meaning*, McGraw-Hill, New York.

Pizzey, E. (1978), *Infernal Child*, Gollancz, London.

Popper, K. (1961), *The Poverty of Historicism*, Routledge and Kegan Paul, London.

Preez, P. du (1982), *Social Psychology of Politics*, Blackwell, Oxford.

Rejai, M. and Phillips, K. (1983), *World Revolutionary Leaders*, Rutgers University Press, New Brunswick, N.J.

Rockhill, K. (1987), 'Gender, Language and the Politics of Literacy', *British Journal of Sociology of Education*, vol. 8, pp. 153–167.

Rogers, J. (1977), *Adults Learning*, Open University Press, Milton Keynes.

Rokeach, M. (1960), *The Open and Closed Mind*, Wiley, New York.

Rozycki, E.G. (1987), 'Policy and Social Contradiction: The Case of Lifelong Education', *Educational Theory*, vol. 37, pp. 433–443.

Rubenson, K. (1989), 'Sweden: Study Circles', in Charters, A.N. and Hilton, R.J. (eds.), *Landmarks in International Adult Education. A Comparative Analysis*, Routledge, London.

Ryan, A. (1970), *The Philosophy of the Social Sciences*, Macmillan, London.

Samarin, W.J. (1972), 'Forms and Functions of Nonsense Language', *Linguistics*, vol. 50, pp. 70–74.

Schofield, M. (1968), *The Sexual Behaviour of Young People*, Penguin, Harmondsworth.

Sharp, R. and Green, A. (1975), *Education and Social Control*, Routledge and Kegan Paul, London.

Shor, I. (1986), *Culture Wars*, Routledge and Kegan Paul, London.

Silverman, D. (1970), *The Theory of Organizations*, Heinemann, London.

Smith, F. (1985), 'A Metaphor for Literacy: Granting Worlds or Shunting Information', in Olson, D.R., Torrance, N. and Hildgard, A. (eds.), *Literacy, Language and Learning*, Cambridge University Press, Cambridge.

Strauss, A.L., Schatzman, L., Bucher, R., Ehrlich, D. and Sabshin, M. (1964), *Psychiatric Ideologies and Institutions*, Free Press, New York.

Tyler, W. (1988), *School Organization. A Sociological Perspective*, Croom Helm, London.

Thomas, W.I. (1923), *The Unadjusted Girl*, Little, Brown and Co., Boston.

Thompson, J. (1980), 'Adult Education and the Disadvantaged', in Thompson, J. (ed.), *Adult Education for a Change*, Hutchinson, London.

Thompson, J. (1983), *Learning Liberation. Women's Response to Men's Education*, Croom Helm, London.

Titmus, C. (1981), *Strategies for Adult Education*, Open University Press, Milton Keynes.

Vincent, C.E. (1964), 'Socialization Data in Research on Young Marriers', *Acta Sociologica*, vol. 8, pp. 118–127.

Vocking, C. (1988), 'Educational Activities with Cultural Minorities', in NCVO — Department of International Relations, *Adult Education in the Netherlands*, Amersfoort.

Wagner, H.R. (ed.) (1973), *Alfred Schutz on Phenomenology and Social Relations*, University of Chicago Press, Chicago.

Walker, R. (ed.) (1985), *Applied Qualitative Research*, Gower, Aldershot.

Wallis, R. (1976), *The Road to Total Freedom*, Heinemann, London.

Walsh, M. (1989), *The Secret World of Opus Dei*, Grafton Books, London.

Weber, M. (1964), *The Theory of Social and Economic Organization*, Free Press, New York.

Weber, M. (1978), *Economy and Society: An Outline of Interpretive Sociology*, University of California Press, Berkeley.

Weick, K. (1976), 'Educational Organizations as Loosely Coupled Systems', *Administrative Science Quarterly*, vol. 21, pp. 1–19.

Wheeler, S. (1966), 'The Structure of Formally Organized Socialization Settings', in Brim, O. and Wheeler, S. (eds.), *Socialization after Childhood*, Wiley, New York.

Whitty, G. (1977), 'Sociology and the Problem of Radical Educational Change', in Young, M.F.D. and Whitty, G. (eds.), *Society, State and Schooling*, Falmer Press, London.

Whyte, J.H. (1984), *Church and State in Modern Ireland 1923–1979*, Gill and Macmillan, Dublin.

Willner, A.R. (1984), *The Spellbinders: Charismatic Political Leadership*, Yale University Press, New Haven, Conn.

Winch, P. (1958), *The Idea of a Social Science*, Routledge and Kegan Paul, London.

Wittgenstein, L. (1961), *Tractatus Logico-Philosophicus*, Routledge and Kegan Paul, London.

Wrong, D. (1961), 'The Over-Socialized Conception of Man in Modern Sociology, *American Sociological Review*, vol. 26, pp. 183–193.

Yarnit, M. (1980), 'Second Chance to Learn, Liverpool: Class and Adult Education', in Thompson, J. (ed.), *Adult Education for a Change*, Hutchinson, London.

Yarnit, M. (1980a), '150 Hours: Italy's Experiment in Mass Working-Class Adult Education', in Thompson, J. (ed.), *Adult Education for a Change*, Hutchinson, London.

Young, M.F.D. (ed.) (1971), *Knowledge and Control*, Collier-Macmillan, London. Young, M.F.D. and Whitty, G. (1978), *Society, State and Schooling*, Falmer Press, London.